Fourth Edition

Elementary Teaching Methods

Paul M. Hollingsworth
Brigham Young University

Kenneth H. Hoover
Arizona State University, Emeritus

Allyn and Bacon
Boston   London   Toronto   Sydney   Tokyo   Singapore

To Kathleen Hollingsworth
and Helene Hoover

Series Editor: Sean W. Wakely
Series Editorial Assistant: Carol L. Chernaik
Production Administrator: Annette Joseph
Production Coordinator: Holly Crawford
Editorial-Production Service: Linda Zuk, WordCrafters Editorial Services
Cover Administrator: Linda K. Dickinson
Cover Designer: Suzanne Harbison
Manufacturing Buyer: Megan Cochran

Copyright © 1991 by Allyn and Bacon
A Division of Simon & Schuster, Inc.
160 Gould Street
Needham Heights, MA 02194

82590714

All rights reserved. No part of the material protected by this copyright notice may be reproduced or utilized in any form or by any means, electronic or mechanical, including photocopying, recording, or by any information storage and retrieval system, without the written permission of the copyright owner.

Previous editions, by Kenneth H. Hoover and Paul M. Hollingsworth, were published under the title *A Handbook for Elementary School Teachers,* © 1982, 1978, 1973 by Allyn and Bacon, Inc.

Library of Congress Cataloging-in-Publication Data
Hollingsworth, Paul M.
    Elementary teaching methods / Paul M. Hollingsworth, Kenneth H. Hoover. —4th ed.
        p.   cm.
    Rev. ed. of: A handbook for elementary school teachers / Kenneth H. Hoover, Paul M. Hollingsworth, © 1982.
    Includes bibliographical references (p.   ).
    Includes index.
    ISBN 0-205-12893-9
    1. Elementary school teaching—Handbooks, manuals, etc.
I. Hoover, Kenneth H.   Handbook for elementary school teachers.
II. Title.
LB1555.H795   1991
372.11′0--dc20   90-22460
                                                                              CIP

Printed in the United States of America

10   9   8   7   6   5   4   3   2   1   96   95   94   93   92   91

Photo credits: Chapters 1–8, 10, 15–17, 19, 20, 23: © Frank Siteman 1990; Chapter 22, Talbot D. Lovering; Chapter 24, FGP, Action.

Contents

SOCIAL SCIENCES DIVISION
CHICAGO PUBLIC LIBRARY
400 SOUTH STATE STREET
CHICAGO, IL 60605

Preface

Instructional processes are the tools of the teacher's trade. Without them, there is no teaching. Although all individuals — especially parents — employ various instructional procedures from time to time, it is the school teacher who is expected to master the art of teaching.

Elementary Teaching Methods, fourth edition, provides a basic framework for a number of instructional procedures. It offers a flexible structure from which each teacher may develop his or her own unique instructional skills so student learning can take place. The techniques and methods described in this book are applicable to the open-school concept, the ungraded school, and the departmentalized school or the self-contained classroom. The degree of emphasis from one technique or method to another will vary depending upon the organizational structure of the school. The wide variety of illustrations will enable the preservice or in-service teacher to perfect a number of instructional methods and techniques for student learning.

The various instructional methods and techniques we describe are designed to be developed within a broad framework of reflective thought, each method emphasizing certain thought processes. However, full concept attainment may not be realized unless individual techniques are supplemented with other instructional methods. Therefore, the treatment of each technique contains many cross-references to related techniques.

In the interest of practical simplicity, little effort is made to provide a full theoretical basis for the methods included. Likewise, relatively little emphasis has been placed on the specific psychological basis for each method. The framework offered in this book, however, is fully consistent with sound psychological principles. It is assumed that the experienced teacher is reasonably well grounded in these areas.

Each chapter features fundamental properties, instructional procedure, values and limitations, and method illustrations. In addition, each chapter has an overview that consists of key concepts and chapter terms that will be encountered in the reading of each chapter. Two new chapters have been added to this edition: "Cooperative Learning" and "Explicit Instruction Method." All other chapters have been updated and revised to reflect contemporary thought.

We wish to express our gratitude to the many teachers, colleagues, and others who have assisted in the development of this book.

P. M. H
K. H. H.

Chapter 1

Planning
for Teaching

Overview

Key Concepts

- The unit concept is fundamental to instructional planning.
- A functional unit concept is broader than specific content material; it embodies a real-life application.
- Unit concepts are not passed along to pupils; rather, pupils develop them as the culminating experience of each lesson.
- Although preinstructional planning is essential, adjustments based upon specific pupil wants and needs are to be expected.
- Lesson plans are generally based upon a single unit concept.
- A lesson plan is a proposed analytical development of a selected problem.
- Since the resolution of a given problem may extend well beyond a single class period, the *daily* lesson plan is a misnomer.

Chapter Terms

- Organizational unit: The Overall subject area plan, consisting essentially of major ideas, problems, and topics that seem appropriate for the subject area.
- Teaching unit: A group of related concepts from which a given set of instructional and evaluational experiences is derived. Units normally range from two to four weeks long.
- Lesson plan: Those specific learning activities that evolve from a given unit concept. Each lesson plan is structured around a problem specifically designed to guide the processes of reflective thinking.

Planning, like mapmaking, enables one to predict the future course of events. In essence, a plan is a blueprint—a plan of action. As any traveler knows, the best-laid plans can go awry. Sometimes unforeseen circumstances even prevent one from beginning a well-planned journey; other times, conditions while on the trip may cause one to alter plans drastically. More often, however, a well-planned journey is altered in *minor* ways for those unpredictable "side trips" that may seem desirable from close range.

Likewise, teachers must plan classroom experiences.[1] They must plan the scope and sequence for learning activities, the subject matter to be utilized, the units to be taught, and the tests to be given. While few teachers would deny the necessity of planning, there is some controversy with respect to the scope and nature of planning. Indeed, methods specialists themselves differ relative to the essential scope of planning. Some seem to feel that unit planning renders lesson planning almost unnecessary. Others stress the importance of lesson plans while minimizing the value of unit plans. While the planning needs of teachers will vary markedly, there is considerable justification for both unit and lesson planning.

The Organizational Unit

An overall organizational unit perspective is achieved by listing major ideas, problems, and topics that seem appropriate for the area of study. The most obvious aids in developing an organizational unit are the selected textbooks and resource materials available. Also needed is a collection of other textbooks, library books, and study aids in the curriculum area. Although organizational units often are prepared by each individual teacher, increased emphasis is being given to joint participation of teachers in the same grade level within the school. This enables teachers to develop desirable commonalities. At the same time, it leaves the individual teacher free to develop each teaching unit in his or her own way.

The organizational unit involves a series of steps leading up to planning a teaching unit. It provides an essential foundation for a subsequent teaching unit and lesson plan. Careless planning at this level endangers the entire educational experience.

Organizational Unit Concepts

After inspecting various resources in the area, the teacher formulates a few basic organizational unit concepts. They will be very broad and suggestive only. There may be as many as a dozen of these. To illustrate from an organizational unit in the area of art for upper grades:

1. Art is a means of communication.
2. Art has cultural and aesthetic values.
3. Art helps children learn arithmetic, science, reading, or any other curriculum area.

After several tentative organizational unit concepts have been stated, they are revised and reworked until four to eight basic ideas remain.

(Some teachers prefer to incorporate these concepts into teaching objectives. This step is not essential, however.)

Organizational Unit and Major Teaching Units

Major teaching units are developed from the organizational unit concepts described in the preceding sections. Teaching unit titles will reflect basic themes implicit in the major concepts. Frequently a need for two or more teaching units may be developed from a single major concept. This suggests the need for more specific concepts. Eventually there will be a teaching unit for each major concept. Appropriate teaching unit titles based upon the illustrated concepts in an area of art follow:

1. Art communicates.
2. Art values.
3. Art enhances learning.

After major teaching units have been tentatively established, an approximate time schedule is established to reflect relative degrees of emphasis to be given to each unit. It may be that time limitations will necessitate basic changes. Sometimes certain proposed teaching units must be deleted. Teaching units are seldom less than two or more than four weeks long; however, the interest and maturity of the pupils will determine the length of the teaching unit.

Organizational Unit Introduction

After major teaching units have been selected, the teacher can develop for pupils an overview of the major aspects for the school year. The purpose of this experience is to give students an opportunity to develop a series of expectations relative to the curriculum area. Basic purposes, at their level of understanding, are offered. Pupils, in turn, are provided an opportunity to ask questions and to offer suggestions. The effect of such an experience is to create initial interest in the experiences to follow.

The Teaching Unit

Unit planning is designed to center the work of the school around meaningful wholes or patterns and to make the work of different days focus on a central theme until some degree of unified learning is attained. The process is one of combining related ideas into some intellectual pattern.

It provides opportunities for critical thinking, generalization, and application of ideas to many situations. Unit themes do *not* correspond to textbook units.

Implicit in unit planning are three different phases: initiating activities, developing activities, and culminating activities. The first phase of unit planning is similar to the steps in planning an organizational unit. Unit planning is necessarily more restricted and specific than the latter. In all cases, however, the process must be consistent with, and fit into, the overall framework established in the organizational unit.

Unit Concepts

From the particular organizational unit concept, a number of teaching unit concepts will be developed. Each of these must contribute to development of the overall unit theme. The teaching unit length will reflect the number and complexity of teaching unit concepts to be developed. To illustrate from organizational unit concept 1, cited on page 3, "Art is a means of communication," the following unit concepts can be developed:

1. Art creates interest.
2. Art presents facts.
3. Art facilitates comparisons.
4. Art expresses relationships.
5. Art presents concepts pictorially.

Teaching Unit Goals

Based upon teaching unit concepts, appropriate unit goals and their accompanying outcomes are developed. Unit goals provide a necessary transition from what the teacher views as the ends of instruction to statements of pupil behaviors necessary for and indicative of the desired learnings. Frequently each unit goal will embody a different unit concept, but sometimes two or more *may* be embodied within a single goal. Indeed, there are usually more concepts than goals. To illustrate from the five concepts cited:

1. After this unit the pupil should have furthered his or her understanding that art presents facts, as evidenced by the following:
   a. The ability to apply appropriate facts in a drawing that he or she makes.
   b. The interpretation of the facts presented in a drawing by a written explanation.

2. After this unit the pupil should have furthered his or her understanding of how art expresses relationships and facilitates comparisons by the following:
   a. The ability to interpret art drawings showing relationships and comparisons in a class discussion.
   b . The ability to apply appropriate relationships and comparisons in a single drawing test.

Goal 1 apparently relates to concept 2, cited on page 5, while goal 2 relates to both concepts 3 and 4 cited on page 5. The behavioral outcomes suggest specific methods and techniques that seem appropriate *means* of goal achievement.

Teaching Unit Introduction (Initiating Phase)

It seems desirable to assist pupils in gaining an overall perspective of the unit by suggesting purposes and activities to be pursued during the unit. It is designed to create a state of readiness for things to come. This is the initiating phase of the unit.

Subject Matter

As an aid in developing a series of cohesive experiences a subject matter outline should be developed. Various activities of the unit rest upon this outline. Some teachers prefer detailed outlines; others favor topical outlines.

Learning Experiences (Developing Phase)

If teaching unit outcomes are stated in specific terms, most of the learning experiences will be identified there. Nevertheless, it is desirable to list all major activities in one place to facilitate adequate preparation for these experiences. This also enables the teacher to develop a desirable sequence of activities and to establish certain priorities. For example:

1. Class Discussion
   Problem: What can we do to communicate to the Russian people details of our way of life?
2. Letter Writing
   Problem: What information can you provide about the U.S.S.R.?
3. Oral Reporting
   Problem: What articles and pictures portray the Russian people and culture?

   4. Construction Activity
   Problem: Which country has the largest land mass, the United
   States or Russia?

   The act of preplanning some of the activities does not mean that
the teacher must assume the role of taskmaster. Pupils may participate
actively in the planning of class activities, but this does not replace the
need for a certain number of preplanned activities *suggested* by the teacher.
As in the sample unit, different pupils often will be involved in different
activities; thus provision for individual differences may become a reality.
For beginning teachers it may be necessary to make a special point of this
in the unit plan.

Unit Evaluation (Culminating Phase)

A unit plan is incomplete without some forecast of progress toward the
teaching unit goals. Teaching unit plans may be rendered ineffective if
pupils anticipate being asked to recall specific facts only from a textbook.
Measurement and evaluation must be consistent with the teaching unit
goals and anticipated behavioral outcomes. Behaviors that are appropriate
as learning activities usually are not adequate for evaluating learning. They
do provide sound bases, however, for development of the needed evaluational experiences. For example, the letter-writing activity (cited in the
foregoing illustrations of learning activities) should help pupils learn the
proper form for letter writing. Thus test items based on another letter
might well be utilized to evaluate their knowledge of the proper form
for letter writing.

Lesson Planning

A lesson plan is an expanded portion of a teaching unit plan. It represents
a detailed analysis of a particular *activity* described in the teaching unit
plan. For example, one of the teaching unit outcomes anticipated in the
sample teaching unit was the pupil's "ability to relate the revolt in Russia
to the Communist Party." This led to the provision for an activity called
learning analysis report. While the activity was stated in the teaching unit
plan, no indication was given as to how the activity would be developed.
In developing pupil activities, careful planning is essential. The lesson
plan serves such a purpose.
   The essentials of a lesson plan are somewhat parallel to those of a
teaching unit plan. Although forms and styles differ markedly from one
teacher to another, a lesson plan usually contains a goal, lesson introduction

(approach), lesson development, and lesson generalization. Depending on the nature of the lesson, it also may include a list of materials needed, provision for individual differences, and an assignment.

The common elements of lesson planning erroneously suggest a standard routine. While it is true that most plans will be structured around the common elements described, significant differences will be observed within this framework. Different teaching methods often are designed for different instructional purposes; they involve different sequences. Thus lesson plans must be modified accordingly. Sample lesson plans prepared for the purposes of illustrating each of the major teaching methods appear in the respective methods chapters. A comparison of some of these plans is recommended. The particular style of lesson planning illustrated in this book is suggestive only.

Teaching Unit Concept

Each lesson plan is based upon a teaching *unit* outcome deemed essential for achievement of a teaching *unit concept*. Thus behind every lesson plan is a concept. Two or more lessons may be essential to ensure the attainment of a single concept. It is desirable to restate the concept prior to development of a lesson plan. Although some authorities feel that in certain contexts the concept may be stated for pupil guidance, most apparently feel that pupils should be guided inductively toward concept achievement. Restating the teaching unit concept in each lesson plan simplifies further planning and helps the teacher focus on one and only one major idea during the lesson.

Lesson Goals

From each teaching unit concept the teacher must decide what major goal domain must be emphasized, e.g., cognitive, affective, or psychomotor. It may be that two or even all three of these should receive emphasis. Usually there will be a different lesson for each major goal domain emphasized. Sometimes, however, more than one domain may be stressed in a single lesson. This applies especially to the method of teacher-pupil planning that involves several unified lessons.

By way of illustration, teaching unit concept 4 is reproduced along with unit goal 2.

Teaching Unit Concept: Art expresses relationships.
Teaching Unit Goal: After this unit the pupil should have furthered

his or her understanding of how art expresses relationships and comparisons, as evidenced by the following:

1. The ability to interpret art drawings showing relationships and comparisons in a class discussion.
2. The ability to apply appropriate relationships and comparisons in a simple drawing test.

Unit outcome 1 suggests class discussion and the cognitive domain (although the affective domain can be stressed in certain types of discussion). Using the teaching unit concept as a guide, the teacher can then derive a lesson goal, with appropriate lesson outcomes. For example, after this lesson the pupil should have furthered his or her understanding of how art expresses relationships and comparisons, as evidenced by (1) the questions asked during the discussion, (2) the ability to offer and/or evaluate hypotheses posed during the discussion, and (3) the ability to derive generalizations from the discussion.

The specific learning outcomes represent behaviors that can be expected during a problem-solving discussion experience.

Lesson Goal and Introduction

Every lesson must be designed to capture pupil interest at the outset. Techniques may range from two or three introductory questions in a class discussion to a five- or ten-minute demonstration in a science classroom. Whatever technique is employed, the purpose is to prepare the learner for subsequent class activities.

Since the processes of reflection demand a constant referral back to the basic problem, it should be placed on the chalkboard. In this way, the problem helps to guide the learning experience.

Lesson Development

Major activities of the lesson are incorporated in this phase of a lesson plan. Subdivisions of the lesson development will vary with the particular method to be used. The teacher must first identify the different aspects of the reflective process germane to the particular method involved. The teacher then writes out points, questions, and/or comments deemed essential in the instructional process. In class discussion, for example, this may consist of only two or three key questions in each area to be explored. At this point the reader should study the illustrated lesson plans provided in the methods chapters.

Deriving Generalizations and Lesson Conclusion

The culminating portion of a lesson is often neglected or rushed. This is particularly unfortunate since it is at this point that pupils are expected to derive concepts or generalizations. The culmination of almost every lesson should involve pupils in the derivation of generalizations based on the current lesson experiences. The lesson generalizations are equal, collectively, to the basic unit concept upon which the lesson is based. Some authorities insist that pupils write out lesson generalizations. In many instances pupils will verbally derive lesson generalizations that are written on the chalkboard.

Basic unit (lesson) concepts, then, are derived by teachers as they plan for instruction. At this level, concepts are discussed during review lessons, treated in a subsequent chapter. As an aid in teaching, the classroom teacher usually writes out one or two anticipated concepts in the lesson plan to be used as an instructional guide only. To illustrate from the cited lesson problem:

1. Relationships can be illustrated in drawings.
2. Drawings can be used to show comparisons.

Values

- Unit planning provides a basic subject matter structure around which specific classroom activities can be organized.
- Through careful unit planning, the teacher is able to integrate the basic subject matter concepts and those of related areas into meaningful teaching experiences.
- Unit planning enables the teacher to provide adequate balance between various dimensions of the subject matter. By taking a long-range look, one is able to develop essential priorities in advance of actual classroom experiences.
- The organizational and teaching unit plans are the best techniques developed to date for enabling teachers to break away from traditional textbook teaching.
- Emphasis upon behavioral outcomes in teaching units and lesson planning results in a more meaningful series of learning experiences.

Limitations and Problems

- A teacher may become a "slave" to his or her plans. This is a special hazard for those who prefer detailed lesson plans.

- Excessive planning may promote an authoritarian class situation. This factor becomes apparent when the changing needs of pupils are largely disregarded.
- Unless adequate caution is exercised, lesson plans may become a mere outline of textbook materials. If practical lesson goals, along with specific behavioral outcomes, are developed *as a basis for* class activities, this situation will not exist.
- Thorough planning takes time—more time, in fact, than is available to some first-year teachers. Furthermore, it is usually impractical to construct lesson plans more than three or four days in advance of the experience. (By making substantial use of marginal notes, a teacher may use effective plans as a basis for subsequent planning.)

Illustrations

────────── **Organizational Unit Concepts** ──────────

I. Useful in the science area (primary grades)
   A. Plants
   B. Animals
   C. Birds

II. Useful in the arithmetic area (kindergarten or first grade)
   A. Personal arithmetic
   B. Money
   C. Counting
   D. Quantity

III. Useful in the language arts area (fourth or fifth grade)
   A. Oral language discussion
   B. Use of the telephone
   C. Story telling
   D. Interviewing procedures
   E. Oral reports
   F. Giving directions

IV. Useful in the social studies area (fifth or sixth grade)
   A. Canada, our northern neighbor
   B. Mexico, our southern neighbor
   C. Our neighbors in Central America
   D. Our neighbors in South America

────────────   **Teaching Unit Concepts**   ────────────

I. Useful in the science area (primary grades)
Unit: Birds
Concepts
A. Birds are helpful because they eat harmful insects.
B. The birds destroy the seeds of weeds.
C. Some birds may be kept in the home as pets.
D. Some birds are beautiful to see.
E. Some birds make delightful sounds.

II. Useful in the arithmetic area (kindergarten or first grade)
Unit: Personal Arithmetic
Concepts
A. Your age is a number.
B. Your family is a group or set.
C. Your house number is a location.
D. Your telephone number is for your safety.

III. Useful in the oral language arts area (fourth or fifth grade)
Unit: Use of the Telephone
Concepts
A. Dialing correctly will get the desired party.
B. Securing special services on the telephone, such as the police department, fire department, or medical doctor in emergency cases, may save someone's life.
C. Telephone standards of speaking will help in communicating with others.
D. Respecting the rights of others when using the telephone is a matter of courtesy.
E. Using a telephone directory saves time.

IV. Useful in the social studies area (fifth or sixth grade)
Unit: Canada, Our Northern Neighbor
Concepts
A. Physical features of the country affect
  1. Weather
  2. Vegetation
  3. Areas of population
  4. Industry.
B. The people of Canada and the United States have many things in common.
C. We are dependent upon the land of Canada for many natural resources.

Lesson plans are provided in each of the chapters dealing with instructional methods.

Endnote

1. Glen F. Lambert, "Lesson Planning and the Experienced Teacher," *OCSS Review,* Spring, 1988 pp. 32–58.

Chapter 2

Organizing for Individual Differences

Overview

Key Concepts

- Pupils differ in numerous ways relative to the school experience.
- Individual enrichment techniques are ideally suited for individual differences; since they often become unwieldy in large classes, however, some form of subgrouping is often necessary to facilitate such practices.
- Subgrouping techniques (within class) are characterized by flexibility in at least three ways:
  a. Pupils can move from one group to another as the occasion demands.
  b. Individual differences within each subgroup must be recognized.
  c. For many activities, pupils from different groups can work with members of other groups.
- Grouping or individualizing instruction gives each child an opportunity to meet the goals of instruction commensurate with his or her capacities.
- Individual instruction allows the child to pace himself or herself in the learning process.

Chapter Terms

- Achievement groups: Children grouped according to their achievement levels.
- Special-need groups: Children grouped together because they share a common problem or difficulty.
- Interest groups: Children grouped together because they share a common interest.
- Team groups: Two children grouped together as a team due to a particular problem common to both.
- Research groups: Children grouped together for the purpose of researching a particular topic.
- Continuous progress: Provides for uninterrupted growth in learning.
- Learning packages: Instructional modules that contain one or more instructional objectives.

Today's teacher is caught on the horns of a dilemma. On the one hand he or she is asked to work with groups of pupils. Recently these groups or classes increased in size as enrollment pressures mounted; present economic pressures are often keeping classes excessively large. On the other hand the teacher is expected to provide for individual differences of pupils. Each year new important differences are discovered, all of which have an impact on learning. The situation is being further complicated by the accelerated mixing of all races, creeds, and different cultural groups and even mainstreaming of handicapped pupils in many cases.

Fundamental Properties

In providing for individual differences within the classroom, the teacher must recognize the unique differences among the children and the varying needs of the pupils assigned to the classroom.[1] An effective program must be organized with appropriate instructional patterns and materials to meet these needs and to match the pupil's different responses to the appropriate teaching method or technique.

The Unique Child

Each child is the product of inherited traits, the environment, and the people with whom he or she comes in contact. Teachers soon learn that the children in their classroom differ from one another in every conceivable way. It is the master teacher who readily admits these differences and goes about the task of assessing the needs of each child and then develops teaching strategies to meet these needs.

A child learns more effectively when presented with learning opportunities in the form of materials and tasks for which he or she is ready. Learning is enhanced when children are appropriately rewarded for their correct responses and when they meet not only the teacher's expectations but their own expectations.

Instructional Patterns

Organizing for individual differences implies some type of instructional pattern that will aid pupils in the learning process. Grouping children together for instruction may be one way to approach individual differences among children. Many teachers avoid grouping while espousing individual instruction; however, the purpose of grouping is to provide for individual differences. If, within a group, attention is *not* directed toward individuals within that group, then grouping loses its purposes.

Organizing instruction on an individual basis is a second fundamental instructional pattern for meeting differences among children. The child essentially works alone without the group. Curriculum materials are made available for his or her use whereby the child paces himself or herself in an instructional manner. As described in the previous chapter, the unit plan combines both group and individual instruction. Unit planning gives the classroom teacher opportunities to provide for pupil differences within the room. Individual competencies and interests are built within the unit structure, and the teacher, through careful planning, is able to involve pupils in activities that are not beyond the child's achievement level.

Instructional Materials

Instructional materials should be selected with the needs of each child well in mind. If the materials are used meaningfully, the selection must be based on the knowledge of each pupil's abilities, achievement level, and interests. This means that the teacher must have available the results of periodic achievement tests, teacher-made diagnostic tests, and pupil interest inventories.

Meeting the problems of differences requires considerable flexibility by the teacher in the use of instructional materials. Sometimes the teacher may adapt the materials for group use. At other times, specific materials should be available so children may work not only individually but also at certain periods without the constant supervision and direction of the teacher.

Grouping

When it becomes necessary for the teacher to initiate grouping within the classroom, there are obvious steps the teacher must follow. Grouping must be based on the knowledge of each child's abilities, achievement level, and interest in the various subject matter areas of the curriculum.

The modern approach to grouping is that it should be as flexible as possible. Children should have an opportunity to work in many different groups throughout the school day. A child may work in one reading group and then shift to work with a different group in social studies and with yet another group in science. The elementary schoolteacher may employ at least six different types of grouping in the classroom plans.

Achievement Groups

Children within the classroom may be grouped according to their achievement levels in one or many different areas of curriculum. For instance, a child could be in several ability groups: one for reading, one for arithmetic, and one for science.

The achievement level of the child would be ascertained by achievement tests, standardized tests, learning aptitude tests, informal tests, plus the teacher's observation. These tests would guide the teacher in selecting the various achievement groups. After the children are grouped, the teacher must maintain group flexibility because some children may function better in a different group. Some children may be adjusted to easier or more difficult groups to approximate more nearly their individual functioning levels.

This recommended grouping procedure is made wholly on the basis of achievement rather than on the basis of ability. If the system works properly, the eventual grouping *actually* will approach one based on ability.

Special-Need Groups

It may be discovered while working with the children throughout the day that several children from various groups are having difficulty in understanding a specific problem. For example, certain children from several reading groups may be called together to form a "special-need group" for learning diphthongs in phonetic analysis.

The special-need group will be disbanded when the children learn the specific technique or solve the problem they have in common. This type of grouping could involve children from each achievement group, and several special-need groups could be organized in the classroom at the same time.

Interest Groups

A third type of grouping within the classroom is the interest group, which is formed among children who share the same or similar interests. Children who are interested in a particular topic such as dinosaurs would share with one another information they have collected from various sources. Class projects, school reports, and construction activities are just a few learning experiences that could be produced in interest groups.

Children who have similar hobbies also could be formed into interest groups. Many hobbies relate very well to various areas of the curriculum and may be an additional source for learning when children are formed into an interest-hobby group.

Team Groups

In team grouping, two children work together as a team concerning a particular problem that is common to both. For example, in the reading area, two children who make omission errors in oral reading could be teamed together. One child could read orally while the second child would circle the omission errors the reader made, thus helping each child become aware of his or her inaccurate oral reading problem.

Research Groups

Research grouping may be used with two or more children. The group task is to research a particular topic. Research groups could be formed for construction activities or classroom reports.

Full-Class Group

Often the entire class should work together as a single unit. Learning activities that are common for all pupils in the classroom could be introduced to the entire class at one time. For example, activities such as listening lessons, choral reading, dramatizations, reporting, and class and panel discussion are appropriate for the full-class group.

Individualizing

Procedures to provide for individual differences in the classroom may be seen in many different forms throughout this country. The concept of *individualized instruction,* which involves a wide range of efforts to tailor the educational program of the schools to the individual learner, has brought about new administrative arrangements and instructional programs.

Each of these programs has been tried with enthusiasm at one time or another as a possible solution to the problem of individualizing instruction. Many of these programs have *individualized* instruction, but many do not have *personalized* instruction—i.e., no one arrangement or program has yet completely succeeded in meeting all the individual needs of the diversity of children in the public schools. Even though all the individual needs may not be met by these approaches, some of these innovations may be utilized in the classroom by the teacher.

Pupil Tutors

Individualizing instruction can be accomplished by using pupil tutors. This program should *not* be simply a matter of allowing advanced sixth grade children to tutor first and second grade children who have experienced some difficulty in learning a specific skill. Pupil tutors should be taught the processes and skills involved in tutoring before they begin.

After the pupil tutors understand their duties, children from upper grades may assist children needing special tutors in the lower grades. This cross-grade tutoring not only aids the child being tutored but also is beneficial to the tutor as more insight is gained in the particular skill taught. Children within the same classroom also may be used as tutors for their fellow classmates. (See Chapter 15 for further details on tutoring procedures.)

Continuous-Progress Plan

A continuous-progress plan provides for the uninterrupted growth in learning of each child without restrictions as to specific materials or modes of instruction. Teachers are encouraged to individually adapt this plan within their own classrooms. The goal of the continuous-progress plan is that each child will receive appropriate learning experiences for his or her individual needs.

In this plan, grade level restrictions are not considered important as long as the teacher and pupil work purposefully from one sequential learning activity to the next.[2] Under the concept of continuous progress, a child does not fail a grade. Each child merely begins work in the new school year where he or she stopped at the close of the preceding year.

Learning Packages

Learning Activity Packages, Contracts, UNIPACS, Performance Criteria Units, Teaching-Learning Units, and many other names are used to identify learning packages. Whatever the name it might have, the learning packages are instructional modules that contain one or more instructional objectives most often stated in behavioral terms. Usually the packages contain a pretest, sample test items, or other criteria that suggest how the behavior will be measured, a bibliography of study references, and a list of instructional materials that are available to help the pupil accomplish the behavioral objectives.

These learning packages are designed to free both the teacher and the pupils from group instruction. The children pace themselves through the learning packages. During the time that a child completes one learning package, another child may complete several packages; thus, no child must pace his or her rate of learning to a group standard.

Many teachers make learning packages to fit their particular requirements for the children in their classrooms. However, commercially developed and tested learning packages are available for teachers and schools who do not have the time or resources to produce their own.

Individually Prescribed Instruction

A goal of individually prescribed instruction is to provide a variety of instructional materials and techniques to meet the individual needs of pupils. The individually prescribed instructional materials are carefully sequenced and empirically developed according to detailed behavioral objectives.

In this program, each child has a thorough diagnosis or diagnostic pretest to determine what the child has mastered in a specific curriculum area and what the pupil has yet to learn. The pupils are then expected to proceed through prepared materials relevant to instructional objectives as determined by the pretests. Ideally, pupils are expected to work at their own rates rather than to work with the whole class. No child need slow down his or her learning to accommodate the rate of a group of other children. Fast learners may move as rapidly as their development dictates. The opposite is also true—slow learners are not pushed beyond their learning intake.

Once the placement test is completed, the teacher determines the starting point for each child. On the basis of this diagnosis of a pupil's weaknesses, a prescription is developed for each child. This prescription lists the materials in which the child should begin the study.

The pupil generally begins work independently on the prescribed materials. Most of the pupils can proceed through these materials with a minimum amount of teacher direction and instruction. As the child is working independently, the teacher is free for instructional decision making, tutoring, evaluation of pupil progress, and scoring of worksheets and tests.

After the pupil finishes work on the prescribed materials, post-instructional tests are administered to determine how well the pupil has mastered them. These tests are also used to prescribe the next instructional unit.

Learning Center

The importance of developing learner self-direction in individualizing instruction has long been recognized. For individualizing instruction and development of independent work habits, school libraries have been an accepted part of the educational scene. What is new is the emphasis on the library as a central part of the educational experience and its expansion to include many types of instructional materials in addition to books. The term *learning center,* or *instructional resource center,* more nearly describes the facility provided in today's schools where films, tapes, filmstrips, programmed materials, recordings, models, and other nonbook materials are incorporated into one collection along with the more traditional printed materials. Some schools have organized the learning center as a separate part from the library. However it is organized, the learning resource center has become a learning laboratory rather than a museum or quiet retreat.

Learning Center Needs

The learning center in the modern elementary school is not the concern of the librarian or audiovisual teacher alone; it is central to the work of all teachers. Therefore, every teacher should have a broad general concept of what is needed to meet the demands of independent study.

A *varied and extensive collection of materials* related to curriculum needs and the personal needs and interests of young people is the first consideration. All types of materials should be available, and they should be organized in such a way that pupils can readily find what is needed. The needs of the slower learner and the poor reader, as well as those of the superior pupil, must be kept in mind. Materials should be selected by teachers and learning center personnel working together, and the budget should be sufficient to allow for replacement of worn and obsolete materials as well as the acquisition of new materials to meet new demands. Duplication of much-used materials is necessary to provide for large numbers of pupils.

The rapid growth of educational technology is revolutionizing the school learning center. The larger machines for classroom use of films, filmstrips, records, and transparencies are being supplemented by smaller and less expensive models that permit pupils to use these materials *as individuals.* Copying machines are now available in many learning centers to eliminate the tedious copying of materials by hand from noncirculating reference works. Teaching machines of all types are appearing in learning centers. The pupil carrel is an elaborate console at which the pupil may hear recordings and tapes, view films and filmstrips, use video tapes, and record his or her responses.

The learning resource center should include sufficient convenient storage space for the present materials collection with room for expansion. Work areas are needed for book processing and for the production of audiovisual materials, and work spaces should be provided for large numbers of pupils and teachers. These spaces should be divided to allow for private individual work, including listening and viewing by the individual and somewhat larger and more elaborately equipped spaces for small-group work. Many schools provide private study areas, or carrels, for from 25 to 40 percent of their enrollment.

The *program of services and instruction* includes much more than the checking out of books and other materials. Skilled reference help must be available at all times, and this should include assistance in using non-book materials as well as in locating material in print. Professional staff members should have time for conferences with teachers; also staff members should be available for classroom visits or instruction of groups of pupils within the resource learning center. There must be a constant flow of materials from the center to the classroom.

Pupil use of the learning center is the final measure of its success. Not only should the pupil be welcome there, but one must have *time* to go there. Pupil schedules must allow for independent study within the school day, and the rules governing his or her movement in and out of the learning center must be as simple and nonrestrictive as possible.

Learning Center Reinforces the Classroom

Many teachers do not realize fully the potential of the learning center and the instructional materials collection for the improvement of their classroom performance—they are content to depend almost entirely upon textbooks. Yet supplementary materials can provide much more information for the pupil than can possibly be presented in the best textbook and, often, in a much more interesting way. Where the text merely summarizes and generalizes, supplementary material particularizes, makes vivid and specific, and adds color and interest to what the text can outline.

The individualization of instruction, now recognized to be the greatest need in education, must be based on a wide variety of available material if it is to be more than a popular catchword. Not only must there be materials for the investigation of many facets of a given subject, but also the materials collection must provide the same information at widely varying degrees of difficulty. There must be something to challenge the brightest student as well as give satisfaction to the dullest and slowest. The needs of a class one year may be quite different from those of a new class the following year. Textbooks and small classroom collections cannot provide for individualization; use of the central materials collection is essential.

Skill in independent study can be attained only through practice on assignments of increasing complexity. As pupils succeed in this area, so does their ability to learn independently and their willingness to assume some responsibility for their own learning. Providing the needed experience in this area is a joint responsibility of the teacher and the learning center specialist.

Interest Centers

In addition to learning centers, which are essentially a total school operation, interest centers in each individual classroom are needed to assist the pupils in the development of independent work habits. Just as a classroom library is supplemental to a school library, so the interest centers are supplemental to a learning center. The term *interest center,* or *learning station,* more nearly describes areas of the room in which the teacher or pupils have established a place in which interests are developed and problems may be more fully explored.

Centers of Interest

Depending upon the interests and the maturity of the pupils in the classroom, many different interest centers may be established. Centers of interest could be the reading center, library corner, play corner, science center, arithmetic center, painting center, sharing center, music center, listening station, and the like.

Interest Center Needs

Elaborate materials and space are *not* needed to develop interest centers in the classroom. A table, some chairs, and bookcases will make an interesting center. A bulletin board will also add to the center if one is available. Cardboard or wooden packing boxes can be remodeled and turned into tables or bookcases when tables, chairs, and bookcases are not available. One side of a cardboard box covered with cloth can make a bulletin board.

Children can make or bring to the center various materials, books, magazines, specimens and exhibits, magnets, aquariums, games, puzzles, etc., which could be shared and add interest in the classroom. For a listening center a record player, tape or cassette recorder, and headphones should be supplied with tapes, records, or cassette tapes.

Interest Centers Reinforce Instruction and Learning

The interest center or learning station reinforces classroom experiences and learning. The centers also develop and extend pupil interests as well as enrich the lives of the pupils in the classroom. Individualization of instruction as well as independent work habits can also be developed through interest centers and learning stations.

Values

- Grouping increases the potential for *individualizing* instruction.
- Through grouping or individualizing instruction, each pupil has an opportunity to meet the goals of instruction commensurate with his or her capacities.
- Competition with one's own progress is possible through individualization of instruction.
- A variety of grouping and individualizing techniques are available for the teacher because no one technique for adapting instruction to pupil differences may be considered superior to others. Rather, a combination of techniques is desirable.
- Individual instruction allows the child to pace himself or herself in the learning process; he or she need not be held to the achievement progress of other children.
- Grouping instruction provides for the children's social and emotional needs.

Limitations and Problems

- Grouping within the classroom *should not* be done just for the sake of grouping; rather, its purpose is to direct *attention to individuals* within the group.
- Subgrouping within a given class must be flexible; however, many teachers do not shift children from one group to another when the need arises.
- Class groups must be handled so as to minimize any feelings of stigma or superiority associated with different groupings.
- Giving identical assignments to all pupils in a given group is little better than no grouping at all.
- Careful advance planning is essential for organizing for individual differences. The teacher who is not able or willing to do careful planning should not embark on such a method of teaching.

Illustrated Grouping Procedures

Organizing for Individual Differences

Initial instruction may be made to a group or the entire class by the teacher or pupil. The children individually experience the learning activity. The group reconvenes for discussion in order that ideas from the entire group may be applied to the problem. The learners must again separate and each pupil must integrate the learning experience; thereby, behavior is changed and the goal for instruction is reached. (See Figure 2–1.)

Group Flexibility

It is conceivable that a child could be with different children in each group to which he or she belongs. A pupil could be with one group of children

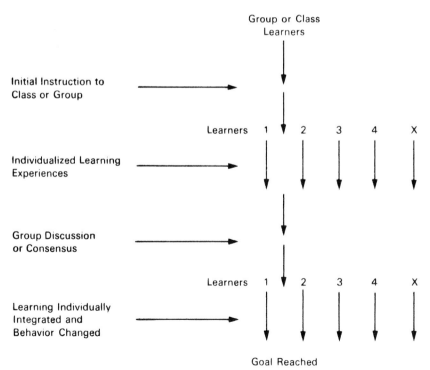

FIGURE 2–1   Combining Grouping and Individualizing Activities

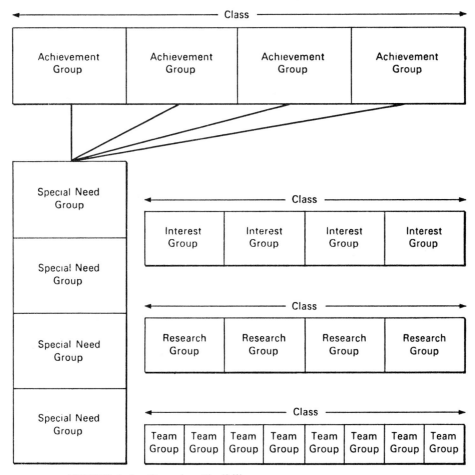

FIGURE 2–2   Grouping Flexibility

in the achievement group, with different children in the special-need group, and with still others in the interest group, research group, and team group. (See Figure 2–2.)

Endnotes

1. Peter L. Bleau, "Kids Who Don't Fit," *Learning,* March 1988, p. 30.
2. In effect, then, the teacher will time and pace the child in accordance with what the teacher knows about the *learning process,* the *learner,* and the *materials* to be learned.

Chapter 3

Teaching Multiethnic Groups

Overview

Key Concepts

- Multiethnic education should include Anglo-American and many other white groups as well as several ethnic minority groups.
- Multiethnic education must become an integral part of the total curriculum.
- Employing the dominant Anglo-American cultural framework exclusively renders multiethnic education ineffective.
- Cultural alternatives should be encouraged so long as they are not inconsistent with the rights, privileges, and responsibilities of citizens in a democratic society.
- Treating the dominant Anglo-American culture as the correct one produces a severe cultural shock for other ethnic groups. Consequently, many such individuals experience serious difficulties in school.

Chapter Terms

- Culture: The behavior patterns, symbols, institutions, and the like that distinguish one group from another.
- Ethnic group: A group that shares a common heritage, including cultural and linguistic characteristics. All Americans belong to some ethnic group; in many cases, however, the group is of little or no importance to the individual.
- Ethnic minority group: An ethnic group that possesses unique physical and/or cultural characteristics that make it easily identifiable.
- Cross-cultural competency: The ability to function effectively in the mainstream of American culture as well as within any other ethnic or ethnic minority subcultural group in this country.

Every young person grows up in a slightly different environment. Quite naturally the individual will attempt to cope with his or her surrounding environment on the basis of those realities. For some (especially ethnic minorities) the school often produces a severe cultural shock. Any and all differences may be treated as "bad" or inferior. Thus the individual is torn between conflicting cultures of home and school.

In preparing young people for competent, satisfying lives in a democratic society, subcultural differences that have not become a part of the dominant culture need not be abandoned. Indeed, in most cases they should be preserved as they play a vital role in the socialization process and help satisfy important psychological needs. Within the particular subculture they may be essential for survival. Moreover, such individual cultural traits often are fully consistent with democratic ideals. Multiethnic teaching attempts to preserve such cultural characteristics and, at the same time, to offer viable alternatives that can lead all pupils into satisfying, productive lives.

Fundamental Properties

The general culture shared by all Americans is a product of a wide variety of ethnic groups. It has been influenced (and is being influenced) by various ethnic cultural elements, some of which eventually become a part of the universal American culture.

In addition to the general American culture, a variety of cultural subgroups exist that contain elements that have not become universalized. The major goal of multiethnic education, according to Banks, is to change the total educational environment to promote a respect for a wide range of cultural groups and to enable all cultural groups to experience equal educational opportunity.[1] This entails helping all pupils develop attitudes, skills, and abilities needed to function effectively in their respective ethnic groups, within the universal American society, as well as within and across different ethnic groups.

Anglo-American Culture

The multiethnic curriculum should help students to develop the ability to make reflective decisions on issues related to ethnicity and to take personal and public action to help solve the racial and ethnic problems in our national and world societies. Effective solutions to the enormous ethnic and racial problems in our nation and world can be found only by an active and informed citizenry capable of making reflective personal and public decisions.[2]

The traditional practice of emphasizing Anglo-American culture only severely restricts one's notion of what it means to be an American. Most of us, for example, studied only the thirteen English colonies. Thus many people implicitly assume that these were the only roots of our cultural heritage. Few realize that long before the first English colony was established in Jamestown, the Spaniards had established colonies in Florida and New Mexico. Moreover, the French established a colony in Louisiana during Colonial times.

The mere addition of this information in the social studies curriculum is of little value when individuals are taught only within the framework of the dominant Anglo-American culture. Rather, ethnic groups and ethnic minority groups must be studied within the total curriculum framework. Under such a system, Anglo-American culture would become no more correct and would receive no more emphasis than any other significant cultural group. Emphasis would be placed upon cultural diversity rather than multicultural groups for their own sake.

Culturally Different

Several years ago, Reissman[3] called attention to a basic difference between "cultural disadvantage" and "cultural difference" that still applies. He pointed out that while culturally disadvantaged pupils are culturally different (diverse), not all culturally different pupils are disadvantaged. So long as today's teachers emphasize and function totally within the dominant Anglo-American culture (or middle-class mold), cultural limitations are likely to be emphasized and cultural positives ignored.

Many ethnic minority pupils are relatively slow in performing intellectual tasks. This "slowness," however, often is not to be associated with dullness or stupidity. Such individuals may be slow because they are extremely careful, meticulous, or cautious. They may be slow because they refuse to generalize easily. Above all, some may be slow because they cannot understand concepts until provided an opportunity to use their hands in connection with ideas. These pupils may also be slow because they speak one language in the home and a different one at school and they are busy translating information in their heads.

Effective Instructional Strategies

Multiethnic instructional strategies must be viewed in at least two different contexts. First, there is an immediate need to correct decades of Anglo-American ethnocentric instruction. Essentially, this portrayed the dominant Anglo-American culture as "right" while all other cultural differences were viewed as "wrong" or at least unimportant. To cope with this immediate problem, a direct approach is needed.

Teachers must adopt a truly multiethnic approach to instruction.

Under such conditions pupils are guided into viewing events, concepts, and situations from different ethnic perspectives. The Anglo-American perspective would still be important, but no more so than several other ethnic perspectives. All would be viewed in terms of duties, privileges, and responsibilities of society as a whole. Under such an approach the dominant Anglo-American norm would receive emphasis as one ethnic group. Other white ethnic groups, such as Jewish American, Italian American, Polish American, and so on, would be emphasized. In addition, various ethnic minorities also would be emphasized. Some of these are Afro-Americans, Mexican Americans, native Americans, Puerto Rican Americans, Vietnamese Americans, and so on.

Obviously each school district and each teacher must select a limited number of ethnic groups for emphasis. This will be determined by the viability of the various cultural traits to be considered. The local clientele to be served must also be considered. In Utah, for example, it makes sense to emphasize American Indian, Mexican American, and Afro-American cultures because of the concentration of such groups.

Incorporating a flexible ethnic approach into instructional methodology will not be easy for those who have never viewed their Anglo-American cultural indoctrination from the "outside." The teacher needs to emphasize different cultures in various subject matter areas, such as:

> *Music:* Along with modern Anglo-American music, music of selected ethnic groups will be emphasized. For example, if the objective is to call attention to the way emotion is expressed, one culture is probably as appropriate as another.
>
> *Art:* People express feeling through art. When this is emphasized, a variety of ways of expressing feeling can be seen from various cultural perspectives.
>
> *Social Studies:* As indicated earlier, cultural roots of various groups should receive emphasis along with the English.
>
> *Physical Education (Playground):* Sports that are favored in other cultures will be emphasized along with Anglo-American sports. These might include soccer, table tennis, and the like.

The objective of multiethnic education is to open up alternatives that can contribute to a full, satisfying life in a democratic society. Multiethnic education can assist the minority group pupils in developing a greater sense of self-identity and pride in their cultural heritage and at the same time provide majority group pupils with an understanding of the contributions of many ethnic groups to our nation.

Values

- Multiethnic education can contribute immeasurably to the basic psychological needs of a substantial number of pupils.
- By employing a multiethnic instructional approach, many desirable cultural alternatives are readily incorporated into the American society.
- A multiethnic approach can minimize achievement difficulties associated with many ethnic minority pupils.
- Specific instructional strategies for such pupils add a new dimension to the age-old problem of providing for individual differences.

Limitations and Problems

- Teachers generally have been educated within the framework of the dominant Anglo-American culture. Thus they tend to project this framework onto their pupils.
- The wide variety of ethnic and ethnic minority groups makes it necessary to select representative groups for study and analysis. Unless carefully handled, this may cause some pupils to feel neglected.
- There is a tendency among some groups to insist that every cultural norm is desirable just because of its existence. Each cultural alternative must be evaluated in terms of the basic tenets of our democratic society.
- Not all ethnic minorities are culturally disadvantaged in today's schools. There is a tendency to consider them as such, however.
- Emphasis on ethnic minorities only tends to divert attention from other equally important ethnic groups.
- Generally teachers have not been prepared for multiethnic education. Adding to the difficulty is the tendency to assign the least qualified and the least experienced teachers to schools and classes with heavy concentrations of culturally different pupils.

—————————— **Illustrated Multiethnic Teaching Ideas** ——————————

I. Useful in social studies (primary grades)

   Children find out from their parents the various nationalities in their background genealogy. Each child then develops a chart using a different color circle for each ancestor who came from a different country. The circle becomes one-half of one color and one-half of another color when parents of a certain ancestor come from two different nationalities or countries until the pupil's circle at the bottom of the chart becomes a circle of many colors.

II. Useful in the health area (first through sixth grades)
Pupils prepare menus particular to various ethnic groups. They then prepare the food and enjoy sampling the various types of food.

III. Useful in language arts (fifth or sixth grade)
Pupils compile bibliographies and cultural contributions made by different ethnic groups.

IV. Useful in social studies (kindergarten through sixth grades)
Children view films and filmstrips on the cultural contributions and the people of different ethic groups.

V. Useful in the reading area (first through sixth grades)
Children read books that emphasize culturally different children. Plays, puppet shows, oral reports, discussions, etc., may be used to illustrate the books read.

VI. Useful in social studies (fifth or sixth grade)
Pupils tape interviews with people from different ethnic backgrounds.

VII. Useful in the music area (kindergarten through sixth grades)
Pupils will participate in learning, singing, and listening to songs that come from different cultures.

VIII. Useful in physical education or playground (kindergarten through sixth grades)
Pupils will learn to play games that are significant game activities from other ethnic groups.

Endnotes

1. James A. Banks, *Teaching Strategies for Ethnic Studies,* 4th ed. (Boston: Allyn and Bacon, 1987).
2. Ibid., pp. 27–28.
3. Frank Reissman, "The Culturally Deprived Child: A New View," from U.S. Department of Health, Education and Welfare, *Programs for the Disadvantaged* (Washington, DC: Government Printing Office, 1963), pp. 3–10.

Chapter 4

Teaching
Mainstreamed Children

Overview

Key Concepts

- Handicapping conditions vary widely, each demanding a different type of intervention program.
- Handicapped pupils are expected to achieve minimum objectives; the manner in which they are accomplished, however, will vary depending upon handicapping conditions.
- Handicapped pupils must be provided opportunities to work and to interact with other pupils directly to the maximum extent possible.
- Evaluation of handicapped pupils must be criterion referenced, without reference to other pupils in the class.
- Speed and number of attempts necessary for completing given tasks must not enter into evaluation procedures.

Chapter Terms

- Handicapped pupils. Those pupils who need special, extra, or unusual assistance to achieve some level of success in a regular school program.
- Mainstreaming: Placing handicapped pupils in regular classes with their nonhandicapped peers to the maximum extent possible.
- Intervention programs: Necessary adjustments for helping handicapped pupils cope with regular class activities.
- Criterion-referenced measures: Measures that are used for evaluating achievement in terms of predetermined standards (criteria), without reference to the level of performance of other members of the class.

One of the most significant but least understood movements in American education today is commonly referred to as mainstreaming. The term signifies a major thrust of recent federal legislation requiring the schools to place handicapped pupils in the least restrictive (most "normal") educational program available. Essentially this means placing handicapped pupils in regular classes to the maximum extent possible. Exceptional pupils are defined as those whose needs differ significantly from those of "normal" pupils to the extent that special educational services must be provided.

Although currently inadequately prepared, teachers are being asked to accept pupils into their classes who have a wide range of physical, emotional, social, and intellectual impairments. Although many such pupils need various types of support services, the law is specific in requiring that they be integrated both instructionally and socially. In short, instructional strategies must be fully adapted to their individual needs.

Fundamental Properties

Coping with the full range of differences demands various types of individualized instruction. Certainly the problem is not new. For many years, teachers have recognized the wide range of pupil differences in terms of achievement, motivation, social, and health problems. Handicapped pupils differ from other pupils in degree only. They bring to the classroom *significant* differences in learning capacity, communication skills, motor development, and social and emotional adjustment. This section is designed to familiarize the teacher with the full scope of the task.

Public Law 94-142

Public Law (P.L.) 94-142, the Education of All Handicapped Children Act, was enacted in 1975. In 1986 another law was passed, P.L. 99-457, which extended the features of P.L. 94-142 to include preschool children three to five years of age. These laws require equal education for all handicapped children between three and eighteen years of age. Failure to meet stipulated provisions of the law excludes the local school district from all federal funds for education.

For the purposes of P.L. 94-142 and P.L. 99-457, handicapped children are those who are mentally retarded, hard of hearing, deaf, speech impaired, visually handicapped, seriously emotionally disturbed, or orthopedically or otherwise impaired or who have specific learning disabilities. In order to qualify as handicapped, these children must need special education and related services as a consequence of their impairments.[1] Public Law 94-142 and P.L. 99-457 call for the least restrictive (most "normal") educational program. Sanctions are provided for noncompliance.

Mainstreaming

The requirement of these laws that calls for placement of handicapped pupils in the least restrictive educational program is often referred to as "mainstreaming." Essentially this means placing such individuals in the regular school program rather than confining them to special classes. It does not eliminate special classes, however. Indeed, if the school can demonstrate that a pupil (with the use of supplementary aids) cannot function adequately in the regular classroom, special classes are required.

The "most normal school setting" has been interpreted as one that combines special and regular classes for handicapped pupils. They are educated with nonhandicapped pupils to the maximum extent possible. It does *not* mean all handicapped pupils will be placed in this manner or that regular classes will be flooded with such individuals. Pupil placement follows careful screening. Various support services are provided.

The basic principle underlying mainstreaming is that handicapped pupils can benefit, both educationally and socially, from being placed in programs with nonhandicapped individuals. Some special education leaders have recommended the Regular Education Initiative to help special education children, particularly those with mild to moderate disabilities, to be taught in regular education classrooms with special services provided to assist the classroom teacher. These leaders feel that the removal of students from regular settings has failed to meet the educational needs of these students.[2] Their mere presence in the regular classroom is not enough, however. The law calls for their social and instructional integration in regular classes. This involves peer relations—an oportunity to gain status as well as instruction appropriate to their level of functioning. In short, it means full integration into the curriculum of the classroom, which results from *personalized* instructional strategies.

Types of Handicaps

All children are different. They possess unequal characteristics on every dimension of life and living, from achievement to physical characteristics. Academic levels of those entering second grade, for example, may range from readiness to fifth grade. Differences for the great majority of pupils, however, are not extreme and have been accommodated with the regular classroom setting. Handicapped pupils possess many of these differences. In addition, they possess one or more handicaps that cause them to differ markedly from other pupils. These include learning capacity, physical differences, communication problems, and emotional/behavior disadvantages. This group often constitutes about 10 percent of the school. Today some of these individuals will be mainstreamed into regular classes. The five topics that follow describe the nature of these differences.

In addition to pupils who recently have been mainstreamed into the regular classroom, there is still another "troublesome" special student called the *gifted.* Although mainstreamed for years, the needs of such pupils frequently have not been met. Often they are "troublesome" to the teacher inasmuch as their thought processes are often well ahead of other children and even the teacher at times. This can pose a constant threat to the teacher. Since the gifted also need special treatment, they too have been treated in this chapter.

Mental Retardation

Mental retardation refers to those who are believed to possess limited ability to achieve in school. Such individuals not only achieve below grade level, but also usually experience difficulty throughout their entire school careers. Their difficulty may range from severe to mild. The mildly mentally retarded are often mainstreamed.

The educable mentally retarded (EMR) pupils characteristically have a short attention span, finding it practically impossible to stay with a task for more than five minutes at a time. Moreover, they forget easily. Even repeated directions may be quickly forgotten. Such persons have often been referred to as "concrete thinkers," as they experience difficulty in deriving concepts and generalizations from learning experiences.

The learning rate of an EMR child is typically slower than that of regular pupils. Thus more practice is required to reach mastery. If, however, the individual is permitted to remain with an objective long enough, some degree of achievement usually can be reached.

Although it is possible that some cognitive disadvantages are congenital in nature, it is recognized that many such disadvantages can be traced to environmental factors. These include malnutrition, poor health, parental deprivation, and the like. Such persons often come to school hungry and sleepy. Thus they may be unable to concentrate on school work. Some pupils have to cope with extreme cultural differences between home and school. In the past, a substantial number of bilingual pupils have been inappropriately labeled and treated as mentally retarded. Even so, they characteristically demonstrate many of the same school-related deficiencies ascribed to this group.

Physical Impairments

Physical impairments vary tremendously. Some stem from the central nervous system. Handicaps are associated with muscles, limbs, joints, and/or chronic health problems. Some may have existed since birth; others may have resulted from accidents and the like. Sometimes secondary handicaps are evident that may influence speech, vision, or mental functioning. Other disabilities may be singular in nature. A severely handicapped person, for example, may sometimes be an extremely able pupil.

The most obvious physical disadvantages are associated with mobility. Such pupils usually will be equipped with special equipment to assist them in moving from place to place. This may require special classroom accommodations. Sometimes the handicap may result in excessive motion, as with those with nerve damage. Other physically handicapped individuals will function at a much slower rate than might be expected. The cause may or may not be readily apparent. Chronic medical problems, such as diabetes, allergies, asthma, and some heart conditions, coupled with prescribed medication often have a profound impact on learning rate and stability.

Many pupils with physical disadvantages must be absent from school frequently for medical care or rehabilitation services. Their absences create further problems in developmental programs in the classroom.

Visual impairment includes the blind (visual acuity of less than 20/200 after correction) and those with partial sightedness (visual acuity of 20/70 after correction). Ability to cope in the regular classroom environment, however, varies widely between pupils, depending upon the individual's ability to use residual vision. Such children are usually provided books and materials that are written in braille. The classroom teacher and faculty support personnel, cooperatively, can do much to alleviate conditions that interfere with learning.

A *hearing impairment* is present when a pupil is unable to hear some or all of the spoken word. Since so much of the classroom experience relies upon the spoken word, such children must be given special consideration. Often hard-of-hearing pupils must work so hard at hearing that they tire quickly. Note taking may be practically impossible. Sometimes such persons will make unintentional noises, interrupt speakers, and speak too loudly or too softly. Thus considerable guidance is necessary.

Learning Disabilities

There is a class of children with *learning disabilities* (LDs). They are usually defined as performing in academic areas at least two grade levels below their school placement. Although normal in other respects, they are often lacking in the basic skills and frequently have poor self-perception, lower self-concept, or reduced motivation. They have a pattern of both strengths and weaknesses, functioning normally in many areas. Since the size of this group depends upon how it is defined, federal authorities usually insist that (for financial assistance) it is limited to 3 to 5 percent of the children in elementary school.

Communicative Disorders

Communicative disorders occur for many different reasons, some of which fall within the realm of mainstreaming. These disorders are classified into language and speech disorders. Language disorders are impairments of comprehension and/or the use of spoken or written language. Speech impairments are articulation, voice, and fluency disorders.

A pupil has a communicative disorder when the disability calls attention to itself or when it interferes with communications. These include enunciation, articulation, voice quality, and stuttering. (Many disappear as the child matures.) Perhaps the most serious of these is stuttering. The individual experiences disruptions in the normal speech flow by prolongations or repetition of sounds and words. Stuttering is often associated with anxieties.

Emotional Disadvantages

Upon entry into elementary school some children display a marked deviation from age-appropriate behavioral expectations. Such behaviors are self-defeating inasmuch as they interfere with further personal and interpersonal development. These are the individuals who may be unable to control their temper, who are subject to sudden outbursts, and who, on occasion, may pose a threat of bodily harm to others. An inadequate self-concept usually forms the foundation for such behavior.

All children have emotional problems from time to time and may even display irrational behavior. A few pupils are constant problems, both to themselves and to others with whom they associate. The first group might be referred to as merely *children with problems;* the latter are truly *problem children.* Problem children have been "hurt" by past experience. They tend to be suspicious, resentful, and overly aggressive. They "cry out" for attention, for success, for love, for security. Such persons, however, may hurt others and often interfere with the learning situation. Although they need and demand attention, they must be stopped when necessary— and then treated with all manner of kindness possible.

Sometimes it is difficult to distinguish between ordinary pupils with problems and these problem children. Usually, however, their consistency of inappropriate behavior provides the necessary clue. Sometimes such persons may not be classified as handicapped children. Nevertheless, their problems are no less than those with more obvious handicaps.

Gifted Children

Gifted children are those who are capable of and have demonstrated high performance in any one of the following areas: (1) general intellectual ability, (2) specific academic ability, (3) creative thinking, (4) leadership ability, and (5) visual and performing arts. They are often identified by unusually high performance on IQ tests (in about the top 3 percent) and by teacher identification.

One way of summarizing the characteristics of gifted children is to examine the behavioral characteristics of children who are gifted and talented. Identified characteristics usually include the following:

1. Cognitive characteristics
   a. Develop formal operations at an earlier age than peers
   b. Are fluent readers
   c. Have strong problem-solving abilities
   d. Recognize contingencies
2. Personal characteristics
   a. Have strong self-concepts
   b. Have internal loci of control
   c. Have less anxiety
   d. Are sensitive
3. Creative characteristics
   a. Demonstrate flexibility
   b. Show originality
   c. Show curiosity[3]

It should be pointed out that not all gifted children are easily identified. This especially applies to culturally different pupils, disadvantaged children, children with concomitant handicaps, and underachievers.

Personalized Techniques for Handicapped Children

With little advance warning, classroom teachers find themselves thrust into a most uncomfortable situation. They are expected to work effectively with pupils who represent the full range of handicapping conditions. Unlike special educators, who typically work with handicapped pupils in special classes of ten or less or in a one-to-one situation, the elementary classroom teachers may have twenty-five to thirty-five pupils in the classroom.

Not only is the classroom teacher unprepared by virtue of his or her educational preparation, but also each special educator has specialized in one or two areas of exceptionality. Almost none of the special educators have directed attention to techniques of working with handicapped pupils in the mainstream of the curriculum. In many instances, this state of affairs has left classroom teachers almost completely on their own.

This section treats survival techniques essential for special pupils who must cope with the classroom environment. They represent commonsense adjustments relative to seating, to speaking and writing, to directed study activities, and the like. Appropriate special educators may be able to provide competent assistance in this realm.

Mildly Mentally Handicapped

Such pupils characteristically are unable to stay with a given task for more than five minutes or so. An indication of this problem usually becomes apparent when the person begins to disrupt the concentration of others. By breaking directions, assignments, study activities, and so on, into very small units or steps, the individual may move through the learning experience rather smoothly. Since such pupils also forget easily, instructions for any given task must be broken down into small, specific segments. It is often desirable to ask the individual to repeat oral instructions as a quick check on comprehension. Demonstration and simulation are especially useful techniques in this respect.

Due to a slower learning rate, EMR children require considerable practice to reach mastery. Thus they simply cannot move from one problem to another as rapidly as other pupils. Since this produces a cumulating effect, the teacher must make adjustments, both quantitatively and qualitatively. Instruction must be limited to the most relevant and functional problems under consideration. For example, in a social studies lesson, the teacher would appropriately focus on local, as opposed to national and international, problems. In language arts, the teacher would ask for a sentence, as opposed to a paragraph, to be written on a particular story. Moreover, the selected story would likely be easier and the basic concept less complicated.

The EMR pupils often will not ask questions about the day's activities. This does not mean that they understand or are not interested. It is more likely that they do not know how to ask a question or are afraid to reveal a lack of understanding since such persons often experience difficulty in both the oral and written word. Whenever possible, however, all pupils should be drawn into regular class activities. This will come slowly and gradually as they develop self-confidence.

Physically Handicapped

Those whose mobility is impaired obviously must be positioned in such a manner as to minimize their handicapping conditions. This may necessitate some rearrangement of seating and the like. Less obvious are secondary handicaps and those associated with chronic health problems. Thus reading, writing, and speaking may be laborious, causing the individuals to tire easily. This often necessitates a reduction in the length of all or most assignments. Many authorities recommend placing a cot or lounge chair in the corner of the classroom to accommodate such pupils.

Visually impaired children should be positioned so as to take full advantage of existing lighting conditions. Above all, this means avoiding glare. Such individuals themselves can offer valuable assistance in this respect. Prior to the beginning of school, visually impaired pupils should be provided a room tour. Using the entrance as a reference point, provide a tactical/verbal description of the room's perimeter, noting reference points such as windows and door openings. Next, emphasize interior placements. A single, nonobstructed wall is an ideal, safe path to travel.

Instructional emphasis for the visually impaired must focus on the remaining senses. Thus full verbal instructions and explanations must accompany visual explanations. This especially applies to material placed on the chalkboard, use of visual materials, and so on. The meaningfulness of certain demonstrations can be enhanced by encouraging touching and manipulating for enhancing size, texture, and shape perceptions.

The *hearing impaired* must be seated to take full advantage of the room's acoustics. This usually means seating such persons near and directly in front of the teacher, as they rely heavily on lip reading. Thus the teacher should remain stationary when talking, face the class as much as possible, and keep his or her face in the light as much as posible. One must avoid standing near a window or other places that may create glare. Exaggerated lip movement, speech rate, or volume should be avoided. Many teachers are learning to use sign language to supplement the spoken word.

The hearing impaired find written outlines, key words on the chalkboard, and easily understood visual material most helpful (This applies to nonhandicapped pupils as well.) Sometimes it may be desirable to introduce the vocabulary of certain lessons ahead of time. A movie can be made more enjoyable if specially captioned.[4]

Learning Disabled

The *learning disabled* are a somewhat ill-defined group of pupils who are usually severely deficient in the basic skills. For example, they may have many reading problems. Thus special books and reading instruction must be provided. Special educators usually work carefully with the regular teacher in this respect. Learning-disabled pupils often suffer from an inadequate self-concept and low motivation. As with all pupils, those with learning disabilities need to experience success in their classroom. Many aspects of instruction must be adapted for this group of children.

Although sometimes posing behavioral problems (due to frustrations), learning-disabled pupils should be distinguished from emotionally disturbed individuals, who may *not* be deficient in the basic skills. Like many other handicapped children, they usually have an inadequate self-concept and low motivation. Again, they need to experience success in nonthreatening situations whenever possible. Special educators can alert the teacher to hazardous situations and how to best cope with behavior problems. Each emotionally disturbed individual tends to follow a recognizable pattern of misbehavior.

Communicative Disorders

Speech and *language problems,* such as articulation, voice quality, and delayed speech, are not uncommon. Most are self-correcting, however, and disappear as the child reaches adulthood. Sometimes the help of special educators is required. Interestingly enough, such problems often recur under stress, often to the embarrassment of the individual involved. This especially applies to stutterers. Under such conditions the harder they try to speak, the more difficult it becomes.

Whenever possible, avoid calling attention to stuttering. Let the person finish, maintaining good eye contact and positive facial expressions. By keeping a record of the circumstances that tend to trigger the affliction, difficult situations can be minimized. Here the child may be able to offer suggestions. If, for example, he or she becomes anxious in class discussion, the teacher can alleviate the problem considerably by aggreeing not to ask for contributions unless he or she raises a hand. The pressure of oral reports can be minimized by utilizing the small group and supplementing presentations with other media.

Gifted Children

Gifted children far excel their classmates in almost all areas of the curriculum. They are usually at least three or four grade levels ahead. For example, at least three-fourths of gifted third grade students will normally excel the average seventh grader in many areas. Moreover, as they advance in school the gap between them and the average pupil becomes greater and more noticeable.

Unfortunately, many teachers cling to the notion that the major program adjustment for gifted children is to give them larger and more extensive assignments than they would give to the average child. The adjustment in the curriculum, however, should be to allow gifted pupils to work at *solving problems* and the *development of problems.* In the science program, for example, they might be challenged to discover and to explain why an experiment "didn't work." Rather than emphasizing the scientific method as an entity, they might be encouraged to study how to use the tool in specific problem areas.

Generally teachers realize that gifted pupils like and need to think for themselves. Oddly enough, such persons tend to become most troublesome when they do just that. Then when they reach decisions that, for the moment, may be counter to "conventional wisdom," they are open to teacher criticism. They challenge, innovate, attempt to modify, and so on. This should be encouraged even though it may be quite unsettling to the teacher.

Methods and Strategies Especially Appropriate for Special Children

Mainstreaming means much more than the mere presence of special children in regular classrooms to the maximum extent possible. It entails both social and instructional integration. Social integration includes an opportunity to gain status and acceptance and feeling comfortable and secure as a full member of the class. It means sharing rights and responsibilities. Instructionally, for example, it means working with other pupils in large- and small-group activities. It does *not* mean working on identical skills and concepts as other pupils.

Certain instructional approaches are especially useful in working with handicapped and gifted children. Often these will involve some degree of individualization of instruction. Generally such individuals must be evaluated on individual progress as opposed to that of the group. This section emphasizes methods and strategies as well as evaluation techniques. It is likely that the ultimate test of instructional effectiveness with this group of pupils rests with the adequacy of evaluation. Often those instructional techniques that are especially effective for handicapped pupils are effective for nonhandicapped pupils as well. The following methods and techniques are helpful for mainstreaming.

Peer Teaching

It has been observed that pupils may learn more from other children than from the teacher. With the advent of mainstreaming, peer teaching (or the buddy system, as it is commonly called) has received renewed attention. (See Chapter 15 for further information on peer teaching.)

Role Playing

Role playing provides practice in how to behave in selected situations. In role playing, hypothetical but representative circumstances involving interpersonal relationships are established. Its purpose is to help pupils understand the attitudes, feelings, or situations of those persons whose roles they assume. By simulating selected handicaps and incorporating them into role-playing situations, nonhandicapped pupils can develop a vivid sense of closeness to such individuals. (See Chapter 11 for further information.)

Learning Centers and Interest Centers

Teachers frequently set aside an area in the classroom where children can go for individual and small-group activities. Through specially provided headsets the handicapped pupil may work on special skills, such as difficult terminology. It may be used as a place to work on assigned projects or any number of related activities. The learning and interest centers may be used by regular students and handicapped students alike. Often the learning center is partitioned off so that work activities do not interfere with other class activities. (See Chapter 2 for further information.)

Small-Group Techniques

A small group is characterized by face-to-face communication between individuals. While the optimum small-group size is usually about five, handicapped pupils may work most effectively in even smaller groups. Although *not* an effective method for covering content, the small group is ideally suited to processes of reflective thinking. In such a microcosm, pupils can easily discuss and analyze practical applications of important issues (See Chapter 2 for further information.)

Evaluation

Effectiveness of a mainstreaming program ultimately rests with the evaluation procedure employed. Traditionally, teachers have expected pupils to compete directly for class grades even though some pupils were less able than others. *Handicapped children as a group simply cannot compete with nonhandicapped pupils for grades.*

Handicapped children should be evaluated almost exclusively on criterion-referenced measures. This involves establishing minimum essentials (criteria) for *each* product of learning, such as exercises, papers, collections, learning programs, and so on. Performance that does not measure up to established standards should be repeated (with remedial assistance) until acceptable levels are reached. Time and number of attempts needed for goal achievement should have no bearing on grading procedures.

Even class tests may be studied and eventually completed by handicapped children. Under such conditions, however, they are used as criterion-referenced (as opposed to norm-referenced) measures. Thus the learner has an unlimited amount of time and may learn from mistakes until all basic items are completed satisfactorily.

Most school systems still expect some form of status marking, whereby a grade indicates relative class standing. In many respects this is an acceptable position, so long as those involved have a reasonable ability to compete. Handicapped pupils, as a group, do not possess this ability for one reason or another. Thus they must be excluded. There is no reason why two systems cannot exist side by side in a given classroom.

Gifted children also profit most from individual evaluation. Since they are likely to rank at the top of the class in all competitive class activities, they can easily develop sloppy work habits. It is just as important to expect maximum effort from gifted children as it is for any other pupil in the classroom.

Values

- Mainstreaming makes the classroom somewhat consistent with society as a whole.
- Nonhandicapped pupils learn to respect and to work effectively with handicapped children only through direct experience.
- Through mainstreaming, some handicapped pupils are able to develop feelings of adequacy and self-worth as they interact with others.
- Mainstreaming, in effect, may force teachers to recognize and provide for the vast range of individual differences among pupils. For

much too long, some teachers have neglected individual differences in their selection of instructional methods and techniques.
- Gifted children may be a tremendous asset to the teacher in working with handicapped pupils.

Limitations and Problems

- Classroom teachers are presently not adequately prepared to cope with handicapped pupils.
- Often special educators are of little help in the broader aspects of instructional methodology. They have been educated to work with handicapped pupils on a one-to-one basis.
- Handicapping conditions often call attention to such persons. This may at times interfere with regular class activities and lead to embarrassment and ridicule.
- Handicapped pupils cannot compete directly for class grades. Thus adjustments in grading procedures are necessary.
- Individualization of instruction is vital when handicapped pupils are present.
- Due to their unusual perceptive abilities, gifted children may pose a threat to the classroom teacher.

Dos and Don'ts

Mainstreaming, for the most part, finds teachers currently ill prepared for the task. Interesting and innovative applications in different curriculum areas are still in the process of being developed. Thus, for this chapter, it seems appropriate to provide some "dos" and "don'ts" in the area.

Dos

1. Expect all special pupils to achieve minimum class objectives.
2. Integrate special children into regular class activities.
3. Adjust the classroom environment to meet the special handicapping conditions of those present.
4. Emphasize criterion-referenced evaluation for such special pupils.
5. Help all children recognize and cope with special handicapping conditions of others.
6. Be prepared to cope with unexpected problems that arise from handicapping conditions, such as epileptic seizures, heart malfunctions, etc.

7. Help special children (along with others) gain social acceptance from their peers.
8. Individualize instruction to the maximum extent possible.
9. Work closely with special education support personnel in helping handicapped pupils cope with regular class activities.
10. Enlist the help of buddies to work closely with handicapped children.
11. Expect and even encourage gifted children to think for themselves.
12. Develop appropriate intervention programs for handicapped children.

Don'ts

1. Don't expect handicapped pupils to achieve the objective level of other children in the classroom.
2. Don't call unnecessary attention to individual handicaps.
3. Don't exempt handicapped pupils from activities they are capable of performing adequately.
4. Don't panic when a handicapped pupil experiences an unexpected difficulty, such as seizures, sudden emotional outbursts, and the like.
5. Don't penalize gifted pupils when they come up with ideas that may pose a threat to your preconceived notions and plans.
6. Don't let handicapped children continue before they have mastered basic concepts being studied.
7. Don't expect handicapped pupils to compete directly with non-handicapped children for grades.
8. Don't permit other pupils to ridicule or embarrass handicapped pupils because of their handicapping conditions.
9. Don't penalize any children (handicapped or nonhandicapped) for their best efforts.

Endnotes

1. Anne M. Bauer and Thomas M. Shea, *Teaching Exceptional Students in Your Classroom* (Boston: Allyn and Bacon, 1989), pp. 14–15.
2. G. Phillip Cartwright, Carol A. Cartwright, and Marjorie E. Ward, *Educating Special Learners*. 3rd ed. (Belmont, CA: Wadsworth Publishing Co., 1989), p. 27.
3. Anne M. Bauer and Thomas M. Shea, *Teaching Exceptional Students in Your Classroom* (Boston: Allyn and Bacon, 1989), pp. 281.
4. For further information: *Captioned Films for the Deaf Distribution Center,* 5034 Wisconsin Avenue, N.W., Washington, DC, 20016.

Classroom Management

Overview

Familiarity with the subject matter and a knowledge of the latest methods of teaching are not all that will be demanded of an elementary school teacher. In fact, other responsibilities seem to require much attention, such as keeping accurate attendance records, collecting the lunch money, maintaining a neat and attractive classroom, arranging areas within the room, and distributing and collecting materials.

Teachers who consider themselves professional individuals may feel that these tasks are menial and possibly unpleasant, but these responsibilities do exist and must be performed. To ignore these tasks would bring chaos and unhappiness into the class environment. Good classroom management will provide more opportunities to teach and a better environment in which children can learn.

Fundamental Properties

Classroom management is essential for an excellent learning environment. Have you ever noticed that children will always choose the longest crayon or pencil, the cleanest or wrinkle-free sheet of paper, and the newest looking book from the shelf? Children, as well as adults, appreciate beauty and newness surrounding them. A teacher must recognize the necessity of a well-managed classroom and try to provide one that is attractive and comfortable. In addition to these factors, the teacher must encourage classroom courtesy, provide for emergency situations, and establish organizational procedures in order that the classroom will be a place for learning.

A Place to Learn

The classroom is an environment in which a child spends many hours each day. The purpose of schools and classrooms is to facilitate learning. Whether or not this purpose is achieved depends on a number of variables the teacher can control.

An interesting and eventful classroom is one variable the teacher can manipulate. This type of a classroom would exhibit contrast and variety. For example, the bulletin boards could reflect ongoing activities within the classroom, yet they could display variety. Representative samples of children's art work would also produce contrast. Centers of interest for reading, science, and social studies also make the classroom more eventful for the children.

A second variable for a place to learn is that the classroom must involve the children in the environment. The classroom should attract the children to it. The pictures, plants, animals, and library corner should stimulate children's questions, curiosity, or need to learn. In order to attract children, the room need not be a work of art, but the bulletin boards should be uncluttered, closet and cupboard doors should be closed, torn books should be mended, pictures without ragged edges should be displayed, and the room should be clean and neat.

The place for a child to learn should be an environment that informs. This third variable, if applied by the teacher, would subtly instruct the child. Applying printed labels to various objects in the first grade classroom would be an example of the environment informing the child. Other examples are placing compass directions on the walls or marking feet and inches on the floor.

Physical Comfort

Ventilation and heating are fundamental properties for good classroom management; they should be a major concern of the teacher. For most activities in the classroom a temperature of sixty-five to sixty-eight degrees is suitable. The room should not be allowed to become stuffy or too warm. Make sure that there is enough air movement to carry away unpleasant odors and that a fresh supply of air is readily available.

It is important that sufficient lighting be maintained in all areas of the room.

The teacher should arrange the various interest centers, tables, desks, and working areas so that glare from chalkboards, furniture, and other surfaces will be avoided. Window shades should be adjusted for proper lighting to avoid glare for the pupils who may be seated near the windows; hence, artificial lighting is essential in many areas of the classroom.

Classroom Courtesy

Through the teacher's example, classroom courtesy and politeness may be taught. The teacher who displays a courteous attitude toward students is encouraging them to be courteous, not only to the teacher but also to others in the room.

If the teacher learns each child's name as soon as possible, this will also add to classroom control and courtesy. The teacher should address the children in a kindly, respectful manner and should insist that the children should address him or her in a like manner.

Classroom courtesy should be extended to visitors to the room. Many teachers appoint children to welcome guests and to assist the guests in finding a place to sit as well as to provide materials or books so that they may follow the particular activity that is in progress.

Outdoor-to-Indoor Adjustment

When children return to the classroom in the morning, after recess, or after the noon lunch period, a teacher should provide a period of time for adjustment. Usually this adjustment period may be only five minutes. A teacher who does not plan for outdoor-to-indoor adjustment may find the lesson plan objectives not reached because the children are not ready to begin.

During these few minutes, many different activities may be planned. In the morning during roll call and lunch money accounting, the teacher could provide for a class sharing time, a current event reporting period, or a library book free-reading period. After recess a musical record may be played or a beautiful picture may be discussed. After the lunch period possibly the teacher could provide for the younger children to rest by telling them to place their heads on the table or desk. Another activity all children seem to enjoy following the noon period is for the teacher to read orally to the children from their favorite story books.

Organization

Classroom organization is another very important facet to good classroom management. Such a mundane task as the arrangement of the tables, desks, and other furniture in the room can have an effect on a child's behavior. If a simple task such as furniture arrangement affects children, then classroom organization becomes even more important for the teacher to consider. Organizational activities such as seating arrangements, attendance and lunch collection, rules and regulations, pupil movement, and a place in the room for learning and teaching devices are a few of the problems a teacher must be willing to solve.

Seating Arrangements

Children in the primary grades (especially first grade) should have their chairs or desks arranged in such a way that they do not see another child's manuscript writing, number activity, or other school work upside down. Many children in the primary grades exhibit orientation problems, and some even have difficulty in left-to-right direction. Comparing their work with the child sitting across the table would compound the orientation problem they may have.

In the middle and upper grades, seating arrangements could be such that children can see each other's face instead of the back of one's head. A few children in these grades could have orientation problems, but it is not as crucial in these grades as the primary grades.

The pupils' desks or tables and chairs should be adjusted to fit their size and physique. Their feet, for instance, should rest comfortably on the floor when seated. The desk or table should not be too high or too low for comfortable table-top work.

Inasmuch as the learner is an active individual, adequate orderly space is needed in the classroom for each child. There should be an open area for dramatizing a story, demonstrating a science project, or other activity. The room needs to be arranged so that there are adequate spaces for movement within the classroom and several interest areas. Traffic lanes in and out of the room should be kept free and open. An orderly arranged classroom seems to have an orderly effect upon children within that room.

Attendance and Lunch Collection

Poor management on the part of a teacher during the roll call or the collection of lunch money will cause behavioral problems in the classroom. As stated earlier in this chapter, this time should be planned for the children. This gives a child an opportunity to share something with the class or report briefly a current event or time to do pleasurable reading. The taking of the class roll or the collection of lunch money can be handled efficiently with a minimum of class time expended.

There are several methods that can be employed to make this task efficient. The teacher could appoint attendance monitors for a row, a group of tables, or a certain section of the classroom. These monitors could make a written or oral report of the children that are absent. The use of a seating chart would also aid in taking an attendance record. By noting the empty desks and comparing them with the seating chart, this task would be handled in a minimum of time. These routine tasks of taking attendance and accounting for children who will be eating in the school cafeteria could be assumed by children, thus freeing the teacher for more important tasks.

Rules and Regulations

The teacher should seek to achieve an attitude of informality and freedom within the classroom that will assist the learning environment; however, rules and regulations are essential to protect the individual child against intrusions into the process of learning. A sufficient amount of rules and regulations are necessary in order to avoid wasted time and energy. Although the precise number and nature of these rules and regulations will vary from one classroom to another, they should be as few and as uncomplicated as possible.

Children should assist the teacher in making the rules and regulations. At a class meeting the pupils *guided* by the teacher could set up the rules and regulations to be followed. When the children are involved and have a voice in making the rules, there seem to be fewer dissenters. The children also learn some important lessons about classroom democracy. Once the rules and regulations are developed, the teacher should be consistent in enforcing them.

Pupil Movement

Some teachers have rather strict regulations about pupils wandering around the school and classroom. Other teachers find that it is not necessary. It seems that the best approach is to use different forms of permissions to suit the occasion. For example, the teacher may give permission to the children in the classroom to sharpen their pencils or place paper in the wastebasket at any convenient time, but to leave the classroom, a child must request permission each and every time.

Problems that can result when children are moving about the classroom can be eliminated before they exist if the teacher is constantly aware of each child at all times. To be aware of each child, the teacher must look every few minutes about the classroom, account for each child, see what he or she is doing, and determine if an individual crisis is approaching. At first, the teacher must constantly and consistently break away from the ongoing activity and check on the children. Later, however, this procedure will become a good habitual response. If the teacher is alert at all times to what is happening in the classroom, he or she is prepared to give extra help at a trouble spot and thus eliminate a behavioral problem.

A Place for Everything

All teachers should avoid having to waste their time or the pupils' time searching for equipment and materials. All classroom equipment, supplies, and teaching devices should be kept in a specific place. Anyone who uses these items should be responsible for their return to the proper place when he or she finishes using them.

Classroom drawers and closets also should be kept in order. A well-ordered closet or drawer makes it easily accessible to select and return teaching equipment. A simple procedure to follow is to have the shelves in the drawers and closets labeled so as to identify the objects to be placed on each.

Materials Collection and Distribution

In addition to organizational abilities, the teacher should also be a manager of the materials within the classroom. Materials collection, distribution, and preparation are all necessarily planned activities in which the teacher must be involved. Not only must teachers be concerned about these planned activities, but they must also provide for library and reference materials and other learning aids in the well-managed classroom.

Materials Preparation

Materials that are necessary for the day's activity should be prepared and ready for use when the activity begins. Children waiting for materials could create many behavioral problems. Not only do the children become impatient, but also they may lose interest in the project if the materials are not ready.

The teacher should not have just the minimum quantities of materials on hand; some extra materials should be available in case they are needed. Problems arise when children make a mistake and need to start over. It is apparent that the teacher should plan ahead and be ready for any type of emergency.

Distribution and Collection of Materials

Much of the teacher's time and energy can be saved if books, materials, and supplies are distributed in a businesslike preplanned system. Children can be assigned to distribute certain books or materials at the proper time. If classroom drawers and supply closets are kept in excellent order, the children will be able to get the materials quickly. The same children who distributed the materials could collect them and return them to the proper places in drawers, shelves, or closets.

When written papers are to be collected, the teacher could select a child from each row, table, or specific area of the classroom to gather these papers. This takes very little time and eliminates the noisy confusion that results when papers are handed up the row or around the table from one child to another. Some pupils, as they pass the written papers, stop to compare answers or other children's work and delay the collection of papers.

Library and Reference Materials

The teacher should provide library books and reference materials in the classroom. Many public libraries, as well as the school library, will allow large quantities of books to be checked out by the teacher at one time for classroom use. These books should be rotated every few weeks. Dictionaries and reference books, as well as maps, globes, and other learning materials, should be readily accessible.

Values

- Appropriate classroom management conditions the behavior in the school.
- Proper classroom management frees the teacher and the pupils for teaching-learning activities.
- An orderly and well-managed classroom environment encourages children to spend their energies in studying and learning.
- Classroom organization provides freedom and informality within the classroom; this is conducive to creating interested and active children in the learning process.

Limitations and Problems

- Many teachers consider classroom management problems as menial and *least* important in planning. Thus, they do not organize and manage their classrooms.
- Classroom management may become so routinized that humanizing of the curriculum and identity of the individual child are lost.
- Rules and regulations may be proliferated to the extent that the teacher may spend his or her entire time in this area rather than in creating a learning environment.

Illustrated Classroom Arrangements

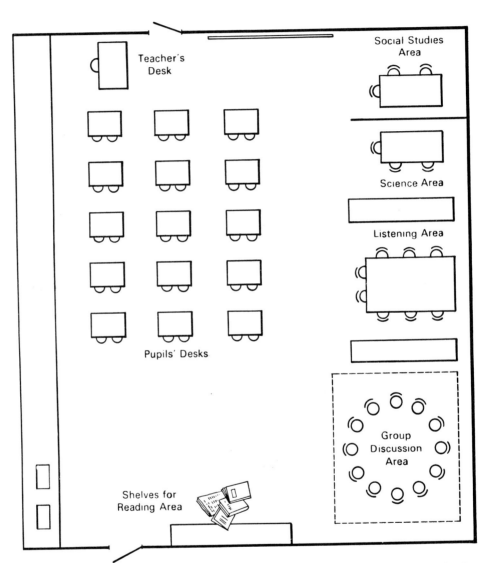

FIGURE 5–1 Room Arrangement for a Primary, Middle, or Upper Grade Classroom

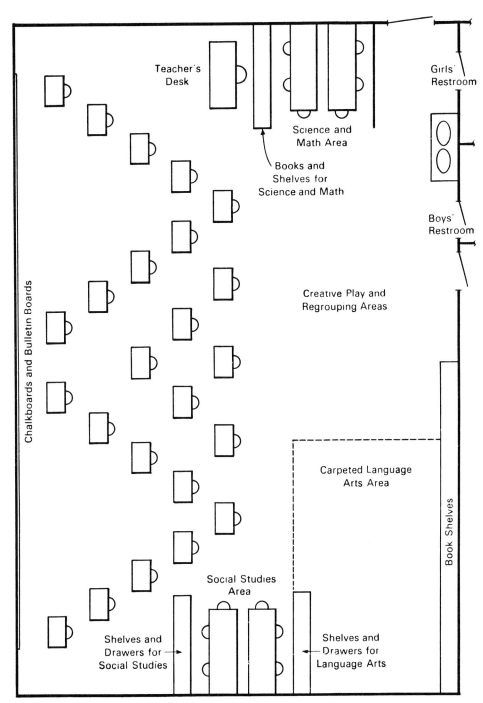

Teacher's Desk

Science and Math Area

Books and Shelves for Science and Math

Girls' Restroom

Boys' Restroom

Chalkboards and Bulletin Boards

Creative Play and Regrouping Areas

Carpeted Language Arts Area

Book Shelves

Social Studies Area

Shelves and Drawers for Social Studies

Shelves and Drawers for Language Arts

FIGURE 5–2 Room Arrangement for a Primary Grade Classroom

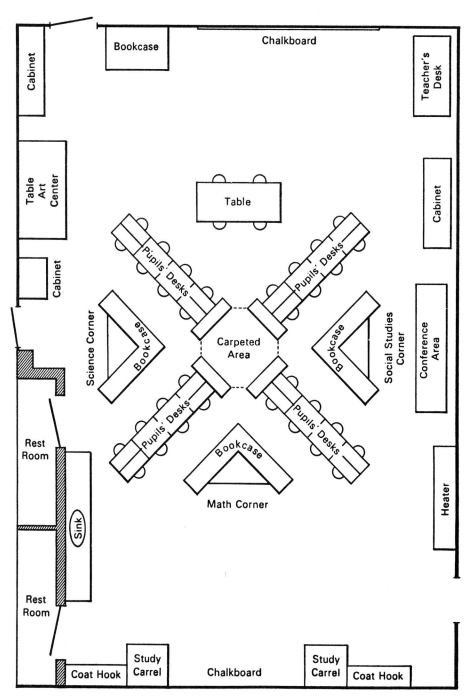

FIGURE 5–3 Room Arrangement for a Middle or Upper Grade Classroom

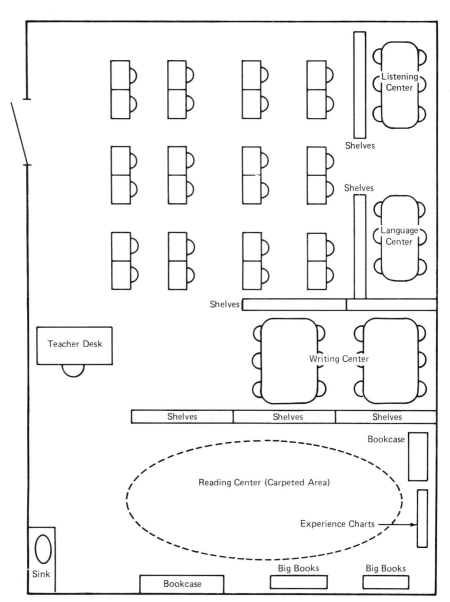

FIGURE 5–4 Room Arrangement for Whole Language Classroom in Primary Grades

Chapter 6

Classroom Discipline and Behavior

Overview

Key Concepts

- Misbehavior is a symptom of other problems.
- Pupils want and have a right to active participation in setting up their own rules of conduct.
- Pupil misbehavior must not jeopardize the learning environment of other children.
- Discipline procedures must be adjusted to individual differences among pupils.
- Appropriate classroom activities will usually result in good behavior.

Chapter Terms

- Discipline: A classroom organization conducive to orderly social conduct, leading to a self-disciplined individual.
- Reinforcement: The process of rewarding (reinforcing) desirable behavior immediately following the act, thereby "stamping in" the behavior.
- Punishment: The process of negatively reinforcing (administering an unpleasant or aversive reward) undesirable behavior or simply withdrawing positive reinforcement (e.g., a privilege or an object). Although punishment can be effective, its effect may be temporary if no new desirable behaviors are learned.

One of the most difficult tasks of teaching is to establish and maintain order in the classroom. Few hours go by without some behavior incident, be it large or small, needing a teacher's attention. All teachers of children have discipline problems.

Teachers must help pupils develop a desire to learn. Learning in today's schools, however, occurs in a social setting. Classrooms are crowded; individuals from all walks of life are thrown together; interests, abilities, and achievement vary tremendously within each class group. Such factors necessarily create problems of classroom order. Thus, the desire to learn must be carefully guided in such a way as to create optimum conditions for all. It is not too difficult to discover discipline techniques that work for the moment. It is more difficult to develop techniques that will eventuate into *self*-discipline. Nevertheless, this is the aim of effective teaching.

Fundamental Properties

The word *discipline* is derived from the Latin *disciplina,* which refers to teaching and learning. It is closely associated with the term *disciple,* which means to follow or study under an accepted leader. Over time, however, school discipline developed various negative connotations. Blind conformity was expected; failure to conform meant harsh, often brutal, physical attacks on pupils of all ages. Today it means many things to people. It is probably the most talked about but least understood of all problems of teaching.

The aim of good discipline is to help the individual adjust to the personal and social *forces* of his or her experiences. First, the child must develop socially acceptable ways of satisfying physical and psychological needs. Second, the child must adjust to the demands of the existing culture and institutions. Finally, the child often will have to adjust to varying standards between his or her home environment and those of the school. The problem of discipline today consists mainly of helping the child develop disciplined and acceptable inner controls.

There are several variables or properties that may cause behavioral problems. These variables can be classified into three broad categories as follows:

1. Teacher-caused problems
2. Pupil-caused problems
3. School-situation-caused problems.

Teacher-Caused Problems

Many discipline problems are teacher caused, such as the following:

1. Inappropriate activity for the time of day or circumstances
2. Sarcasm
3. Inconsistency
4. Being impolite and inconsiderate
5. Having favorites
6. Gossiping about pupils in public places
7. Failure to make class and lesson purposes clear to pupils
8. Using the same method day after day

9. Failure to provide for individual differences
10. Talking "over" noise
11. A classroom that is either too hot or too cold
12. Taking time out for calling roll, taking lunch money, and the like
13. Confusion resulting from disruption of class routines
14. Vague assignments
15. Emphasizing factual-type tests

Pupil-Caused Problems

A second variable contributing to disorder within a classroom can be considered to be pupil caused. Pupils are usually quick to exploit an unfortunate situation. Some of them dislike school and most teachers associated with it. Others, just like all human beings, react in terms of health, emotions, and passing interests. Certainly the home, family, and culture of the child can also affect the perception of the school and the classroom. The child's perceptions can ultimately establish priorities, values, and needs for learning, which can contribute to pupil-caused disorders in the classroom. A number of pupil-caused situations that tend to contribute to possible disorder in the classroom are as follows:

1. The child who "clowns" for attention in the classroom
2. The child from an emotionally unsound home
3. The child who is sick
4. The child who does not have space to do school work at home
5. The child who watches TV all night
6. The child who lacks reading skills needed for an assignment
7. The child who comes from a culture that feels it is "sissy" to read or go to school

School-Situation-Caused Problems

A typical elementary school may have all kinds of activities that disrupt the school day, such as the following:

1. The last few minutes of the day
2. The last few minutes prior to lunch
3. The last few minutes of the day on Friday
4. The first part of the class following recess or a fire drill
5. Before a holiday or classroom party
6. The first few days of school
7. Appearance of a substitute teacher

8. The last few days of school
9. Inflexible schedules
10. Disruptive announcements over the public address system
11. Unregulated visitor behavior
12. Poorly planned school activities schedules
13. Poor lighting and ventilation
14. Food smells from the cafeteria
15. Band and chorus practice next door

Development of Discipline within Children

Discipline is hard for children to learn because it is composed of innumerable specifics. Truth, honesty, dependability, respect for property, privacy, personality, helpfulness to others, and protection of smaller people are just a few of the rules of society that each new generation must learn to uphold. Some children learn such lessons at home and need only *apply* them at school. Others must *learn* the rules of the game. The acquisition and alteration of attitudes and values take time. Patience is essential. One's teaching task in discipline is similar to the task in any other field. Children learn some things by listening, but they are more likely to remember and act on their *own words and ideas*. They need to solve their own problems — to make proposals, seek out and analyze the available data, test their own hypotheses, and examine their own results.

Children will learn more quickly if they are permitted to assist in setting up their own rules of conduct. However, the teacher must retain the right to determine what action is needed when rules are broken. This is made necessary because behavior results from many *different* causes. The action to be taken must be determined by the causes and the individual involved. For instance, a class may decide that late assignments should not count as much as those turned in on time. There are times, however, when such action would be most inappropriate (sickness, special emergencies, etc.). The teacher must weigh each case separately.

How does one respond to misbehavior of stable children? One must first determine the causes. If the teacher decides that the individual does not yet know or understand what is expected, he or she should *talk, discuss,* and *explain.* This is effective at times; however, the problem may need more action than discussion and explanation.

Punishment and reward may be necessary at other times — both are effective and both are appropriate techniques to use. Whenever possible, though, reward (the positive approach) should be used. Punishment causes one to remember because of pain, discomfort, or fear, whereas reward gives pleasure or satisfaction.

Guidelines for Handling Class Disturbances

There are a number of general guidelines that many teachers have found to be effective. However, the reader is cautioned against assuming any fixed procedure in class disturbances.

Disturbing Conversation

Sometimes such a disturbance can be ignored. If it threatens to spread, the teacher can move to the area of disturbance. One may offer to help the pupils get started on an assignment. If the teacher is talking to the entire group, a pause or a question to one of the disturbing pupils can effectively solve the problem. Although some teachers are quick to separate pupils who disturb, this is often an inadvisable procedure. The practice may create resentment and serve to spread the problem to other parts of the room.

Passing Notes

Such activities are symptomatic of a boring experience or lack of appropriate challenge. Frequently a change of pace takes care of the situation. It is not appropriate to read notes aloud to the class.

Overdependence of One Child on Another

This is a problem that usually will work itself out. Such pupils sometimes need each other until wider social acceptance is possible. Wider social acceptance is encouraged through emphasis on group work in which pupils are grouped sociometrically.

Hostility between Individuals and/or Groups

Talk with each of the participants individually. Try to find the cause prior to any drastic attempts at reformation.

Cheating

Cheating may occur as a result of overemphasis on grades or the establishment of unrealistic standards. In Chapter 2, the importance of making assignments and tests commensurate with pupils' abilities was emphasized. If the task is too hard, pupils may be forced to cheat in order to meet the requirement.

Tattletales

Children should be taught the difference between tattletales and reporting. A tattletale is one who tells *personal* things, whereas a child who *reports* about another child has been given the responsibility to do so because the child being reported is breaking a *school* or *classroom rule.* Children need to learn and be helped to distinguish between tattling as a busybody operation and reporting as an essential group function. Tattling deals with the insignificant; reporting deals with consequential information regarding the health, safety, and welfare of the children in the class and with a particular classroom routine or regulation essential to effective classroom operation. Teachers need to treat tattling and reporting with consistency. Young children need many opportunities to consider the subtle differences between these two items.

Temper Tantrum

When a child in the classroom has a temper tantrum, everyone in the classroom should avoid giving the child an audience. The teacher should move the child to his or her desk or table, or the teacher may need to remove the child from the classroom altogether so other children will not give him or her an audience. The teacher may find out what caused the child to have a temper tantrum and then try to help the child see the behavior in a different way. This may prevent it from happening again.

Refusal to Comply with a Teacher Request

Sometimes a teacher makes a simple request only to discover that the child refuses to obey. What should be done under the circumstances? The action to be taken will, of course, depend upon the nature of the request. Refusal to comply with simple requests usually is associated with high emotional tension. Don't argue with the child; continued argumentative dialogue makes things worse. Don't make statements or threats that cannot be enforced or that give the teacher or the child no alternatives for subsequent behavior. Usually the teacher can take the child by the hand and direct him or her toward that which was requested; however, it may be necessary to take the child from the room to discuss the problem. It is very important, however, that teacher requests be followed. Failure to comply should be subject to certain consequences. Unreasonable requests should be avoided. A reasonable request for one pupil may be unreasonable for another. Provide a cooling-off, reflective period to allow both child and teacher to reduce emotional levels and to become more objective; then the problem may be more easily handled by both teacher and pupil.

Isolation

Separating a child from peers tends to reinforce the craving that induced the behavior in the first place. It may be necessary to isolate a pupil *temporarily* as a stopgap measure, but continued use of this technique can only lead to greater frustration and deeper feelings of guilt and resentment.

Removal from the Situation

While there will be times when a child must be removed from the classroom, it should be used only as a last resort. In such instances the teacher is admitting that one cannot handle the situation. When it becomes necessary, the offender should be sent to a specific member of the teaching or administrative staff. In other words, the child should not be sent from the room without adequate provisions for supervision.

Selected Discipline Approaches

Many classroom discipline attempts have been made by teachers throughout the years, from the *hickory stick approach* to a very complete and elaborate discipline program. Several discipline approaches have been selected to be reviewed so one can choose an approach or utilize a combination of discipline approaches that will meet the needs of the children and the teacher in his or her classroom. The selected discipline approaches to be reviewed are Canter's assertive discipline, Dreikurs's logical consequences, Glasser's reality therapy, Kounin's management skills, and Skinner's behavior modification.

Canter's Assertive Discipline

Lee Canter developed an approach to discipline called *assertive discipline*.[1] This approach has become very popular throughout the country during the past few years. The major strengths of this approach are that it is competency based and transfers responsibility for behavior from the teacher to the child. Canter stresses the following objectives for discipline:

1. Teachers have the right to teach. Teachers clearly communicate to their students their wants and needs in teaching. The teacher will not tolerate children who keep them from teaching.
2. Students have the right to learn. The teacher will not tolerate children who keep other children from learning.
3. Students will not be allowed to engage in activities that are not for their best interests or the best interests of other children.
4. When students respond appropriately, they will be rewarded immediately for that behavior.

The teachers use assertive responses that are clearly understood, short, and to the point. Consequences are established before the misbehavior occurs and are understood clearly by the students. Canter suggests that the first time in the day that a child misbehaves, his or her name is placed on the chalkboard; at the second offense a check is placed after the name; at the third offense a second check is given; and so forth. For each check, a certain length of time is spent after school. For the fourth offense, the child not only stays after school but must also go to the principal's office; at the fifth offense of the day the child must stay after school, go to the principal's office, and call home. For the sixth offense, the child is taken home or the parents are asked to take the child home.

Dreikurs's Logical Consequences

Rudolf Dreikurs views discipline as an ongoing process in which children learn to be responsible for their own behavior and to respect not only themselves but also others.[2] Children need to develop self-control. In developing self-control, he suggests that the teacher deal with the children in the classroom through the use of logical consequences. These consequences are established before the misbehavior occurs so the child may choose to act properly or choose the consequence of his or her misbehavior. In order for the solution to be logical rather than punishment, the consequence must be related to the misbehavior, be respectful, and be reasonable. He maintains that if any of the "three R's" are missing from the solution, then it is no longer a logical consequence but becomes a punishment. He also describes mistaken goals that motivate children to act as they do. The four mistaken goals identified by Dreikurs are (1) attention, (2) power, (3) revenge, and (4) assumed inadequacy. These goals that lead to misbehavior can be diffused or lessened by the teacher's actions, thus helping the child to develop self-control. His discipline approach would have teachers organize their classroom in a democratic way that allows students to be involved in establishing the standards of conduct in the classroom. In this approach, it is important to maintain the classroom with order, definitive limits, firmness, and kindness and allows the child to choose his or her classroom behavior.

Glasser's Reality Therapy

William Glasser developed a discipline approach called "reality therapy" to deal with children's personal problems.[3] The thrust of this approach is to help students develop better self-control and make important steps toward self-discipline. Glasser advocates a control theory to help students determine their needs and explore alternative choices for satisfying these needs. Schools cannot succeed at teaching the basics without attending to children's needs.[4] The emphasis in using reality therapy is upon establishing helpful relationships to accomplish tasks successfully. Reality therapy involves a teacher and a student in a mutual attempt to solve the student's problem. After showing the student that the teacher really cares about him or her and wants to help, the following steps are followed to solve the discipline problem: Help the student (1) identify his or her inappropriate behavior; (2) make a value judgment on his or her inappropriate behavior; (3) formulate a plan to improve his or her behavior; and (4) commit to a plan and follow it. If the child does not follow the plan, then the steps need to be reconsidered and possibly a new plan devised.

Kounin's Management Skills

Through research in the public schools, Jacob Kounin found that the teachers who exhibited two important management skills were very successful in classroom control.[5] These two skills were called "withitness" and "overlapping" behaviors. He defined "withitness" as the skill of knowing what is going on in the classroom at all times. A teacher with this skill is very much aware of what activity each child is involved in at any given moment. It almost follows the saying that many children use, "My teacher has eyes in the back of her head." The second important skill is that of "overlapping" behavior. Overlapping behavior is the ability of the teacher to deal with more than one issue or problem simultaneously. Although these two management skills do not constitute a complete discipline program, they can be developed by teachers to help them to be more successful in the classroom.

Skinner's Behavior Modification

B. F. Skinner's research has led to student control through what has been referred to as *reinforcement theory* or *behavior modification*.[6] An individual who is rewarded for what he or she is doing will continue doing what was rewarded. Conversely, if a student is punished for doing what he or she is doing, that person tends to discontinue the behavior. These rewards and punishments are called reinforcers. Thus behaviors of students are shaped through negative or positive reinforcement. The *token economy* has been used successfully for classroom control. Students are rewarded by being given tokens (such as chips, phony money, punch cards, etc.) for proper behavior. These tokens can then be traded for toys, books, food items, and so forth. Social reinforcers, such as praise for behaving properly, are used extensively by classroom teachers. In fact, most theories of classroom discipline depend upon reinforcers in one form or another.

Values

- Appropriate classroom activities will cause good behavior.
- Proper control and assistance will help the child to operate ultimately under his or her own initiative and direction.
- Positive motivation will decrease discipline problems. A close relationship between motivation and discipline is evident.
- The individual child's well-being will be enhanced through good practices in discipline. Techniques of discipline will be varied for each individual in the classroom.
- Good discipline will help the child adjust to the personal and social forces of his or her experiences.

Limitations and Problems

- Discipline problems probably are the most subtle and least understood in all aspects of teaching.
- Teachers assume that the disciplinary measures that seem reasonable to them should appear reasonable to children.
- Poor behavior is caused.
- The mere process of keeping pupils busy and orderly is not enough.
- Consistency on the part of the teacher in handling discipline problems is difficult to maintain.

Illustrations

Discipline and Motivation Guidelines

The principles that follow are basic to the problem of discipline. Guiding principles for effective motivation are essentially the same for effective discipline.

1. Reward is more effective than punishment.
2. Motivation that originates with the individual is more effective than that which is imposed from without.
3. Immediate reinforcement of a desirable response is needed.
4. Motivation is contagious; that is, a highly interested and motivated teacher tends to produce highly interested and motivated pupils.
5. A clear understanding of purpose enhances motivation.
6. All children have certain psychological needs that must be met.
7. Self-imposed tasks tend to create more interest than do teacher-imposed tasks.
8. "External" rewards sometimes are necessary and effective in stimulating initial interest.
9. Varied teaching techniques and procedures are effective in maintaining interest.
10. It is economical to capitalize on existing interests.
11. Activities that stimulate interest for the less able may be inappropriate for the more able, and vice versa.
12. High anxiety makes learning difficult or impossible.
13. Anxiety and frustration in mild form can be beneficial to learning.
14. If the task is too difficult and if assistance is not readily available, frustration quickly leads to demoralization.
15. Each pupil has a different level of frustration tolerance.
16. Peer group pressure is much more effective in promoting discipline than adult-imposed pressures.
17. All human beings need and expect the imposition of reasonable limits to guide their conduct.

Endnotes

1. L. Canter and M. Canter, *Assertive Discipline* (Santa Monica, CA: Canter and Associates, 1976).
2. R. Dreikurs et al., *Maintaining Sanity in the Classroom,* 2nd ed. (New York: Harper & Row, 1982).

3. W. Glasser, *Schools without Failure* (New York: Harper & Row, 1969).
4. W. Glasser, "On Students' Needs and Team Learning: A Conversation with William Glasser," *Educational Leadership,* March 1988, pp. 38–45.
5. J. Kounin, *Discipline and Group Management in Classrooms* (New York: Holt, Rinehart and Winston, 1970).
6. B. F. Skinner, *The Technology of Teaching* (New York: Appleton-Century-Crofts, 1968).

Chapter 7

Questioning Techniques

Overview

Key Concepts

- The questioning level employed in large measure determines the level of thinking elicited.
- Appropriately phrased problem questions (e.g., policy questions for class discussion) set the stage for use of higher order questions.
- Through appropriate probing techniques the learner may be encouraged to indulge in the higher process of reflective thought.
- Higher order questions necessarily incorporate the lower levels of cognition.
- Since evaluation questions call for personal reactions, they necessarily overlap with the affective domain.

Chapter Terms

- Recall questions: Questions that call for the recitation of specific facts, principles, or generalizations. Usually characterized by such key words as *who, what, when,* and *where.*
- Comprehension questions: Questions requiring understanding and manipulation of data through interpretation, summarization, example, and definition. Usually characterized by such key words as *how* or *why.*
- Analysis questions: Questions that call for taking apart data for the purpose of discovering hidden meaning, relationships, or basic structure. Characterized by using *established criteria* for discovering assumptions, motives, implications, issues, logical fallacies, and so forth.
- Evaluation questions: Questions that call for judgments, opinions, personal reactions, and criticisms, based upon the *learner's own criteria.* Usually characterized by such key words as *should, could, would, in your opinion,* and so forth.
- Problem (policy) questions: Open-ended questions, often *preplanned* by the teacher, that form the basis for an instructional experience. They often begin with the word *what* but sometimes may begin with such key words as *why* or *how.* The word *should* or *ought* is stated or implied in the question.

- Probing techniques: The method of asking intermediate questions, providing cues or hints, or asking for clarification after the pupil indicates an inability to respond effectively to an initial question. The technique is designed to lead the learner to the original question by capitalizing upon existing knowledge and understanding.
- Redirection: A method of involving more than one pupil in the answer to a question. Such questions often involve several reasons or factors, differences of opinion, and so forth.

Questioning is the heart of teaching and is involved in some way with every method and technique described in this book. Indeed, one might say that a teacher is (or should be) a professional question maker. Asking questions is one of the most effective means of stimulating thinking and learning. This chapter provides assistance in questioning techniques.

Fundamental Properties

Each instructional method is developed within a framework of critical thinking processes. The classroom question constitutes the teacher's major tool for encouraging thought processes. Critical thinking may be conceived as including all thought processes beyond the memory level. Thus it seems appropriate to treat questions from the vantage point of *levels*. Recall, comprehension, analysis, and evaluation provide such a frame of reference.

Recall Questions

The process of critical thinking begins with the knowledge of data or facts. Factual questions often involve the key words *who, what, when,* and *where* and have only one correct answer. The pupil is required merely to recall or recognize information or facts such as dates, events, persons, and places. Also included is *recall* of basic principles and generalizations.

Obviously such information is needed, but too often teachers never expect students to go beyond this level. The greatest problem involves determining what knowledge is worth remembering and how to structure learning around this so that it becomes a means rather than the end of instruction.

Though the recall of specific facts is essential to all levels of thinking, it must be remembered that unrelated facts are quickly forgotten.

Moreover, memorized knowledge may not represent a very high level of understanding. Above all, concentrating on memory neglects other intellectual processes learned through practice. Solving problems is learned by actual practice rather than by memorizing the inductive conclusions derived by others.

Comprehension Questions

After the learner gives evidence that he or she has the essential facts well in hand, questions to determine *understanding* are asked. Comprehension questions characteristically require the learner to *manipulate* information. One must relate facts, generalizations, and definitions. Key words in this category are *how* and *why*. Whereas recall questions require remembering, comprehension questions call for manipulation and modification in some way. To illustrate:

1. What factors contributed to the westward movement in the 1800s? (Involves recall of text materials.)
2. Why did the pioneers seek new lands? (Involves an understanding.)

Although the foregoing illustrations appear to be characteristic of the two levels cited, the first question could be comprehensive in nature if the pupil must draw inferences from various media sources. If, however, the answer is to be found in the textbook or if the information has been previously presented in the classroom or in a report, the question is merely one of recall. Likewise, the second question may be a memory item if the answer has been previously given to the pupil. Thus the *conditions* of a question must be known before it can be accurately classified. Question classification is a tool for recognizing the thought processes involved in answering them. For convenience, application-type questions are included as a form of comprehension. The same kind of reasoning is involved except that the pupil is not informed relative to the specific idea or concept to be applied.

Comprehension questions may be subdivided into four groups: interpretation, summarization, example, and definition. The first of these, interpretation, asks the pupil to show relationships between facts or ideas such as likenesses, differences, cause and effect relationships, or comparisons. Summarization merely requires the pupils to restate ideas in their own words. Examples call for an illustration of the idea involved. Definitions require pupils to develop their own explanations of an idea. (It cannot be one that has already been given.)

A major element of questioning tactics is knowing when and how to introduce higher order questions. A comprehension question, for example, may elicit a recall response or perhaps a personal reaction. In such cases the teacher should probe for the analysis expected. Thus a series of questions may be initiated.

Analysis Questions

The process of analysis involves taking apart information and making relationships in order to discover hidden meaning and basic structure. The pupil is able to read between the lines, to distinguish between fact and opinion, and to assess the degree of consistency or inconsistency. In science, for example, the pupil is able to distinguish between relevant and extraneous materials or events. Likewise, in the social studies area, a pupil is able to detect unstated assumptions.

Whereas comprehension questions emphasize *understanding,* analysis questions involve seeking out *underlying relationships* and *organizational patterns.* Certain key words suggest analysis. Among these are *assumptions, motives, implications, identification of issues, fallacies,* and processes of *induction* and *deduction.* Analysis questions ask the pupil to solve a problem by conscious observance of *established criteria* that follow established rules of logic and must be consistent with the known facts.

Analysis questions follow questions of comprehension. The reader will recall the comprehension question cited earlier: "Why did the pioneers seek new lands?" An analysis question could then be asked: "What *implications* can be drawn concerning their old farm lands?" (This question assumes that implications have not been drawn by others.)

Evaluation Questions

Included here under evaluation are two categories in the Bloom taxonomy labeled *synthesis* and *evaluation.*[1] Synthesis is the process of reassembly of ideas to develop new ones. At this point in the critical thinking process the learner offers proposals for solving the problem under consideration. Closely followed is the related aspect of evaluation in which the learner critically examines the proposals offered. Evaluation may be deferred if the objective is to generate as many ideas as possible. Frequently, however, evaluation follows immediately after an idea is proposed. Often this is accomplished in a *single pupil response.* For this reason the processes of synthesis and evaluation are treated as a single aspect of the questioning technique.

Evaluation questions call for comments involving judgments, opinions, personal reactions, and criticisms that are judged on the basis of stated criteria. These criteria may be imposed by the questioner or by the respondent. Such questions usually include or imply such key words as *should, could* or *would*. Questions such as "In your opinion . . . ," "What is your personal reaction . . . ," "How would you evaluate . . . ," "Do you think . . . ," tend to call for evaluations. Unless otherwise indicated, the pupil should state his or her opinion and then provide a basis for such views. It becomes apparent that there is no one right or wrong answer to such questions. Answers are judged on the basis of how well the response was defended. Sometimes a teacher may ask a pupil to state his or her views. In such cases the views are defended and judged on the basis of the pupil's frame of reference. "If you had an opportunity to move west with the pioneers, *what do you think* would be the problems you would face?" In this case the pupil would be expected to *state* and *support* his or her views. The question could be stated in another way, however. "If you could have moved west with the pioneers, how would the Indians affect your journey?" In this case the answer must be defended from a provided frame of reference of the teacher.

Evaluation questions involve both intellectual and emotional considerations. Accordingly, some responses will tend to be highly biased and opinionated. While this is to be expected on occasion, continued emphasis on acceptable criteria is needed to maintain objectivity.

Problem Questions

Although evaluation questions are considered to represent the highest order of complexity, some attention should be directed to those problem questions used as a starting point for most instructional methods. The various methods treated in subsequent chapters are developed within a broad framework of critical thinking or problem solving. Those that embody the entire problem-solving process are developed from broad problems of policy. A problem of policy is an open-ended question that implies a needed change from the status quo. Often it begins with the word *what*, but it may begin with such key words as *why* or *how*. The words *should* or *ought* also are stated or implied in the question. For example, "What action should be taken to keep the school yard cleaner?" It is assumed (by the wording of the question) that some further action is needed.

A problem of policy is most effectively treated when certain definable steps are followed. Each instructional method has its own unique problem-solving approach. Each level of questioning, previously described, usually will be employed. To illustrate from the preceding example:

1. What have we done to keep the school yard clean? (Recall question.)

2. Why is it necessary to keep the school yard clean? (Comprehension question.)
3. What are the benefits of a clean school yard relative to us in the school? (Analysis question.)
4. In your judgment, how has keeping the school yard clean helped us? (Evaluation question.)

Several or even all the questioning levels may be employed in each phase of the problem-solving process. Greater emphasis will be placed on certain questions at each level, however. For example, during the earlier part of a discussion recall questions will receive considerable emphasis.

Problem questions must be carefully preplanned. If such questions are ill conceived, the subsequent problem-solving experience is of limited value. The most common error results from confusion between certain types of evaluation questions and questions of policy. An evaluation question tends to deal with one possible solution to a problem, whereas a policy question opens the door to any number of possible solutions. In the preceding illustration, for example, one possible solution could be to make each class of pupils clean up and police the school yard by their room. Sometimes the teacher, due to his or her own advance understanding and/or existing biases, may word the problem as an evaluation-type question. To illustrate: "Should each class of pupils clean up around their own room?" Under such conditions, discussion tends to be limited to the merits and limitations of the one proposal.

Enhancing Pupil Answers

An understanding of question levels is but a small part of the art of questioning. As previously indicated, questioning techniques are directly or indirectly associated with all the "logical areas" of communication.

Probing for Answers

Probing for more adequate answers is a well-known but often neglected technique. Socrates, who lived in the fourth century B.C., became famous for his skill in eliciting correct responses through probing procedures. Probing, used when an initial response is inadequate, involves asking the *same* pupil a series of questions. There are two principal types of probing: prompting and clarification.

Prompting involves asking a series of recall questions designed to elicit those things the pupil knows relative to the original question. Prior to the prompting sequence it may be desirable to rephrase the question to be certain that the pupil understands what is being sought. The procedure is used when the pupil is suspected of possessing the necessary background knowledge for handling the question. It is designed as a guide in the critical thinking processes. To illustrate:

> *Teacher:* How does the principle of immunization work?
> *Pupil:* I don't know.
> *Teacher:* Using a smallpox vaccination as an example, what happens if the vaccination "takes"? (A different question, recall in nature.)
> *Pupil:* One usually gets sick and has a high temperature.
> *Teacher:* Good. Are there any other problems? (Recall question.)
> *Pupil:* One develops a sore at the place of the vaccination.
> *Teacher:* Fine. Now what does this suggest to you about smallpox? (Comprehension question.)
> *Pupil:* If one had smallpox, there would be sores all over his or her body; so I guess the one sore is a little bit of the disease.
> *Teacher:* Your answer is basically correct. Why is an individual made immune to the disease? (Analysis question.)
> *Pupil:* One's body, with the one sore, builds up defenses against the disease.

As the illustration suggests, the pupil is not told that the answer is wrong. Instead he or she is encouraged or reinforced at every step to help build confidence. Generally one should avoid interpreting or rephrasing the pupil's response. In addition, a teacher should not give up on a pupil if an answer is not immediately forthcoming. Doing this tends to eliminate an individual from the discussion. In some cases about 10 percent of a class may make 90 percent of the contributions.

Clarification is a probing technique that calls for a restatement or expansion of a response. It is usually used when the response is correct but still does not measure up to the teacher's expectations. Instead of giving hints, the pupil is asked to improve his or her response. Such comments as the following are often used: "Explain"; "Would you restate your answer in another way?"; "What else can you add?"; "Are there other reasons?" To illustrate:

> *Teacher:* What happens in the body when a person is immunized?
> *Pupil:* Well, we are usually immunized against such diseases as smallpox and measles.
> *Teacher:* These are good examples but what actually happens in the body when we are immunized against such diseases?

It may be necessary to do some prompting if the pupil is unable to clarify the original response satisfactorily.

Effective Techniques in Questioning

Most teachers and certainly pupils recognize that the teacher and a few individuals tend to do most of the talking in class. Although there are many psychological forces at work in any given class, there are certain techniques that may greatly reduce teacher talk and expand the number of participating pupils.

The most obvious technique is the practice of calling on *nonvolunteers*. When pupils realize that they are not likely to be called upon unless their hands are raised, they are likely to keep their hands down. The few pupils who do raise their hands tend to monopolize the experience. Usually, they are the ones who have a good grasp of the problem and who like the reinforcement answering provides. The teacher, in turn, is reinforced by the apparent group progress suggested by the volunteer respondents. Nonvolunteers, however, most need the experience of active participation. Pupil participation is enhanced when both volunteers and nonvolunteers are asked to respond. The teacher can simply announce that all individuals will be called upon.

Another effective technique to enhance questioning effectiveness is through *redirection*. Teacher talk can be minimized by asking questions that elicit several responses. This may involve a question in which several reasons or factors may be requested, or it may be one in which differences of opinion exist. Thus different pupils are expected to offer reasons or opinions. It may be necessary to cue the group to what is expected by saying, "This question has many parts to it. Please give only one when you answer." Redirection has the added advantage of encouraging pupils to respond to each other. (All too often the pattern is teacher-question-pupil response.)

Another rather obvious technique is stating a question prior to calling upon the individual. The teacher should pause for a few seconds after asking the question and before calling upon someone for an answer. If the teacher designates a respondent *prior* to asking the question, the rest of the class will tend to relax and may not even "hear" the question. By pausing, the teacher gives each pupil time to organize his or her thinking for a thorough answer. The higher level questions usually demand a few seconds for meditation.

Still another technique for enhancing question effectiveness is the practice of allowing adequate time for an individual to formulate a response. Some pupils need more time for expression than others. A teacher who habitually cuts a pupil off before he or she is finished tends to discourage the shy individuals. The teacher should avoid interpreting a pupil's response to fit his or her own criterion of acceptability. Clarification is in order here. Those pupils who tend to ramble on and on without actually saying what they mean can be encouraged to write out their thoughts before responding verbally.

Too often neglected is the relationship of questions to individual differences. Although dull pupils can handle higher order questions, they cannot be expected to bring in the degree of association expected of bright pupils. Likewise, some pupils tend to be more adept at divergent thinking than others. By adapting questions to the individual, greater attention to different approaches to an issue can be gained.

Values

- Questioning techniques apply to all instructional methods. The success of any given instructional experience is dependent largely upon how questions are handled.
- Critical thinking is encouraged through artful questioning above the recall levels.
- Questions calling for multiple answers cause a questioning pattern that is most helpful for pupil growth. The questioning pattern may be teacher-question-pupil response, pupil-respoonse, pupil-question-pupil response, and so on.
- Effective questioning tactics depend upon a climate in which participation is encouraged and answers are reinforced.
- Probing techniques enable the individual to judge the adequacy of his or her own response.
- Wide participation is achieved because the teacher calls on both nonvolunteers and volunteers.
- Individual differences among pupils in the classroom may be handled in questioning sessions by the effective teacher. Some children can handle thought-provoking questions while others can provide recall answers. Thus, all children may participate and contribute to a discussion.

Limitations and Problems

- Teacher behaviors of repeating questions, answering one's own questions, and repeating pupil responses tend to be major obstacles to effective questioning processes.

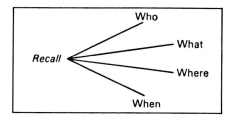
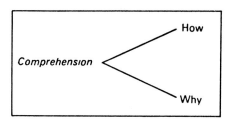

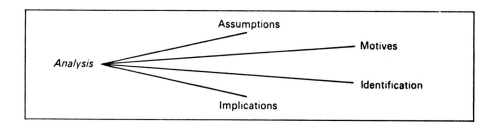

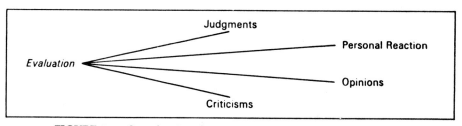

FIGURE 7–1 Question Levels

- Many teachers encounter difficulty in developing reflective thought in pupils because of the way they phrase their questions. A question that calls for a yes or no answer discourages discussion.
- The foremost problem associated with questioning techniques is the tendency to emphasize recall only.
- There is a tendency for teachers to "rush" pupil responses and to expect answers that fit the teacher's preconceived notions.
- A common problem among teachers is to involve relatively few pupils in the questioning process.

Questioning Illustrations

I. Useful in the reading and language arts areas
   A. Comprehension questions
      1. Explain Mary's plan to find her dog in the story you just read.
      2. How do you know in the story that Tom tried to do his best?

3. Why do standards for discussion sometimes prevent proper sharing in the classroom?
4. How does a study of language skills contribute to an understanding in the classroom?

B. Analysis questions
1. What was the author's purpose in writing the story you read?
2. What assumptions are suggested when the writer of the story said, "No one could go down in the cave"?
3. What are the main reasons for establishing punctuation rules for writing?
4. Which are the facts and which are the opinions in that report?

C. Evaluation questions
1. Which of the stories in this unit would you consider to be the best story?
2. What do you think of the character William Tomet in the story?
3. In your opinion do the *standards for interviewing* help you to make better interviews?
4. What is your personal reaction to the suggestion that research techniques be used in preparing for class reports?

II. Useful in science and arithmetic areas
A. Comprehension questions
1. Compare the moon, Mars, and Earth with respect to their sizes.
2. Give an example that suggests our mountains are constantly changing.
3. How would you define a cardinal number?
4. What does the fraction 4/3 mean?

B. Analysis questions
1. How are common respiratory diseases related to weather conditions?
2. What techniques can be used to determine if plants need air?
3. What must you know for that answer to be correct?
4. Which are the facts and which items are irrelevant to the arithmetic story problem?

C. Evaluation questions
1. In your opinion why do so many people talk so much about the weather?
2. For what reason would you favor doing a laboratory experiment over reading about an experiment done by someone else?
3. Which decimal fraction method would you consider to be better?
4. How would you judge the plausibility of your answer to that arithmetic story problem?

III. Useful in the social studies area
   A. Comprehensive questions
      1. What comparisons can be made between clothing in Colonial times and clothing today?
      2. What does that political cartoon mean?
      3. Explain the need for community helpers.
      4. State in your own words the reasons for different types of housing.
   B. Analysis questions
      1. In the story of Davey Crockett which activities are facts and which activities are the opinions of the writer?
      2. What was the author's purpose in writing those things about Abraham Lincoln?
      3. What were some of the motives that influenced the U.S. government to have people migrate to the Oregon Territory?
      4. What assumptions seem evident from pleas of the southern states to withdraw from the Union prior to the Civil War?
   C. Evaluation questions
      1. In your opinion should George Washington's birthday be celebrated on Monday even though it is not February 22?
      2. Of these two rules, which rule will result in the greatest good for the greatest number in our class?
      3. What is your personal reaction to the study of South America in our social studies class this year?
      4. Do you think we should celebrate a Betsty Ross Day?

Endnote

1. Robert T. Kloss, "Toward Asking the Right Questions: The Beautiful, the Pretty and the Big and Messy Ones," *Clearing House,* February 1988, pp. 245–248.

Chapter 8

Drill or
Practice Procedures

Overview

Key Concepts

- Drill or practice is an effective method for polishing mental or motor skills; it is often ineffective for cognitive and affective learning.
- Drill or practice basically is an individualized (rather than a group) method.
- Modeled demonstrations are essential in the development of mental and motor skills.
- To avoid monotony, the setting for drill and practice must be varied constantly.
- Practice does *not* make perfect; it makes permanent. Unless it is corrective in nature, usually requiring supervision, it may be worse than useless.

Chapter Terms

- Drill: Commonly used in connection with the teaching of mental skills. In this chapter the terms *drill* and *practice* are used interchangeably.
- Practice: Commonly used in connection with the teaching of motor skills. In this chapter the terms *practice* and *drill* are used interchangeably.
- Initial learnings: Basic cognitive understanding or perception of the rudiments of the skill to be learned.
- Varied contact: Preliminary practice of the skill being developed.
- Repetitive practice: That practice designed to correct minor details (problems) associated with a skill. Often referred to as adding "polish" to the skill.
- Kinesthesis: Usually used in connection with motor skill development, the term refers to muscular sensation or the "feel" for a desired movement. Verbal and visual kinesthetic cues are most useful in the early stages of learning, gradually giving way to internal cues as the skill develops.
- Overlearning: Learning beyond the point of bare mastery.

Ask almost any secondary teacher what training deficiencies, if any, are apparent in freshmen, and the response is likely to be direct and to the point. "They tend to be weak in the basic skills: reading, writing, and arithmetic." The solution: More drill or practice in these areas! Likewise, the lay public has repeatedly accused the schools of reducing or even eliminating drill from the schoolroom. Some teachers, however, dare not admit the use of drill as a teaching method, fearing they will be associated with a traditional approach to teaching. Although the technique has undoubtedly been misused in the past and accordingly is associated with a memoriter type of instruction, the modern school does *not* advocate the elimination of drill or practice. In fact, current teaching techniques demand even *more and better* practice than did those in the earlier schools.

Skill deficiencies, apparent among many pupils, usually can be more accurately attributed to *improper* drill procedures than to inadequate amounts. Following are some instances of *misuse* and *misapplication* of practice or drill:

A teacher asked pupils to memorize formulas.

A teacher required pupils to repeat verbally the steps of a problem-solving process.

A teacher asked pupils to commit to memory safety regulations.

A teacher requested pupils to memorize the state capitals and a series of important dates.

A teacher expected pupils to memorize selected passages of prose and poetry along with the names of important authors.

A teacher required that pupils memorize the rules of a game before participating in the activity.

The foregoing illustrations represent but a few of the inappropriate uses of practice or drill. What is there about these experiences that renders them inappropriate? Each of them violates at least one of the necessary conditions of effective practice. In the first place, practice or drill must be contained within the framework of a functional situation. Although pupils do need specifics, they are useful only as a means of deriving generalizations. Furthermore, drill prior to initial understanding is a waste of time. Finally, practice or drill must be restricted to the acquisition of skills. Drill applied to the development of understandings and attitudes is a useless endeavor.[1] Perhaps a thorough understanding of the meaning and function of practice or drill procedures will somewhat clarify the point.

Fundamental Properties

Drill or practice is an old, time-tested technique of teaching. It is essential to every subject area. Unfortunately, however, the method has been grossly misused. It seems likely that this state of affairs reflects a basic misunderstanding of the place for drill in teaching. This section emphasizes those fundamental processes that have a critical bearing upon this issue.

Necessary Initial Learning

Prior to engaging in any form of practice, an individual must develop a cognitive understanding of the basic function or purpose and the rudiments of the skill to be mastered. This usually involves some preliminary reading, participation in a discussion, listening to an oral presentation, and the like. In the motor skills area the importance of basic cognitive understanding is readily apparent; in the mental skills area, however, the problem is much less obvious. Drill without basic understanding is often confusing and usually a waste of time.

The Role of Demonstration in Drill or Practice

The processes of skill development involve both the cognitive and the psychomotor domains. This means that a basic understanding must be translated into verbal responses or motor movements appropriate to the skill. Thus it is almost essential that the learner have an opportunity to observe a modeled demonstration of the skill involved. Such an experience must be as consistent with basic cognitions as possible. All minor discrepancies should be clarified. The learner is then able to mimic his or her observation in the preliminary stages of application.

Drill or Practice as an Individualistic Process

In translating any cognitive learning into somatic movements, each individual is unique. In skill development orthodox approaches are encouraged. Ultimately, however, those practice exercises necessary for learning the "correct strokes" become an individual matter.

Occasionally it may be necessary for an entire class to sound out certain words in unison in the early stages of drill. Otherwise, drill is something that each learner must perform on his or her own. The same principle holds for a motor skill. Even though several pupils may be working or playing at the same time, the teacher must observe the progress of each pupil as the skill is perfected. For this reason drill or practice outside of the class setting is usually encouraged.

R00885 84868

Feedback in Skill Development

Skill development basically consists of solving mechanical problems. Basic to this process is immediate knowledge of results. In the early stages of skill development the learner should receive such feedback from one exploratory trial to the next. In a motor skill, for example, he or she must realize what the muscles *are* doing and what the muscles *should* be doing in order to perform the skill properly.

Although verbal feedback is reinforcing, visual perception is even better. Videotaped exploratory trials with immediate playback facilities are most desirable. Thus the learner is able to analyze his or her own performance and make necessary adjustments. Once an adequate perception of the movement is established, the learner is able to rely upon memory as a guide to performance. Verbal and visual cues, accordingly, are gradually eliminated.

Efficient Drill or Practice Sessions

Frequent, short drill or practice sessions are preferred. Especially in the area of mental skills the learner soon becomes exhausted. Fifteen- to thirty-minute sessions are most efficient. When an individual becomes exhausted, the frequency of mistakes increases. If repeated often enough, the mistakes may become "stamped in," rendering them especially difficult to dislodge. Although the same principle holds true in the area of motor skills, it may be necessary to lengthen practice sessions gradually for the purpose of developing "polish."

Daily practice is recommended. Less than once a week is probably not often enough for maintaining efficiency. The polish phase of skill development represents *overlearning* (learning beyond the point of bare mastery). Drill up to 50 percent is recommended for overlearning. A vocabulary skill, for example, that requires thirty minutes to learn may be efficiently drilled for forty-five minutes.

Kinesthetic Sense in Motor Learning

In the early stages of skill development motor pathways are developed through "trial turns." Varied tries at performing the skill call attention to certain patterns. Accuracy is not important at this point. With practice, however, each movement is refined partially by "feel"; for example, the learner begins to internalize the movements. Less conscious effort is required for the task than was originally experienced. This process varies with the individual and the particular skill involved.

As skill development progresses, the feel or "touch" for various

SOCIAL SCIENCES DIVISION
CHICAGO PUBLIC LIBRARY
400 SOUTH STATE STREET
CHICAGO, IL 60605

movements becomes increasingly evident. In order to enhance this experience, continued use of visual cues is desirable. Films, demonstrations, and the like help the learner "sharpen" his or her mental image of the skill to be mastered. In the advanced stages of motor learning kinesthetic sense becomes internalized.

Motor skills sometimes are developed inappropriately prior to any organized instruction. Relearning thus becomes extremely difficult, as a new set of guidelines (cues) must be established for developing the correct feel for the movement. The learner may revert to his or her old (outmoded) patterns without even becoming aware of the process. Even so, this kinesthetic sense accompanies learning and provides necessary feedback for the learner.

Appropriate Areas for Drill or Practice

Practice is appropriate whenever a more or less fixed pattern of automatic responses is needed. It is designed to extend or polish *skill* learning by adding meaning and associations to original learnings. Motor skills, habits, and mental skills are made more useful and meaningful through appropriate practice procedures. Many lessons in today's elementary schools are concerned principally with the acquisition of skills. Such skills as required in reading, spelling, and arithmetic make heavy demands on practice or drill procedures.

Drill especially has been subjected to severe criticism due to its misuse. Except in a few specialized cases (e.g., developing sequences or patterns), its use must be restricted to the area of mental and motor skills. The traditional practice of asking pupils to memorize (drill) specific facts in history, for example, represents a misuse of the method.

Drill or Practice Differ from Review

Practice and review are alike in that they both add to or supplement initial classroom learnings. Moreover, there is a substantial amount of practice or recall in review procedures. It must be remembered, however, that in review a minimum of time is devoted to the recall of basic concepts and that these concepts serve as a *means* to the major issue to be resolved: "What related problems seem to bear upon the things we have learned?" Furthermore, both practice and review, when properly used, ensure more permanent learning. The deeper understandings and associations gained through review, like the polish developed through practice, tend to make learning more functional, thus increasing retention.

As previously indicated, one of the major differences between practice and review has been too often overlooked. While practice techniques are most effective in the teaching of skills, they are not effective in the teaching of understandings, attitudes, and appreciations. In these areas, reviews are needed. Whereas review involves the processes of *group* deliberation or problem solving, practice techniques for the most part do not rely on group processes. Practice or drill can be considered an extension to the group problem-solving process—one of refining the *products* of deliberative processes. Another important distinction between the two techniques is that whereas a review may involve the entire class group, the practice or drill procedure must be individualized. In a review lesson, for example, the relationships and associations developed by one member can be especially helpful to the other class members. Practice or drill, however, usually is much more effective when individualized. Most of us can remember instances when the class was asked to repeat something in unison. Perhaps it was the letters of the alphabet or a rule in phonics. Recent investigation, however, has discredited such practices when used for this purpose. (See Chapter 20 for more information on the review method.)

Drill or Practice Techniques

As in any other method of teaching, there are certain steps that, if followed closely, will greatly accelerate the development of effective skills. Although the perfection of motor skills depends to some degree on innate ability, these skills seldom will be fully realized in the absence of an effective training program. Playing various games, for example, may be limited by native endowment, but the difference between one who has been taught properly and one who just picked up the game skills is obvious. The same principle holds true for other skills. Teaching, likewise, is a complex of *skills* that can be developed. Although some individuals possess more natural abilities than others, appropriate instructional procedures can be of invaluable assistance to most of them. The cliché that "teachers are born and not made" has been thoroughly disproved. Perhaps as a consequence of the earlier and false notion that skills cannot be taught, they were for a long time left to chance. Even today some teachers make relatively little systematic effort in the development of mental skills among pupils.

As a result of extensive investigation, educational psychologists have been able to offer many useful clues to the effective development of skills. Three steps contribute greatly to the development of skills: development of initial learning, varied contact, and repetitive practice.

Initial Learning

A skill, like all learning, is first introduced by explaining to the learner its purpose. Once the purpose is thoroughly understood, verbal instruction on the rudiments of the skill is given, often accompanied by a demonstration of the skill, in order to promote full comprehension of the purpose of the activity and the general form and sequence of events to be followed.

Detailed explanations or demonstrations should be avoided at this point. If more than the rudiments of the skill are presented, thinking processes may become confused. A teacher, for example, would introduce an arithmetic computation problem by going through the steps completely and by demonstrating how to do the problem. Later, if necessary, detailed explanation may be helpful.

Varied Contact

After being briefly introduced to a skill in a functional situation, the learner must have direct contact with the activity in a variety of meaningful situations. The learner must be given an opportunity to engage in exploratory trials, ask questions, observe skilled performers, inspect diagrams, and so on. In terms of the problem-solving process this phase might be called *evaluation of alternative proposals* since during this phase pupils develop and test their own way of performing the skill. This is indeed the *creative* aspect of skill development.

The teacher can be especially useful in the exploratory phase of mastering a skill by helping pupils capitalize on strengths and minimize weaknesses. By pointing out their strengths and weaknesses, the teacher can aid learners in diagnosing their own problems. Recognizing the importance of reinforcement or reward in learning, the teacher should make critiques as positive as possible.

One of the greatest problems a teacher will encounter in skill development is that of getting learners to see their mistakes. The mere act of telling a person that he or she is omitting words while reading orally, for example, may have absolutely no effect on the learner for the simple reason that he or she has developed an internalized habit of omitting words while reading orally. An audiotaped playback of a selected reading, however, may produce almost immediate corrective efforts.

Oddly enough, some teachers assume that verbal instruction is all that is needed to develop skills. The assumption is made that once a person understands how a skill is performed, he or she can complete the process through individual initiative. An excellent example of such a fallacy can be found in the teaching of instructional methods courses at some colleges and universities. The complaint is often heard, "We tell (or less commonly, show) prospective teachers how to teach, but they tend to forget these learnings when they start teaching." A more accurate statement would be that the learners simply have not been prepared to utilize the skills involved. They need varied contacts with skills under controlled and closely supervised conditions that approach actual situations as nearly as possible. Simulated teaching experiences in a methods course cannot produce proficiency in the skills needed, but they can broaden understanding and perception of the intricate relationships involved. If a teacher is to use review, drill, dramatic play, class discussion, and the like effectively, verbal explanations, demonstrations, *and* varied direct contact with the skill prior to practice teaching are needed. It is only in practice teaching and later that polish is achieved.

Repetitive Practice

A skill must be repeated often for the purpose of refining it. The condition under which it is performed, however, should be *varied* as often as possible in order to prevent boredom and, more importantly, to enhance the likelihood of its transfer to related situations. Let us take an example from the area of reading. A group of pupils in beginning reading could practice a phonic sound by hearing the teacher make the sound; they might sing a song containing the phonic sound; they could say words containing the sound; they could hear rhyming words containing the same sound. The drill is similar, but the situations have been varied.

Although repetitive practice is essential in the perfection of a skill, forcing pupils to practice will have little positive result. The pupils must be self-motivated to improve their skills through practice.[2] Following a period of accelerated learning that results from early practice sessions, many learners reach a *plateau* on their progress. This probably indicates a need for a more thorough understanding of the relationship of certain details to the total skill. At this point added encouragement and direction from the teacher are extremely useful. A chart showing the individual's progress tends to contribute to continued interest and improvement.

Practice or repetition can become monotonous very quickly, even under the most favorable circumstances. When individuals practice for a purpose very important to them, motivation can remain high for long periods of time. Too frequently, however, classroom problems are more remote to the learner than might be desirable. The very nature of the materials sometimes accounts for this difficulty. Drill in important terminology and sequences of events, for example, may be important but not in itself very interesting. Short games offer excellent opportunities for motivating pupils. Games can be created in which winning is not essential in order to encourage those pupils who really need the practice.

Planning for Drill or Practice

Development of motor skills has long been a familiar aspect of formal education. The technique is relatively easy to apply simply because the learner quickly becomes overtly active. The individual asks questions; difficulties can be observed and corrected as the skill is developed.

In the realm of mental skills, however, the task is much more complicated. Although the *processes* are comparable, there are fewer observable activities that are useful for effective guidance. While memorization is frequently stressed (sometimes inappropriately), seldom are memory techniques provided.

In teaching a specific skill, whether it be in a game or subject matter area, the teacher should consider an outline with the following steps:

1. The teacher diagnoses the child's need in the skill area.
2. The teacher instructs or demonstrates the skill to the child.
3. The teacher organizes an activity that he or she directs with the child participating in the skill.
4. The child works on the skill with the teacher "spot checking" his or her performance in the skill.
5. The child continues to work on the skill with a variety of materials in order to develop overlearning of the skill.
6. An evaluation is made by the teacher or child to determine the mastery of the skill.

After the steps in this outline are completed, the entire process would be repeated with a new skill.

The sequence of experiences is based upon much careful investigation in the area of skill development. It is as equally applicable to the development of motor skills as it is to the development of skills in reading, language arts, social studies, science, and arithmetic.

Values

- Drill or practice is the basic instructional method for polishing mental and motor skills.

- The individualistic nature of the method is conducive to direct pupil involvement. Especially in the motor skills area interest is maintained.
- Drill or practice, when spaced appropriately, can reduce the rate of forgetting and contribute to continued development of the skill.
- Practice develops habits. Thus desirable habits developed during the elementary school years tend to become a part of one's life style.

Limitations and Problems

- Drill or practice in the cognitive domain often is inappropriate. It is in this realm that the method has been widely misused.
- Since early drill or practice is largely exploratory, diagnosis is essential. Misguided drill or practice may impede appropriate skill development.
- In the early stages of skill development accuracy rather than speed is emphasized. Skill development being largely individualistic in nature, it is sometimes difficult to achieve this balance.
- Repetitive drill or practice may become monotonous unless a variable learning environment is provided.
- Overlearning in the latter stages of skill development is desirable. Since the degree of overlearning will depend somewhat upon the learner's purpose, it may be difficult to work out appropriate practice sessions with each individual learner.

—————— **Illustrated Drill or Practice Techniques** ——————

I. Useful in any motor skills area
   Videotaped Explorations Set up your class into five-minute microteaching sessions. (This assumes basic understanding of the rudiments of the skill.) Provide opportunities for pupils to select either a progressive or a repetitive task sequence.

   Immediately following the experience, replay for study and analysis. Have the pupils critique themselves in terms of delivery, continuity and sequences, and specific techniques and styles used. Finally, ask the pupils to identify different ways of performing key phases of the experience. (This tends to expand thinking, thereby encouraging new insights in the area.)

II. Useful in the reading area
   The teacher places many different two-syllable words on the blackboard that follow the pattern of two consonants between two vowels, such as *butter*.

The teacher pronounces each word and then encourages the children to examine the words in order to see the pattern. After examining the words, the children recall from memory other words that fit the same pattern.

The teacher then leads the children in generalizing the rule for syllabication and they then verbalize the syllabication rule.

The pupils should practice this rule by using syllabication in contextual situations.

III. Useful in movement education

The individual nature of drill provides an excellent opportunity for the use of pupil teams (in both mental and motor skills areas).

After the basic rudimnents are understood, gross body movements follow. The participant must progress through a stage of body movement in a particular sequence. Another pupil or the teacher can be extremely useful in providing much needed feedback and diagnosis.

Following short practice sessions, critiques may be made until the entire sequence can be completed successfully. The teacher will concentrate on common problems and unusual difficulties as he or she moves from one group to another.

IV. Useful in the language arts area

Set up a role-playing opportunity. Assign pupils specific roles, such as hosts and hostesses, visiting celebrities, young and old adults, children, etc. Have each participant plan an aspect of courteous behavior required at a party for the role played.

V. Useful in career education, arithmetic, or social studies areas

Develop a mock business firm that employs skilled workers. With imagination, roles can be established for a variety of skill levels.

Endnotes

1. A possible exception involves drill for mastering patterns, sequences, or order of arrangement.
2. Debra Baird Rooks, "Repetition: Catalyst for Motivating Student Success," *Reading Improvement,* Winter 1988, pp. 258–262.

Brainstorming Techniques

Overview

Brainstorming literally means using the *brain* to *storm* a problem. It is a technique by which a group attempts to find a solution for a specific problem by amassing all the ideas spontaneously contributed by its members. Brainstorming is a technique of applied imagination or creativity.

The precise relationship between creative imagination and problem solving is not fully understood. Most writers suggest, however, that too much emphasis on the formal structure of analytical thought processes is detrimental to creative (sometimes called intuitive) thought. Routinized activities of any sort seem to be detrimental to the process. However, ideas reached intuitively must be checked and refined by analytic methods. The procedure described in this chapter enables the learner to exercise considerable creativity within the broad framework of the problem-solving process.

Fundamental Properties

Brainstorming embodies the fundamental aspects of creative thought. An idea is creative when it possesses an element of novelty that can be applied to a given situation. The process includes the ability to produce ideas that are relevant and unusual, to see beyond the immediate situation, and to redefine the problem or some aspect of it. The properties described in what follows are basic to creative thinking. Techniques of brainstorming seem to encourage and nurture many of these concepts.

Originality

The ability to produce unusual ideas, to solve problems in unusual ways, and to use things or situations in an unusual manner is the essence of originality. Sometimes it is viewed as uncommonness of response—the ability to make remote or indirect connections. Creative individuals, being skeptical of conventional ideas, are willing to take the intellectual risks associated with creative discovery.

Persistence

Creative people are usually persistent individuals who are willing to devote long hours to a given task and to work under adverse conditions, if necessary. Above all, creative people are willing to face failure. Frustrations seem to motivate them on to increased effort.

Independence

Creative individuals are independent thinkers who look for the unusual and the unexpected. Such people notice things that other people do not, such as colors, textures, and personal reactions. Frequently, these people explore ideas for their own sake to where they may lead.

Unlike the nonconformists who flout convention because they feel a compulsion to be different, independent thinkers maintain a balance between conformity and nonconformity. Unlike conformists, creative persons are open to experience and confident in the worth of their ideas, although they are their own most severe critics.

Involvement and Detachment

Once a problem has been identified, creative persons quickly become immersed in it, first researching how others have tried to solve it and becoming acquainted with its difficulties and complexities. Thus involvement sets the stage for their own creations. Creative individuals soon become detached enough to see the problem in its total perspective. By setting work aside temporarily, creative people give freedom to develop.

Deferment and Immediacy

Creative people resist the tendency to judge too soon. They do not accept the first solution but wait to see if a better one comes along. This tendency to defer judgment seems to be an attribute of an open-minded person—one who is unwilling to reach a decision prematurely.

Incubation

By putting the problem aside temporarily, creative people allow the unconscious to take over, making various associations and connections that the conscious mind seems to impede.

The incubation period may be long or short, but it must be utilized. Sleep or almost any change of activity helps to encourage illumination. This period of purposeful relaxation permits the mind to run free.

Illumination

After a period of frustrated effort, creative people may sometimes suddenly solve a problem. This sudden flash of insight is believed to be the fruits of unconscious inner tensions. It may be that the powers of association are enhanced when the mind runs freely on its own. The flash usually occurs after a period of incubation when individuals are not actively pursuing the problem.

Verification

Although illumination provides the necessary impetus and direction for solving a problem, the solution must be verified through conventional objective procedures. Sound judgment must complete the work that imagination has set in progress. Indeed, a flash of insight may be partially, if not totally, unreliable and merely serve as a catalyst for liberating the creator from a restricted approach to the problem. Sometimes one flash of inspiration will precipitate others that must be verified.

Brainstorming Procedure

Basically creativity is an individualized process, but as with analytical thought, it can be encouraged and enhanced through group ideation processes. Brainstorming techniques have been especially effective in this regard.

Identifying the Problem

In preparation for a brainstorming session the leader (a pupil or the teacher) selects a *specific,* as opposed to a general, problem. The problem "How should we behave on a field trip?" is too broad. To narrow the problem, two or three subproblems might be formulated: How should we behave on the bus? How should we behave going to and from the bus? How should we behave at the water station?

When the problem has been reduced to its lowest common denominator, the selected subproblem(s) is posed as a concise, definite question. Questions of what, why, where, when, who, and how serve to stimulate the creation of ideas. For example: Why is it needed? Where should it be done? Who should do it? How should it be done?

Preparing the Group

New participants need to be conditioned for their initial session. A warm-up practice session on a simple problem will stimulate the production of ideas. Primary grade children may need this warm-up practice session each time the brainstorming technique is used.

Leading the Ideation Session

In preparation for the actual brainstorming session, the leader explains and writes out four basic rules that must be faithfully followed:

1. Criticism is ruled out: Judgment of ideas must be withheld until later.
2. "Freewheeling" is welcomed: The wilder the idea the better; it is easier to tame down than to think up.

3. Quantity is wanted: The greater the number of ideas, the greater the likelihood that the idea will be useful.
4. Combination and improvement are sought: In addition to contributing ideas of their own, participants should suggest how ideas of others can be turned into *better* ideas or how two or more ideas can be combined to form still another idea.

The setting for brainstorming is informal and relaxed. The leader begins the session by explaining the problem, writing the four basic rules on the chalkboard, and indicating that when a rule is violated, a specific signal will be used to stop the violator, like a knock on the desk. Only one idea is offered at a time. The leader especially encourages ideas precipitated by previous ones. If several children desire to speak at once, the participants are encouraged to jot down ideas before they are forgotten. Because ideas tend to be contagious and many persons often desire to speak at once, groups of about eight to twelve are preferred. Much larger groups, however, have been effective under the direction of expert leaders.

Sometimes the leader may need to repeat ideas to encourage additional creative thinking. The objective is to "milk the group dry of ideas." In addition to opening up new channels of thought, the leader keeps prodding with statements such as "What else?" "I cannot believe that you have expressed all your ideas." Short, silent periods are to be expected as children try to think up new ideas. It is usually in the final stages of the session that the most unique and useful ideas emerge. Most ideation sessions will not exceed fifteen minutes. If the group is large and/or if more than one subproblem needs exploration, two or more subgroups may be utilized.

Utilizing Afterthoughts

In closing the brainstorming session, ideas generated should be counted and reviewed. This serves to stimulate individuals to think further on the problem. The recorder(s) or teacher can quickly scan the ideas for categories. A glance at the full list usually indicates from three to five classifications. The leader (a pupil or the teacher) asks the participants to keep the problem on their minds until the next day, when they will be asked for afterthoughts. This can be made as a definite assignment. Such an incubation period sometimes produces some of the most valuable ideas.

Processing Ideas

After all ideas (including afterthoughts) have been reviewed, they are screened, edited, and placed in appropriate categories. While this may be done by the entire group, it is usually preferable to have a committee of three to five pupils do it. Usually the teacher will want to assist in this process. It is desirable to establish a list of criteria for evaluation of ideas. One group established the following:

1. The idea must be stated in a short, clear manner.
2. It should be possible.
3. It should have some element of the unusual, the novel.

The committee or teacher must exercise due caution in the elimination of ideas. Some of the "wildest ideas" may contain elements of imagination that are not obvious at first glance.

Implementing Ideas

How a group uses the ideas of a brainstorming session is largely dependent upon its purpose. For example, the purpose may involve techniques of oral or written expression in art, literature, or music. It may involve novel ways of playing certain games, of memorizing, of doing some chore. It may even deal with certain aspects of human relations, such as how to keep calm when one is angry. Whatever the purpose may be, ideas must be implemented. This may be accomplished on an individual basis or in subgroups. Sometimes the results of brainstorming sessions may be shared with the children in the classroom. On other occasions they may be of a private nature and may not be shared with anybody else except the teacher.

Deriving Generalizations

As a concluding experience, the group may draw generalizations based upon various action programs. This enables all members to profit from the experiences of many. Certain experiences may set the stage for the enactment of one or more selected situations for further study and analysis. Dramatic play (described in Chapter 11) has been most useful in this connection.

Planning for Brainstorming

Although the brainstorming session is an informal one, it must be carefully planned. The following plan indicates one way of stimulating a group to creative activity. Since the creative act is in itself a unique experience to the individual involved, the brainstorming method will take on many different dimensions depending upon the purpose being served.

─────────   **Lesson Plan Illustration (language arts area — fifth grade)**   ─────────

Concept   Book reports can be imaginative and interesting.
Problem   What different ways are there to make book reports?
Goals   After this lesson the pupil should be able to make different book reports, as evidenced by:

1. The variety of book reports he or she used.
2. The use of these ideas in his or her own book reports.

Lesson Approach   As has been previously pointed out, book reports can be different from the written-type book reports we are using now. Is it necessary to write out the book report by putting down the title of the book, the main characters in the book, and then a short synopsis of the story? Have you ever thought of other ways to report on a book? Is it possible to report on a book other than by writing about the book? Today we will attempt to determine other ways to do book reports.

For the next few minutes we are going to "storm the brain" for ideas concerning how we might report on a book we have read. This experience will be fun for all of us if we follow four simple rules. (Put on board.)

1. Criticism is ruled out.
2. "Freewheeling" is welcomed. (The wilder the idea, the better.)
3. Quantity is desired.
4. Combination and improvement of ideas are sought.

(Appoint recorders from opposite sides of the room.)

I will knock on my desk when one of the rules seems violated. Just raise both hands when you desire to express a "hitchike" idea.

Lesson Development   What different ways may we make book reports? Suggested categories for book reporting (to be inserted as the flow of ideas diminishes):

1. Drama: A child could dramatize the book read by using puppets as principal characters in the book and acting out an important incident in the book.
2. Drawing: A pupil could report this book by drawing comic strips to report the important sequences of the story in the book read.
3. Machine reporting: A child who had read the book could report a dramatic scene by use of the tape recorder and present it to the class members.

4. Discussion: Several people who had read the same book could meet together and discuss the book with one another.

Reviewing Ideas (first day)   Now that it seems as if our group is "dry" of ideas, let us determine how many have been produced in the last fifteen minutes. (Ask the recorders to give the number and to suggest categories.) Do you suppose that we *could* produce even more ideas if we were really to try? That is just what I want you to do.

Utilizing Afterthoughts   Let us each write out our problem and the categories suggested by our recorders. Keep the problem in mind until tomorrow when I will call for your additional ideas. Just keep your mind open, jotting down ideas as they occur to you. Such afterthoughts may occur to you when least expected, so keep pencil and paper near you at all times.

Processing Ideas (second day)   (Take up lists of additional ideas and pass along to the recorders.)

I am appointing a committee of five to screen, edit, and categorize your ideas of how we can report on books read. (The teacher will assist the committee as needed.) We will each receive a reproduced list of this master list.

Implementing Ideas (third and fourth days)   Study our list of ideas and check two or three of these that you wish to use for reporting a book you have read.

Assignment   Your task is to report on a book you have read utilizing a suggested idea. Keep in mind that the idea may be expanded and altered as you apply your imagination. You should write out the original idea, however. We will then let the class try to relate your book report to our list of ideas.

Deriving Generalizations   As a result of this experience, a number of principles or ideas are evident relative to book reporting. Let us list some of these.

Suggestive Ideas (to be derived by pupils)
1. Book reports can be fun.
2. Variety in book reports is interesting for everyone concerned.
3. We learn about drama and art when making book reports.

Values

- Brainstorming helps prepare pupils for truly creative individual effort.
- The ideation session tends to minimize existing inhibitions that ordinarily tend to block creativity.
- Brainstorming is useful for generating alternatives to the resolu-

tion of problems. It is also useful in the processing and implementation stages of creative experiences.

- The brainstorming experience generates enthusiasm for learning. Once their imagination is activated, most pupils progress at an accelerated rate.

Limitations and Problems

- Despite the many values of group brainstorming, individual ideation usually is more valuable and can be just as productive. Actually the process incorporates both individual and group ideation in a three-stage approach: individual creation of an idea, group verification of the idea, and then development of the idea to its conclusion.
- The effectiveness of a brainstorming session is dependent upon the appropriateness of the problem employed. There is a decided tendency among teachers to select problems that are too complex.
- Production of ideas through brainstorming sessions is merely an initial phase of creativity. Analytical problem-solving techniques must complement this process.
- Brainstorming places the leader (teacher) in a new role. Instead of passing judgment and giving direction, he or she must develop an atmosphere free from inhibitions. Some teachers (as well as pupils) experience difficulty in making such a transition.

Illustrated Brainstorming Memos

I. Useful in social studies area (first or second grade)
   Concept   Safety rules of school prevent accidents.
   Problem   How can we prevent accidents on the school grounds?
   Suggested Categories
   1. Playground equipment: Use styrofoam- and rubber-protected playground equipment.
   2. Children: Wear protective clothing.
   3. Automation: Have "people-movers" that keep children from falling or running into others.

II. Useful in the science area (third or fourth grade)
   Concept   Plants, properly displayed, will interest people in seeing our work.
   Problem   How can we display the plants we have grown for open house?

Suggested Categories
1. Colored lights: To make display pretty.
2. Labeling: Paper placed behind the plants to label the plant parts.
3. Grouping: Place the same kind of plants together in a separate display throughout the room.

III. Useful in the music area (upper grades)
Concept Music portrays moods to the listener.
Problem In what ways are moods reflected in music?
Suggested Categories
1. Loud: Music that is loud may show excitement.
2. Soft: Music that is soft may show calmness.
3. Rhythm: Music rhythm may show action.
4. Instruments used: Various individual instruments are used to show various moods.

Chapter 10

Discussion Methods

Overview

When individuals engage in discussion, they ponder or meditate; they think critically.[1] They reflect on their ideas along with those of their peers. Such individuals are searchers and inquirers; in effect, they say, "Here are my ideas. How do they relate to your opinions and the facts of the situation?" They are willing to alter views that seem inadequate under the scrutiny of thoughtful analysis. Views are not changed, however, on the basis of peer pressure or emotion. If the objective evidence seem to warrant reassessments of tentative ideas and assumptions, the participants are ready to adjust accordingly.

Discussion is most appropriate when areas of controversy exist. Although a rather poor means of disseminating information, discussion is ideal for evolving, sorting, and sifting facts and values essential for the resolution of problems. Discussion is ideally suited to attaining the higher cognitive and affective goals.

Fundamental Properties

Discussion essentially embodies the basic properties of the democratic process. Discussion is based upon the assumption that individuals, when sufficiently informed on an issue, are capable of decision making in an atmosphere characterized by a free interchange of ideas and expressions. It is the responsibility of the discussion leader to create an appropriate environment for open reflection.

Open-Mindedness

Discussants are receptive to new ideas. They examine or ponder new ideas alongside their own notions, making objective comparisions and contrasts. Above all, the discussants must cultivate the ability to look at themselves and their ideas objectively and dispassionately. First of all, they seek to identify their own biases and prejudices. They must seek to avoid either-or thinking, recognizing the possibility of middle ground. This does not mean, of course, that they must change their attitudes. It does suggest, however, that each participant probably will see his or her own notions as not quite as good and the ideas of others as not quite as bad as he or she had originally seen them.

Flexibility

As implied in the foregoing, the discussants are willing to change their minds on the basis of logical, objective evidence. They do not necessarily do so, however. If, on the basis of his or her considered judgment, other ideas must be rejected, the individual makes a stand.

Even then discussion evolves into opposing camps, the discussant must be flexible enough to understand other views from the frame of reference of those involved. In rare instances a discussion group may merely agree to disagree.

Objectivity

Although the spirit and life of a discussion is projected through basic human emotion, intellectual processes of objectivity are emphasized. Ideas advanced by others are accepted on their own merits. Sources of information are frequently cited; evidence that might discredit certain facts or evaluations is brought into the open forum of reflection. Emotionalism, through persuasive language and gestures, is definitely discouraged. Even in a teacher-led discussion, contributions or inferences by the teacher must be open to careful scrutiny.

Reflective Process

The basis purpose of discussion is to reflect upon information and ideas that lead to the resolution of a stated problem. Accordingly, there are no speeches in a discussion. The discussants make their points, contribute a bit of information or ask a question, and then wait for somebody else to react to their contribution. The discussion leader (a pupil or teacher) reflects questions back to the group for analysis. Even in a teacher-led discussion the teacher must be viewed as one of a panel of equals. In attempting to accomplish this "impossible" task, the teacher should develop skillful questions designed to encourage penetrating analysis and evaluation of ideas.

Discussion Procedure

When people associate with each other, they usually discuss. Individuals often find solutions to their daily problems by talking them over with others. Ask your neighbor what he or she thinks of the slate of candidates for the school board and he or she will probably respond with, "I don't know; what do you think?" After some *discussion* it is quite likely that both you and your neighbor will have clarified your views on the problem. Such informal discussion goes on continually in and out of the classroom. Indeed, it is basic to the democratic process.

To be effective as an instructional method, however, discussion must be carefully planned and executed. Although there are a number of variations and interesting modifications, the basic aims of discussion are to stimulate analysis, to encourage interpretations, and to develop or change attitudes. In this section a technique that embodies all these aims is described. Through appropriate leadership, evidence is brought to bear on the crucial aspects of a selected problem; the evidence is evaluated and analyzed by the *group*; certain proposed solutions are introduced and evaluated; and finally, generalizations are derived from the experience.

Identifying the Problem

Discussion often breaks down because of the wording of the discussion problem. Four major types or kinds of questions have been identified. All may become involved during the discussion process. The *policy* question, however, is basic to the problem-solving type of discussion emphasized in this chapter. It should serve as a major problem for discussion. The four kinds of problems that lend themselves to varying degrees of reflective thinking are described next:

1. Fact: Problems of fact are concerned with the discovery and evaluation of factual information. Answers to such questions can be verified directly or indirectly. Fact questions are emphasized during the analysis phase of the problem. For example: "What are the rules, if any, concerning making noise in the school hallway?"

2. Value: Problems of value (opinions) concern matters involving value judgments. Answers to value questions cannot be verified as either true or false, but they can be examined for consistency and should include supporting reasons and implications. Value questions arising during the latter part of discussion often call for application of accepted standards in determining the appropriateness, rightness, or effectiveness of an issue. For example: "How well are our school rules being followed?" Questions of value arise frequently during the early phases of a discussion. They are related to the *evaluation* of facts.

   Problems of fact and problems of value usually can be identified by the presence of some form of the verb *to be*. Indeed, they are sometimes referred to as *is* or *are* questions.

3. Advocacy: As the term implies, problems of advocacy focus on finding one specific solution. Since only one solution is considered, advocacy questions tend to encourage argument rather than discussion. They often emerge in discussion when hypotheses or tentative solutions to a problem are being evaluated. It is for this reason that establishment of accepted criteria should be developed prior to weighing the alternatives. To illustrate: "Should more school rules be added concerning noise in the school hallway?" The question can be answered by yes or no. Wording of the question precludes consideration of other alternatives. Such questions usually begin with the word *should* or *ought*.

4. Policy: Problems of policy (advice) deal with matters necessitating decisions or action. Implied in the problem is the importance of exploring all possible solutions. Policy questions often begin with the words *what* or *how*. The word *should* or *ought* is also stated or implied in the question. For example: "What should be the policy about making noise in the school hallway?"

In resolving a problem of policy, questions of *fact, value,* and *advocacy* will be involved. The reverse does not follow, however. In formulating problems for discussion, teachers often confuse policy with advocacy questions. Advocacy questions immediately direct attention to one particular solution. Furthermore, they tend to divide a group into opposing camps.

Analyzing the Problem

As a preliminary step in decision making, the various components of a problem must be introduced and evaluated. The process leads the learner from definition of important terms to an inspection of important facts and circumstances associated with the problem. In this phase of discussion the seriousness of the problem is examined.

A discussion guide is offered for the problem, "What steps should be taken to get pupils to eat better foods?"

1. What foods are nutritious?
2. How common are poor diets among pupils?
3. What are the effects of poor diets?
4. What evidence indicates the problem is likely to persist? Are there evidences to the contrary?

Establishing Hypotheses

After all the pertinent facts and values have been carefully examined, the learner is ready to offer possible solutions to the problem. The advantages and disadvantages of each proposal are fully explored. While some of the alternatives will be suggested in various background reading references, pupils are encouraged to offer ideas of their own. Such ideas often are prompted during the analysis phase of the discussion. In this way, creative thinking is encouraged. To illustrate:

1. Television should advertise only nutritious foods.
2. It should be against the law to manufacture nonnutritious foods.

Deriving Generalizations

Sometimes the outcome of a problem-solving discussion is a definite plan of action. By weighing each of the suggested hypotheses, the pupils reached some decision concerning one or more preferred courses of action. In most classes, however, the scope of the problem will be too broad to achieve such an end.

Most class discussion experiences conclude with the derivation of generalizations. To illustrate:

1. Poor diets can affect a person's health.
2. Nutritious foods help an individual to grow and develop properly.

Role of the Teacher as Discussion Leader

Basic to effective class discussion is the appropriate use of questions. Both student and teacher questions must be stated clearly and impartially. It is relatively easy for a biased leader to influence the discussion process by interjecting slanted questions from time to time. The question "Why are nonnutritious foods dangerous?" for example, merely calls for support for a preconceived point of view. A better question might be "What are the effects of nonnutritious foods?"

An effective discussion leader must know how to handle nonrelated or remotely related questions. In the spontaneous interplay of individual reactions to issues, a variety of questions tends to emerge. The teacher must continually make quick decisions as to the desirability of pursuing given questions. Pushing the group too forcibly can impede or even block group reflection, while entertaining all questions can lead to a myriad of blind alleys, resulting in little or no progress. Sometimes the wise leader-teacher may simply ask the questioner, "Would you tell us how that is related to our problem?" Some teachers practice putting both the problem and the key questions on the board *in advance* of the discussion. This practice tends to keep the issue constantly before the group.

In class discussion, pupil questions usually are redirected to the group. Answering questions for pupils tends to emphasize the teacher's role as an "expert." Few individuals do their best thinking when they are constantly reminded that the leader already "knows" the answers. Under such conditions they are inclined merely to let this person think for them. Redirection of pupil questions tends to bring out new relationships and interpretations.

Skillful teachers generally accept pupil responses to questions. If, however, a response obviously is in error, pupils themselves can handle the situation if adequate time for reflection is provided. Inaccurate responses may stimulate further questions and analysis designed to evoke reappraisal of the issue. Undue pupil embarrassment should be carefully avoided, however, if reflection is to continue. A teacher sometimes accepts an inaccurate response temporarily, simply by calling for other ideas pertaining to the issue. Usually subsequent responses will clarify the inaccuracy. (Occasionally the matter may have to be clarified before the group is permitted to advance to the next point.)

Reflection demands time! The teacher-leader can inadvertently encourage glibness by rushing responses unnecessarily. As one pupil expressed it, "He doesn't care what you say so long as you say it in a hurry." There are times, however, when, because of sudden insight, an individual needs to make a quick response. This is usually evidenced by the unusual eagerness of the respondent.

Planning for Discussion

Class discussion often breaks down as a result of inadequate preplanning by the teacher. Although pupils themselves often suggest the need for a class discussion by the questions they ask, the teacher assumes responsibility for formulating the problem for discussion. Furthermore, the teacher must develop a structured discussion guide that incorporates the essential dimensions of the discussion process. The lesson plan that follows is suggestive only.

———— **Lesson Plan Illustration (health area—fifth or sixth grade)** ————

Concept   Poor diets may affect an individual's health.

Problem   What steps should be taken to get pupils to eat better foods?

Goals   After the lesson the pupil should have furthered his or her understanding of the effects of poor diets on an individual, as evidenced by:

1. Contributions and questions posed during the discussion.
2. Ability to draw conclusions during the follow-up discussion of the problem.

Lesson Approach   Show a ten-minute film, e.g., *Foods for Better Living*. Ask pupils to jot down questions immediately following the film presentation.

Lesson Development
- A. Analysis of the problem
  1. What foods are nutritious?
  2. How common are poor diets among pupils?
  3. What are the effects of poor diets?
  4. Is the problem likely to continue? Why or why not?
- B. Establishing hypotheses: In view of our discussion of this problem, what steps should be taken to get pupils to eat better foods? Possible solutions (suggestive only):
  1. Organize an educational program designed to inform all pupils concerning nutritious foods.
  2. Pass laws against the manufacture of nonnutritious foods. (Advantages and disadvantages of each proposal will be treated fully.)
- C. Deriving generalizations: From our discussion, what important generalizations seem apparent? Examples of points that may be advanced are as follows:
  1. Poor diets can affect a person's health.
  2. Nutritious foods help an individual to grow and develop properly.

Values

- Discussion involves the processes essential to a democratic system.
- Prejudices and biases are frequently modified when subjected to the scrutiny of the peer group.
- When individuals in a group pool their ideas, they are much more likely to correct deficiencies in evidence and reasoning than they could on their own.
- Group discussion tends to make the leader and participants progressively less dependent upon the teacher.

Limitations and Problems

- Discussion presupposes adequate preparation. It is impossible to reflect effectively upon facts and concepts that are unknown or incompletely understood.
- The permissive characteristic of discussion tends to encourage digression.
- The discussion leader may be unable to maintain an open mind.
- Even when carefully organized, class discussion is unpredictable.

- Group agreement or consensus does not ensure accomplishment of goals.

Illustrated Discussion Outlines

I. Useful in the science area (primary grades)
Unit Weather
Concept Cloud types indicate weather changes.
Problem How can clouds help us to know what the weather will be like?
Sample Analysis Questions
1. What does a cirrus cloud tell us about the weather?
2. What does a cumulus cloud tell us?
3. What do stratus clouds indicate?

II. Useful in the language arts area (fourth through sixth grades)
Unit Written Communication
Concept Writing autobiographies enable a child to be observant of the things that go on around him or her.
Problem What is the best way to author a story of one's personal experiences?
Sample Analysis Questions
1. What made the autobiography *Ben and Me* interesting?
2. What makes autobiographies different from other stories?
3. What kinds of events take place in autobiographies?
4. What words make the autobiography more real?
Some Possible Solutions to Consider
1. The things that happen are everyday events.
2. The autobiography tells the story of a person.
3. The autobiography is about yourself.
4. Words such as *I* or *we* make the story more real.

III. Useful in the health area (seventh and eighth grade)
Unit Microorganisms
Concept Respiratory diseases are transmitted in many ways.
Problem How can the transmission of respiratory diseases be minimized?
Sample Analysis Questions
1. What are some common respiratory diseases?
2. What are airborne microorganisms?
3. How are they transmitted?
4. Why is the problem more important today than in the past?

Some Possible Solutions to Consider
1. Pass strict laws on air pollution.
2. Require inoculations against disease.
3. Require medical checkups.
4. Require regular chest X-rays.

IV. Useful in social studies area (fourth or fifth grade)
    Unit Pioneers
    Concept Pioneers were motivated to move West for various reasons.
    Problem What reasons did the pioneers have for moving West?
    Sample Analysis Questions
    1. What was happening to the fertile lands in the eastern part of the United States?
    2. Why did Mark Twain and people like him move West?
    3. Why did miners and prospectors go to the western part of the United States?
    4. Where were the population centers in the United States?
    5. What freedoms were enjoyed by the pioneers who moved West?
    Sample Possible Solutions to Consider
    1. Many pioneers moved West for new lands.
    2. Some pioneers moved to the western part of the United States for adventure.
    3. Gold enticed many pioneers to go West.
    4. Many moved West because they felt the cities were too crowded.
    5. Some moved West to escape jail sentences and to make a new life.

Endnote

1. David W. Johnson and Roger T. Johnson, "Critical Thinking through Structured Controversy," *Educational Leadership*, May 1988, pp. 58–64.

Chapter 11

The Dramatic
Play Method

Overview

Key Concepts

- A simulation of reality may be superior to reality itself for instructional purposes.
- Role playing is merely a vehicle for portraying a selected life situation.
- Dramatic play problems must be immediate to the lives of those involved; one does not play his or her own life role, however.
- "Success" or lack of success in the dramatization has no bearing on the usefulness of the experience for class analysis.
- Analysis of the dramatized situation emphasizes factors that contributed to actual feeling reactions.

Chapter Terms

- Dramatic play: A spontaneously enacted situation (usually five to ten minutes long) depicting an actual life problem that is used for study and analysis.
- Role playing: The enactment phase of a dramatic play, sometimes referred to as a *skit*.
- Verbal and nonverbal cues: Subtle hints that suggest emotional reactions to events during the dramatization.

In dramatic play, role playing is used as a vehicle to portray a situation for study and analysis. It involves the spontaneous enactment of a realistic life problem in the realm of interpersonal relationships. When used effectively, it may enable learners to improve their response to a situation, to increase their repertoire of responses, and to increase their sensitivity to the feelings of others.[1]

Fundamental Properties

Any meaningful portrayal of a selected life experience depends upon its immediacy and relevancy to the lives of those involved. Almost any concept can be related to problems of everyday living so long as the learners are able to project themselves into the situation. The properties that follow are essential to a realistic setting.

Determining Pupil Readiness

When the learner recognizes inadequacies of previous behaviors, he or she is challenged to seek new ways of coping with situations. Various techniques can be used to create an awareness of inadequate understanding of a concept. For example, the following concept may be involved: Empathic ability aids in the resolution of different points of view. To test readiness or to determine the present level of understanding, the learner may be shown a film and asked to cite evidence of empathy or lack of it and to identify factors that appeared to block the empathic process. Other techiques might include an analysis of a story, written examples from past experience, or an open-ended problem situation. The learner may be asked to indicate how he or she would react to a problem situation and then to designate those behaviors that show empathic ability. Such experiences help the learner realize the need for expanding his or her understanding of the concept and for improving one's skill in applying appropriate principles in the area.

Affective Considerations

Problems of interaction usually are associated with an individual's inability to understand the impact of human emotions. Thus a dramatized situation can be structured around a conflict situation, the resolution of which demands some insight into the basic needs of the other person. The objective is to determine the impact of specific events upon feeling reactions of those involved.

Realistic Situation

A situation close to the lives of the pupils is a basic essential of the dramatic play experience. Unlike drama, which often re-creates scenes far removed from pupil experiences, a dramatic play situation is developed from the everyday lives of those involved. For example, one does not play a role of George Washington or the Queen of England or even some local adult figure. A youngster plays roles that are within the realm of his or her personal experience. The child does not play an identifiable life role that might be embarrassing in any way.

Simplicity

Although human interaction varies from the simple to the complex, analysis is greatly facilitated when the situation is kept as simple as possible. Situations involving two pupils are preferred. Additional players not only complicate the analysis, but may also place one member of the cast on the defensive unnecessarily. There seems to be a tendency to "gang up" on the underdog. Sometimes additional players may be added if the situation is replayed.

Spontaneity

The situation for enactment is not rehearsed. Indeed, the participants are selected immediately after the situation has been developed. After one has been projected into his or her role, the way it is played is not a critical issue. The individual is instructed to react to the situation as he or she feels at the time. If certain comments or inferences have a positive reaction, for example, the participant will reflect this through his or her behavior just as any individual might behave. Likewise, feelings of indifference or even negative reactions are reflected through various behaviors. One makes no effort to telescope such feelings, however. They are allowed to develop in as natural a manner as possible.

Dramatic Play Procedure

Dramatic play should be conceived as a series of steps with each step necessary to a successful learning experience. Inasmuch as the method focuses upon human emotions, careful planning is essential if a sound psychological climate is to be maintained.

Problem Identification

The teacher formulates a problem to be solved. After pupils are made aware of their present inadequacies in the area, the problem is placed on the board for all to see. From the concept "Empathic ability aids in the resolution of different points of view," the following problem might be evolved: "How can we further appreciate another person's point of view?" In this manner, pupils are made aware of the concept to be learned in language that they can understand.

Defining the Situation and Roles

The specific situation for enactment is based upon the felt needs of the learner. For example, the teacher may ask, "What instances can you recall from your own lives that illustrate lack of empathy?" The teacher then suggests that one of these be acted out through a skit. The broad situation may be developed by pupils (with teacher guidance), or it may be preplanned by the teacher. If the broad situation is preplanned by the teacher, pupils should assist in developing details of the situation.

To illustrate, using the problem of empathy, someone (or the teacher) may suggest a situation where a new child has moved into the neighborhood school. The broad situation is then placed upon the board.

> Susie, a fourth grader, has moved into a new school.
> Her father is in the service.
> She moves quite frequently.
> Susie needs to make new friends.

At this point, pupils fill in some details of the situation, such as Susie's problems of getting acquainted with new children, Susie's characteristics, and possibly some characteristics of Ruth, who lives near Susie.

After assuring the group that one's acting ability is not to be evaluated, a volunteer cast is selected. Susie (the one who is to lead the conversation) is then asked to leave the room while the class adds additional points relevant to the situation as seen by Ruth, who lives near Susie. These would be factors and feelings that would definitely influence the situation but would not be fully appreciated nor understood by Susie. For example: Ruth has not gone out of her way to meet Susie. Susie may not want to get acquainted with Ruth. Ruth has her other friends.

Preparing the Class for Observation and Analysis

The class is asked to watch for clues that are indicative of the situation as it develops. What questions or comments seem to contribute to or detract from the development of empathy? What clues are (or are not) pursued? What behaviors indicate that Susie (or Ruth) did or did not understand each other's feelings? Why did you identify with either Susie or Ruth? How else might the situation be handled to show empathy?

Dramatic Play

Prior to the return of the leading character, the teacher assists the other players in identifying their roles. The teacher may briefly summarize the situation or may ask two or three leading questions, for example, "What do you think of Susie?" "What plans do you have to help Susie feel welcome?"

Susie is called into the room. The teacher then prepares Susie for the role she is to play. How old are you? How long have you lived in this town? How will you make new friends?

The players are instructed to react to their role situations just as the events make them feel. The dramatic play continues uninterrupted for about five or ten minutes. Action is cut when enough of the scene has been portrayed to enable the audience to analyze the situation.

Analyzing the Situation

When the drama is stopped, the teacher will want to ask three or four key questions designed to draw attention to the situation. The following are suggested:

1. Might this situation actually have occurred? (A yes answer is expected.)
2. To those reacting to the situation: How did you feel as the situation developed?
3. To the leader of the situation: Did you feel as if you were making progress?
4. To the class: What clues did we get that may account for these feelings?

The class then recalls comments and nonverbal expressions that reflected changes in feeling reactions. The players are used as resources to substantiate various forms of the analysis. Attention is continually directed to the processes of interaction; criticism of how the roles were played is forbidden.

Finally, after the enacted situation has been thoroughly analyzed, some attention is directed toward other approaches that might have been employed. Sometimes it is desirable to replay the situation.

Related Situations

Following the analysis, pupils must be made aware of the variety of similar situations that could have been selected for analysis. Thus they recognize the generalizability of that concept. Empathic ability, for example, is needed in a wide variety of interaction situations. These include other children groups, older groups, and contacts with younger children.

Deriving Generalizations

As a culminating activity, pupils are asked to formulate generalizations from the experience. Generalizations should apply equally well to any number of related situations. Pupils may be asked to perform this task individually by writing them out, or they may do it jointly through class discussions and make an experience chart. In any event, generalizations represent the basic learnings that result from the dramatic play experience. To illustrate:

1. A feeling for another person is increased when you put yourself in his or her place.
2. Friendship may be developed when one is willing to be a friend.
3. Words, phrases, or body movements sometimes reveal hidden feelings.

Planning for Dramatic Play

The illustrated plan is designed to clarify further the essential steps of employing the dramatic play method of teaching. Although each teacher eventually will develop his or her own techniques in the area, none of the steps included in the lesson development can be safely omitted.

———————   **Lesson Plan Illustration (health area)**   ———————

Concept   Empathic ability in assisting someone to get acquainted in an unfamiliar place.

Problem   How can we help a child who moves into our school?

Goals   After this lesson the pupil should have increased his or her sensitivity to the feelings of others, as evidenced by:

1. Ability to detect clues to hidden feelings
2. Ability to identify specific ways to help a person get acquainted in a new setting
3. Ability to derive valid generalizations as a result of the experience

Lesson Approach   Our health class mentioned the problem people have when they move to new places. Because we have a lot of new pupils moving in and out of our classroom, perhaps we can take this as our problem situation, act it out, and then analyze it in relation to our feelings for others. (Pupil) Let's take a situation in which a girl moves into our class. (Other pupils give approval.) Fine. We will develop the situation that follows:

Lesson Development

A. Broad situation
   1. Susie, a fourth grader, has moved into a new school.
   2. Her father is in the service.
   3. She moves quite frequently.
   4. Susie needs to make new friends.
B. Details of the situation (class develops): Concentrate on general aspects of Susie and Ruth who lives near Susie.
C. Threat reduction: In this type of experience no one is to be criticized on acting ability. There is no right or wrong way of doing this.
D. Selection of players: Volunteers (One should not be permitted to play his or her real-life role.)
E. Send leading character from the room.
F. Fill in additional details (by class)
   1. How may Susie feel in the new school?
   2. Why does Ruth want to know Susie?
   3. What about Ruth's other friends?
G. Preparation of class observation and analysis
   1. Remember to jot down key words and phrases that seem to affect feelings—either positively or negatively.
   2. Note expressions on pupils' faces.
H. Warm up the players
   1. Who are you?
   2. What time of day is it?
I. Play (no more than ten minutes)
J. Analysis of the situation
   1. How did the play come out?
   2. How did you feel? (to each of the players in turn)
   3. What clues did we get that may have accounted for these feelings?
K. Related situations: What similar situations can you recall that illustrate this feeling or a lack of it?

Deriving Generalizations   What generalizations can we draw from this experience that might also apply to many other related situations? For example:

1. A feeling for another person is increased when y
in his or her place.
2. Friendship may be developed when one is willing to b

Values

- Dramatic play provides the learner with new insights into possible responses to social situations.
- The dramatic play method increases one's sensitivity to the feelings of others in conflict situations.
- Through dramatic play, individuals are able to project themselves into the shoes of others. Realism is maintained without the usual threat to one's personality that characterizes analysis of actual life situations.
- The enactment of selected situations provides a rare opportunity for discussion of actual feeling reactions.

Limitations and Problems

- The dramatic play experience demands meticulous planning of a series of steps. A breakdown at any point may block the learner's ability to portray a realistic situation.
- The problem must be of immediate concern to those involved. In some subject areas realistic parallels are difficult to visualize.
- Discussion analysis must focus on the situation at all times. When rapport in the situation is not effectively established, there may be a tendency to criticize the players.
- As employed in the dramatic play experience, role playing is merely a tool for developing understanding. Therapy—emphasizing the motives behind the roles played—has no place in the classroom.

Illustrated Dramatic Play Situations

I. Useful in language arts area (fourth through sixth grades)
Unit Telephone Courtesy
Concept Courtesy in answering the telephone is appreciated.
Broad Situation
1. People call on the telephone. John shouts "Hello."
2. John keeps his lips too close to the telephone.
3. People dislike calling because John is rude to them on the telephone.

reading area (primary grades)

eading

sideration of others who are reading orally.

n

or oral reader.

read because others laugh at him.

nscious when he reads his experience stories to class

social studies area (kindergarten, first or second grades)

Unit   Work in Home

Concept   Everyone in the family must share the work.

Broad Situation

1. Mary does not pick up her clothes or put away her toys.
2. Mary's parents scold her for not doing her share of the work in the home.
3. Mary screams and cries when she is told to pick up her clothes.
4. Mary throws her toys around the house.

IV. Useful in spelling and handwriting areas (first through sixth grades)

Unit   Written Communication

Concept   Must spell and write in an acceptable manner for written communication to take place.

Broad Situation

1. Frank does not feel he needs to practice handwriting or spell words properly.
2. Frank dislikes it when his teacher corrects his handwriting and spelling.
3. Children in Frank's class cannot read his reports or stories.

V. Useful in the science area (upper grades)

Unit   Procedures for Science Experiments

Concept   Responsibility is necessary to eliminate accidents.

Broad Situation

1. Kenneth and Jane were "goofing around" during their science experiment.
2. Their teacher told them that accidents can occur when pupils are not careful with scientific experiments and equipment.
3. Kenneth and Jane felt their teacher was unreasonable concerning the rules.

Endnote

1. Stephen H. Yaffe, "Drama as a Teaching Tool," *Educational Leadership,* March 1989, pp. 29–32.

Chapter 12

Simulation Game Method

Overview

Key Concepts

- A simulation game is an approach to problem solving.
- A basic element in a simulation game is conflict or clash of opposing forces.
- Simulation games present lifelike problems or situations.
- The simulation game method provides a means of combining theory and practice.

Chapter Terms

- Simulation model: An artificial, condensed representation of reality that incorporates both role playing and dramatic play and the element of a game.
- Simulation cycle: A phase of the game that is structured around a crisis. Several cycles may occur in one game.
- Game resources: Items or symbols of power used in the game situation, such as raw materials, play money, and votes.

Any number of complex social problems confront the pupils in this nation today. Usually such problems possess many variables that bear upon appropriate solutions. Most instructional methods are designed to approach a given problem from a single framework of decision making. Nevertheless, it is recognized that a wholly appropriate solution might be rendered wholly *inappropriate* when other parties or frames of reference are considered. This has led to the development of the simulation method, which is currently creating considerable attention among elementary school teachers everywhere.

Fundamental Properties

A *simulation* is an artificial, condensed representation of reality. It may reproduce the essential details of either a model or an actual situation. Governing the conduct of a simulation are rules that limit or proscribe the actions of players. Rules are incorporated into a *game* of some type for the purpose of introducing the elements of competition, cooperation, and conflict as they normally occur in real life.

Game Rules

Rules of a simulation game perform three distinct functions:

1. They specify the distribution of resources among the players as the game begins.
2. They state relationships among the various elements of the game, including players, resources, moves, and winning or losing.
3. They describe the mode of sequence of play.

Role Playing and Dramatic Play

Simulation incorporates both role playing and dramatic play in addition to a third element—a game.[1] Instead of seeking solutions to a single problem, several interacting problems are involved. Like dramatic play, simulation is based upon some element of social conflict. Solutions must be acceptable to the majority of the members of the group represented. Unlike dramatic play, the game is the element that determines the winner or loser.

Representation of Reality

A simulation *model* is a simplified representation of reality reduced to manageable proportions. It attempts to include those elements of reality that are essential to the processes under investigation. Simulations or operating models have been in use for some time.

Resource Materials

Currently simulation games are being enthusiastically developed and used by teachers. Commercially developed games are available that depict historical events, economic development, consumer behavior, and city life.[2] There are games of world trade and games involving principles of developing nations, buying, the money system, and life in a society near the survival level. Many teachers (and pupils) are developing their own simulation games.

Simulation Game Procedure

Too often the design and use of simulation games are left to hit-or-miss procedures. Many people are currently writing about their experiences in general terms, but few have bothered to suggest the specific steps followed. Like dramatic play (and indeed most methods of teaching), the simulation game is another approach to problem solving. Unlike other methods, however, this involves a complex situation necessitating *resolution of several problems* as the situation develops. The steps identified in this section should greatly facilitate the appropriate application of the method.

Identifying the Problem

A simulation game embodies at least two or three closely related unit concepts. Basic to the development of a simulation game is conflict or the clash of opposing forces or desires. As with any other method, concepts provide the basis for development of goals and anticipated behavioral outcomes. For example, behaviors that would suggest added tolerance and respect for those who hold opposing or differing social attitudes might be identified.

Developing the Model

Using the identified basic concepts as a guide, the teacher must develop a rough outline of the game to be portrayed. It may be hypothetical or a replication of an actual process. In any event, it must be a selective representation of those elements necessary to achieve objectives. If too complex, pupils will become frustrated and may lose sight of the purpose entirely. If overly simple, the game may have little motivational value and may result in basic misconceptions concerning the complexities of actual events.

Above all, the teacher must explore in depth the essential elements to be utilized in the simultation. In evaluating the potential value of the proposed simulation, one might ask, "Do the elements to be portrayed look like the real thing?" The simulation need not look like the real thing in all respects but does need to resemble those elements that are relevant to the study at hand.

Creating the rudimentary outline of a simulation game is the "giant step" of the process. It is at this point that creative imagination is essential. Once the broad aspects of the experience have been created, the details can be readily developed.

Identifying Teams

The identification roles to be played can be inferred from the model to be portrayed. They are built around the basic concepts previously identified for the situation. Class size, of course, is a practical consideration that will influence role assignments. It has been found that subgroups of four to six children are ideally suited for such purposes.

Role assignment may be made on a purely random basis, pupil choice, child's ability, or sociometrically. Perhaps a combination of all the foregoing should be considered, dependent upon the nature of the group and simulation involved.

Game Resources

The relations of the elements in a simulation game are made realistic through resources (raw materials, money, votes, etc.) to exchange in competition with other players. Although a precise quantification of power is not always evident in real life, most educational simulations attempt to assess precise values of resources exchanged.

Basic to any simulation game is appropriate use of audiovisual materials. Such media are most useful in creating the simulated environment. In a production line simulation game, for example, the raw materials are essential for the activity.

Identifying and Developing Sequence of the Play and Final Payoff

A game is played in well-defined cycles, each structured around a crisis. Pupils must know the precise goals to be achieved and fully understand the rules of procedure to be followed. Rules limit the range and define the legimate actions of the players.

Action begins with a "crisis" of some kind. In the illustrated simulation the crisis is to demonstrate the efficiency of the production line as compared to the output of the individual workers. The first phase of Cycle I involves planning for the production line groups and the individual worker groups. The second phase is carried out by actual assignment of duties for the production line groups and the completed task necessary for the individual worker groups. The third phase usually involves group action of some kind. In effect, the strategy, planned and developed in the previous phases, is now put into action. In the illustrated model, this phase is called the actual work load for production. The final phase focuses upon the work completed and the organizational advantages of the production line groups and the individual worker groups, which is a logical consequence of the work project.

Other cycles can be planned that logically follow Cycle I as the occasion demands. Some games may consist of one cycle; others may incorporate three or more such cycles. The nature of the phases within a cycle depends somewhat upon the nature of the game. Usually they will involve a sequence of planning, assignments, action, and consequences.

Postgame Discussion

A thorough postgame discussion is potentially the most valuable aspect of simulation. Each participant, having made one or more important decisions during the game, has been rewarded with a certain number of points (e.g., money, products completed, votes). One way to begin the discussion is to ask the highest and the lowest scoring players to describe their activites. By contrasting, general principles begin to emerge.

Since a simulation game represents an *abstract* of reality, a comparison of the experience with the actual or parallel situation is essential. In the illustration, for example, rewards were based upon products actually completed. Since a simulation cannot include all aspects of reality, the experience must be analyzed thoroughly for distortions of reality.

Finally, pupils should be guided in a critical derivation of concepts or generalizations. The process of becoming thoroughly involved in a conflict situation may cause the learner to temporarily lose sight of basic purposes involved. Pupil concepts will not necessarily correspond with those identified by the teacher during preplanning, but they should be similar to them.

Planning for Simulation Games

As with any other method, the use of simulation games demands careful planning. The experience may be completed in one period of time but may extend for four or five days or longer. Since considerable preparation and warm-up is essential, a sufficient amount of time should be allowed. The following plan is suggestive of the intricate relationship involved.

——————— **Lesson Plan Illustration (social studies area—second grade)** ———————

Concepts
1. Assembly line production requires workers to cooperate with one another to achieve their goal.
2. More items are produced per worker in assembly line production than an individual worker making the product alone.

Problem Which method will produce more decorations, the assembly line groups or the individual worker groups?

Goals   After this lesson, the pupil should have furthered his or her understanding of assembly line production and individual worker production, as evidenced by:

1. Ability to work effectively in the group
2. Ability to resolve the problem and follow through in making the decorations
3. Ability to analyze the problem of decoration production between the two major groups

Lesson Approach   In our study of various workers in our community we have seen that each group of workers has special functions to perform.

Today we will work two different ways to determine the production difference of assembly line workers as compared to individual workers making the same product.

Each of us will be given a job and certain rules to follow. The game involves definite steps to follow with a time limit. The "winner" will be that group that succeeds in making the most decorations that are made a specific way.

Lesson Development   The teacher will inform the groups as to the "crisis" or problem to be solved. Background information from the textbooks and various trade books is used. (Charts may be enlarged and reproduced for clarity. Use of an overhead projector may be most useful in this connection.)

A. Phase I: The situation begins with a planning session for the assembly line groups and the individual worker groups. Six groups of five each will be designated. Three groups will be individual worker groups and three groups will be production–assembly line groups. In addition, two or three reporters will be designated. The strategy for production line groups will be to delineate the specific jobs for each worker to perform, thus leading to the completed decoration. The strategy for individual worker groups will be that each will make the entire decoration by himself or herself.
B. Phase II: The assembly–production line groups will make specific assignments to children for the tasks to be performed. Each child will perform one task on each decoration. The individual worker groups also will become familiar with the steps each must follow to complete the decoration.
C. Phase III: Groups will assemble to make the decorations. All materials, scissors, paste, etc., will be available for each group. The work will continue until a specific amount of time has elapsed.
D. Phase IV: The groups will reflect upon the advantages of the

assembly line production and the individual worker production. (Length of each phase will vary, depending upon size and maturity of the group. The illustrated problem might consume additional time if additional cycles are introduced.)

Postgame Discussion   What groups have the least and most completed decorations? Would you describe your activities? For example:

1. What happened in the assembly line worker groups?
2. What happened in the individual worker groups?
3. Why do we have assembly line workers in our community?
4. Why do we have individual workers in our community?

Values

- Simulation games involve the pupil in an active, realistic problem-solving process. Simulation presents lifelike problems or situations that challenge the participants to develop appropriate response.
- The simulation game method leads pupils to the development of conceptual learnings.
- Simulation offers a procedure for bridging the gap between theory and practice.
- Participants consider the simulation experiences stimulating and highly motivating.

Limitation and Problems

- Even though the simulation game is lifelike, not *all* factors can be simulated. By limiting the variables, simulation may lead to improper conclusions.
- The time factor is important for simulation games. Teachers sometimes underestimate the number of hours needed for successful simulation games.
- Choosing games beyond the child's maturity or qualifications will lead to frustration for the child and teacher.
- Preparation for the simulation activity is essential. The teacher must prepare the children thoroughly and must understand the theoretical bases for the problem.
- During the simulation game activity, children may become highly competitive and tempers may erupt. The teacher is cautioned to aid the child who develops these difficulties.

——————— **Illustrated Simulation Game Situations** ———————

I. Useful in social studies area (fourth and fifth grade)
   Unit   Geographical Features and the Growth of Cities
   Concepts
   1. Geographical features help or hinder the growth of a city.
   2. Industrial forces and competition for workers affect the growth of cities.
   3. Planning and cooperation by city leaders and citizens affect the growth of cities.
   Problem   What geographical features and forces work together in the development of large cities?
   Goals   After this lesson, the pupil should have furthered his or her understanding of geographical features and forces that help in developing cities by:
   1. Ability to work effectively in committees
   2. Ability to resolve a "crisis" problem of competing forces between cities in the development of a city
   3. Ability to critically analyze geographical features and determine how these features may hinder or help in the growth of a city

II. Useful in the arithmetic area (fifth or sixth grade)
   Unit   Fractions in Daily Life
   Concepts
   1. Fractions are a useful part of the child's daily life.
   2. Whole numbers and fractions written together are mixed numbers.
   3. Mixed numbers are used in the stock market quotations in the local newspaper.
   4. Prices of stock fluctuate from day to day.
   Problem   Which group can choose the shares of stock that go up the most on the stock market?
   Goals   After this lesson, the pupil should have furthered his or her understanding of mixed numbers as a useful part of daily living by:
   1. Ability to work effectively in a group
   2. Ability to resolve the problem and figure price fluctuations of a group's selected stock
   3. Ability to determine the stock fluctuation among the groups within the class
   4. Ability to make trades with other groups and pick the best stock

III. Useful in the social studies area (upper grades)
   Unit   Inflation of a Money System
   Concepts
   1. Supply of money influences prices.

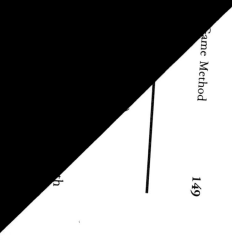

ials to buy influences prices.

oup could make the most finished products in the
ime?

esson, the pupil should have furthered his or her
nflation of money by:

y for needed materials to finish certain product

gold certificates when these certificates were scarce
or needed materials

yze the relationship between supply of money and
rials as they influenced prices

Endnotes

1. In the context of this chapter the terms *simulation* and *simulation games* are
   synonymous.
2. Kathlene R. Willing, "Computer Simulations: Activating Content Reading,"
   Journal of Reading, February 1988, pp. 400–409.

Chapter 13

Teacher-Pupil Planning Techniques

Overview

Key Concepts

- Teacher-imposed activities and assignments are replaced by problems and projects suggested by pupils themselves.
- A set for planning is established when the pupils are guided and supported without unnecessarily imposing the teacher's wishes or authority upon them.
- The teacher's role may vary from one of guidance to one of offering suggestions and advice.

Chapter Terms

- Teacher-pupil planning: Teacher and pupils work together in planning and directing a learning experience.
- Inquiry processes: An approach to learning that emphasizes pupil initiated and direction of one's own learning experiences.

The art of living and working together harmoniously is the ultimate task of all humankind. That humanity has thus far failed miserably in achieving this goal is evident on all sides. From the highest levels of international relations to the person on the street, one sees evidences of humanity's inability to work together.

Traditionally, the role of the teacher has been conceived as that of a taskmaster. Pupils have been expected to conform, to know *about* subject matter, to compete with one another for grades that all too often become the ends of education. The situation still exists in many elementary school classrooms—*not* because the instructional approach is considered sound, but frequently because those involved simply are unable to break from years of conditioning when they themselves were students.

Democratic instructional procedures are probably best characterized through joint teacher-pupil planning. This procedure involves teacher and pupils working together. It is one of freedom, creativity, and self-direction. With teacher guidance, critical thinking is developed as pupils themselves set up their own problems for exploration and analysis. Thus tasks become self-imposed, activities become self-directed, and evaluation becomes self-competitive.

Fundamental Properties

Teacher-pupil planning, like most other instructional approaches, involves the processes of inquiry. Unlike some other approaches, however, this technique is based upon current pupil needs and interests rather than upon organized bodies of subject matter as a starting point. Indeed, the processes of reflective thought are applied by the entire group. The topics that follow represent essential conditions necessary for effective application of the method.

Democratic Framework

Teacher-pupil planned experiences are conceived within a framework that may be new to both child and teacher. Teacher-imposed activities and assignments are replaced by problems and projects suggested by pupils themselves. A competitive class climate is replaced with a climate of children working together as they pursue different aspects of a complex problem. All legitimate areas of choice must be identified and then resolved by the class group. The teacher's role is relegated to that of a participating guide — guiding pupils in their objective consideration of issues, sometimes by acting as a resource person, by discouraging or even rejecting suggested actions that would carry children beyond the particular problem under investigation, or by offering suggestions and advice. The basic objective is that of supplying guidance, assistance, and support at every step of the way *without* unnecessarily imposing his or her wishes or authority upon the group.

Immediate Applications

In selecting an appropriate topic for teacher-pupil planning, attention must be directed to the immediate concerns of children. Some areas of school work are more directly related to the group than others. There are areas within almost all subject areas in which immediate parallels can be found. If such parallels can be made apparent to pupils, *prior to a thorough investigation of the topic,* a teacher-pupil planned experience may be effective.

Flexibility

Children feel real concerns in many areas of their daily existence. If the teacher-pupil planned experience successfully touches their lives, the quantity and quality of questions will be almost overwhelming. Textbook units no longer will seem adequate, as questions tend to cut across topical areas. Some questions may seem more directly related to certain curriculum areas than the one under consideration. The answers to other questions will be difficult to find. A few questions may be embarrassing or even appear to go beyond the realm of prudence acceptable to school authorities.

Both teacher and pupils must be flexible is such matters. The teacher must be willing to revise his or her thinking with respect to units, recognizing that conventional lines often are extremely arbitrary. Questions that seem inappropriate for class consideration can be reworded to incorporate the basic idea in a more acceptable form. Sometimes a teacher will find it necessary to exclude questions that may be treated more appropriately in a different context or that are remotely related to the area. An explanation of such matters is desirable.

Resource Materials

The diversity of questions will render textbooks inadequate. One must search through library books, magazines, encyclopedias, yearbooks, and the like. Frequently, personal interviews with individuals knowledgeable in the area are appropriate; sometimes school trips and individual experimentation are needed. The teacher, anticipating such needs, must make preliminary arrangements for study groups in a variety of settings. Key books must be placed in the room; potential resource people must be contacted. Since pupils will be working somewhat independently of the teacher, expected rules of conduct must be clearly established.

Time Requirements

The processes of planning, researching, and reporting take time. Developing questions, establishing study groups, and researching a given area necessitates a time span of at least a week. Reporting, review, and evaluation activities will likely involve another week. On the other hand, most teachers have found that children vary greatly in their interest in a given problem area. The maturity of the children and their sustained interest in the problem must determine the time requirements.

Teacher-Pupil Planning Procedure

The processes of teacher-pupil planned experiences follow a logical sequence of problem solving. The basic objective is to guide learners in their exploration at every step along the way. Above all, the learners must anticipate each phase of the experience well in advance of the activity and plan accordingly. The procedure that follows is suggestive only.

Identifying the Problem

In teacher-pupil planning as here conceived, the teacher identifies the problem *area*. He or she then attempts to develop interest in the area by using such techniques as a discussion, film, resource speaker, or oral report. For purposes of illustration, a specific example from the science area is employed. Let us assume that the unit is entitled "Conservation."

> *Creating interest:* The pupils have read about conservation in their textbooks and weekly newspaper. The suggestion of a day for a field trip to see what they have been studying will create the interest to plan.

Clarifying the Issues

Once the proper foundation has been established, pupils are urged to formulate questions they would like answered. Emphasis is placed upon realistic, practical problems rather than upon questions they think the teacher wants them to ask.

> *Teacher:* From our general study of conservation what sub-headings or division seem appropriate? What are some areas that might be worthy of exploration?

The class then suggests appropriate groups. Some of them might be as follows:

1. Identification of conservation practices
2. Identification of good policies controlling pollution
3. Identification of poor pollution policies
4. Can we stop pollution?
5. Ways to aid in conservation

> *Teacher:* Now we will list specific questions you would like to have answered as we study and go on a field trip. Your questions will determine what we will see and study, so make sure they represent what you really want to know. To assist us in organizing our thoughts, we will refer to the general areas listed. Some may develop questions in each area, while others may be interested primarily in only one area.

Questions are grouped and refined. To save time, it may be desirable to appoint a committee for this purpose. When the list of questions has been compiled, the teacher should make copies available to each person.

Planning and Developing the Learning Activities

At this point pupils are assigned to subgroups, usually on the basis of choice. Subgroups of five are preferred. Each subgroup is expected to select a leader and a recorder and to develop a study plan. Each subgroup considers informational sources along with methods of investigation, reporting, and evaluation. Pupils should give some consideration to all phases of the project so that they can grasp more fully the total task ahead. The teacher moves from group to group to guide and direct as necessary. For example, pupils may need guidance in rephrasing and expanding some of the questions. "Why do we want to know about the problem of pollution? How can we use the information in our daily lives?" The teacher may find it necessary to assist some groups in developing an appropriate division of labor. Does each person know his or her specific responsibility? Are the tasks appropriate for the individuals involved?

At the outset the teacher will want to suggest the amount of time available for the project. Time allotments for each group must be established early. By providing for some flexibility in this respect, pupils are encouraged to use their own imaginaton relative to unique and creative ways of reporting to the class. They will then need assistance in carrying out such plans.

Collecting Data

The teacher, well in advance of need, should have placed key library references in the classroom, made arrangements for some of the class to be in the library each day, and looked into the possibilities of field trips and other resources.

While investigating a variety of problems, the groups will have different resource needs. These require careful supevision, a great deal of trust in pupils, and a supportive attitude on the part of other teachers and administrators. The wise teacher will set the stage carefully. The first five minutes of class time might well be devoted to brief progress reports and plans for the day's activities. Copies of the reports should list problems needing attention. The teacher quickly determines which problems need immediate attention. A short class discussion on how to find information may be in order, especially for groups inexperienced in the procedure.

Reporting Procedures

Although a group may have accomplished a great deal in planning and research activities, the value to the class group depends on how well findings are shared with others. Somewhere in the process the entire class might profitably set up standards for this phase of the project. Each group can be asked to consider the problem before planning its specific method of reporting. A master list is then distributed to the chairman of each group. One class listed eight points essential to an appropriate presentation.

1. Material presented should relate to the goals established.
2. Presentations should involve all members of the group in some way.
3. Presentations will be brief, preferably not exceeding fifteen minutes.
4. Presentations should not be read.
5. Other class members should be alloted time for questions. If a key question cannot be answered, some member of the group should be designated to find the answer.
6. As a general rule, technical material should be omitted from presentations. When it is necessary, however, it should be reproduced for the class.
7. Sources of information should be available.
8. Contradictory evidence should be presented as impartially as possible.

Following each presentation the teacher may lead the class in a general review for the purpose of expanding, clarifying, or correcting important points. It is seldom appropriate to have more than two group presentations in one day. However, sometimes keen interest may be indicated, suggesting the desirability of having more group presentations.

Establishing Generalizations

As a culminating activity the teacher will want to conduct a review of the entire project. This will involve recalling the major concepts and procedures employed and expanding to related areas. (See Chapter 20, "Review Methods.") The activity serves the important function of organizing and clarifying basic ideas that have been developed gradually over a period of several days.

Evaluating the Experience

Early in the teacher-pupil planning experience, pupils are asked to give some consideration to evaluational techniques. As indicated previously, they assist in establishing standards of reporting. They may want to participate in some sort of group evaluation. Whatever procedure is employed, it should be developed jointly by teacher and pupils.

The Planning Experience

A detailed lesson plan is needed if the teacher-pupil planned project is to develop smoothly. The illustration that follows incorporates the essential steps of the procedure. It is designed to serve for the entire project.

───────── **Lesson Plan Illustration (science area—fifth or sixth grade)** ─────────

Concepts
1. Conservation helps save our natural resources.
2. Pollution policies may be good or bad depending upon how they affect our environment.
3. Our living habits directly influence the policies concerning conservation and pollution.

Problem   How can we better understand conservation practices and pollution policies?

Goals   After this experience the pupil will know how to identify conservation as evidenced by:
1. Identification of conservation practices he or she sees on the field trip
2. Group report concerning conservation

After this experience the pupil should have furthered his or her knowledge of pollution as evidence by:

1. Identification of pollution he or she sees on the field trip
2. Group report concerning pollution

After this experience the pupil will understand more fully how to cooperate with others of his or her peer group in planning as evidenced by:

1. Cooperation during the planning
2. Cooperation and acceptance of responsibility while on the field trip and within the subgroup

Lesson Approach

Creating Interest   The pupils have read about conservation in their textbooks and weekly newspaper. The suggestion of a day for a field trip to see what they have been studying will create the interest to plan.

Lesson Development

Teacher   From our general study of conservation what subheadings or divisions seem appropriate? What are some areas that might be worthy of exploration?

The class then suggests five or six groupings. Some of them might be:

1. Identification of conservation practices
2. Identification of good policies controlling pollution
3. Identification of bad pollution policies
4. Ways to stop pollution
5. Ways to aid in conservation

Teacher   Now we will list specific questions you would like to have answered as we study and go on a field trip. Your questions will determine what we will study, so make sure they represent what you really want to know. To assist us in organizing our thoughts, we will refer to the general areas listed. Some may develop questions in each area, while others may be interested primarily in only one area. (Reproduce question list for each pupil. Add two or three questions if this seems necessary for accomplishment of major objectives.)

Formulation of Buzz Groups   At this time we will form a separate buzz group for each identified area of our problem for the purpose of correlating our questions. (Ask for volunteers.)

Select a leader and a recorder. List and rework questions, cutting out duplications. *Then* add other questions that are prompted during this activity. (Reproduce question list for each pupil. Add two or three questions if this seems necessary for accomplishment of major objectives.)

Development of Learning Activities   Now that you have studied the list of questions in each area, you see the task before us. We will ask for an indication of preference for committees to be formed for each area.

Committee Buzz Groups   Our task is to find the answers to our list of questions and to somehow provide the class with these answers. What are some possible sources of information? (List on chalkboard.) For example:

1. Field trip
2. Books
3. Magazines
4. Resource people

Now let us move into our committees and organize for action, selecting a leader and a recorder. Work out an appropriate division of labor. I will visit each group for the purpose of answering questions.

Collecting Data   At the conclusion of each days' activities I want you to indicate progress for that day and to suggest problems (if any). The recorder should submit this report after each work period.

Field Trip Standards What rules of behavior will be established for our field trip? (List.)

Looking Ahead—Anticipating Reporting Techniques Now that we have had an opportunity to work on our projects for two or three days, let's turn our attention to reporting techniques. What are some possibilities? (List.) For example:

1. Oral reports
2. Skits
3. Discussion

Standards What standards should we establish for the presentations? (List.) For example:

1. Not to be read
2. Limit to ten minutes long (teacher suggests this one)
3. Separate findings from your own opinions

Organize for Reporting At this time you should decide upon a technique(s) for group presentations. Leaders will discuss plans with your teacher, pending final approval.

Evaluation How should the presentations be evaluated? Let us list some possibilities. (List.) For example:

1. Teacher rating scales
2. Group evaluation of individuals; class evaluation of groups
3. Written tests

From this list (as groups) decide upon preferences.

Class Presentations Each individual should list questions as they arise. (Ask during question periods.)

Deriving Generalizations Now, as a result of our experiences, let us formulate major ideas or concepts that have emerged from these experiences. (List.) For example:

1. Conservation is everyone's responsibility.
2. Pollution control is important.

Values

- Teacher-pupil planning is democratically conceived, resulting in increased pupil independence in his or her own learning activites.
- The self-imposed tasks inherent in the procedure result in intrinsic motivation. Inded, discipline problems are rare if real choices are provided.
- The procedure emphasizes *processes* as much as *products* of learning. Thus *discovery* of new ideas and concepts are sought as a *means* of giving meaning to further performance.
- In teacher-pupil planning, competition tends to shift from individuals to small groups and self-imposed standards.
- The instructional approach emphasizes an active pupil. Indeed, the method often has been called "project work," calling attention to the inherent nature of the activities involved.
- Development of creativity is encouraged, since the learners must assume responsibility for solving problems in their own ways.

Limitations and Problems

- In some areas it is difficult to find legitimate areas of choice. Especially in skill areas, a minimum of opportunity for joint teacher-pupil planning activities may be available.
- Sometimes individual pupils are not prepared to accept the freedom essential for self-direction. The break from conformity in learning teacher-imposed tasks may, on occasion, create anxieties and tensions. These in turn may be reflected in class misbehavior. A pattern of gradually increased responsibilities is usually preferred.
- Teachers sometimes lack the ability to relinquish control necessitated by teacher-pupil planning. This seems to be the greatest single deterrent to democratically conceived classes. Although one is, to a marked degree, a victim of personal school experiences, the cycle can be broken by a process of gradually increased pupil involvement.
- A criticism occasionally voiced by experienced teachers is the time required in teacher-pupil planning processes. Unfortunately, the necessity of "covering the text or subject" is often implicity assumed to be the teacher's basic task. Today, however, the advancement of knowledge is expanding at a geometric rate. Facts soon become outdated. An implicit assumption associated with the democratic classroom is the importance of ideas and concepts in an orderly process of exploration and discovery.

─────────── **Teacher-Pupil Planning Illustrations** ───────────

I. Useful in the social studies area (primary grades)
   Unit   The home
   Concepts
   1. All homes have certain similarities.
   2. Climate affects the type of homes that are built.
   3. Some homes have certain differences.
   Problem   How might we understand more about various homes?
   Possible Areas of Interest
   1. Apartment home
   2. Single-family home
   3. Indian home
   4. Farm home
   5. Trailer home
   6. Eskimo home

II. Useful in the reading area (middle grades)
   Unit   Oral Reading
   Concepts
   1. A child reads orally to share information.
   2. Oral reading is a cooperative effort.
   3. Good oral reading requires preparation.
   Problem   What aspects about oral reading should be explored?
   Possible Areas of Interest
   1. Purposes for oral reading
   2. Abilities needed for good oral reading
   3. Standards for the oral reader
   4. Preparation for oral reading
   5. Standards for the audience during oral reading

III. Useful in the health area (upper grades)
   Unit   The Human Body
   Concepts
   1. A healthy body provides its own defenses against disease.
   2. An organ *not* functioning properly tends to influence all body systems.
   3. Early diagnosis and treatment of disease are essential.
   Problem   What factors about the human body as it fights disease should be explored?
   Possible Areas of Interest
   1. Body defenses against disease
   2. Disease influences upon the body
   3. Keeping the body healthy
   4. Diseased body needs
   5. Immunization

Chapter 14

Cooperative Learning

Overview

Key Concepts

- Cooperative group learning provides for both academic achievement and interpersonal skill development.
- Cooperative group learning can unite children with varying backgrounds, ethnic differences, and learning styles.
- Cooperative group learning leads to higher achievement levels among pupils.
- Divergent thinking, problem solving, and creative tasks can be enhanced through cooperative learning groups.

Chapter Terms

- Cooperative structured group: A group of children working together on an assignment with emphasis on the development of interdependence and interpersonal skills.
- Interdependence: Children dependent upon one another for the outcome.
- Interpersonal skills: Skills used to enhance affective positive relationships between or among children in the cooperative learning group.
- Monitoring: The teacher watching and observing for the purpose of determining whether the group of children are achieving the tasks needed for the activity.
- Processing: Children reflecting upon and reacting to what took place during the cooperative group activity.

Working together in a cooperative activity is certainly not new in our schools. Different kinds of grouping have been used by teachers for many years to effectively develop lessons so learning will take place. However, cooperative learning as described in this chapter has a definite structure that assists the teacher in reaching the various goals of education. This approach is yet another move toward a more democratic classroom that brings into focus the value and worth of each child in the learning process.

Fundamental Properties

Cooperative structured learning involves more than merely placing children in groups to work together. What distinguishes a cooperative learning group from other groups is that it must function with five elements: (1) development of positive interdependence, (2) teaching of interpersonal skills, (3) monitoring, (4) processing, and (5) evaluation of the group work.[1] The fundamental properties of cooperative learning are treated within this general framework.

Positive Interdependence

Children must realize that they all succeed together as a group. One child cannot succeed without all of the others in the group also succeeding. This group success can be accomplished by determining common group goals, sharing the resources available (both human and materials), and receiving the reward, which is the same for everyone in the group.

Interpersonal Skills

Interpersonal skills do not just happen when you put children into a group. They need to be taught like any other skill. The teacher needs to help children learn to communicate better, to trust each other, and to handle conflicts within each group. Interpersonal skills are also developed within the group. For instance, the leader is not assigned this role by the teacher. In cooperative learning groups, leadership is shared with each member of the group taking responsibility for the leadership role. Shared leadership increases the effectiveness of the group because each child in the group has more of a commitment to the group goals.

Leadership in a cooperative group deals with task functions and maintenance functions. Task functions deal with setting the goals and doing whatever is needed to meet these goals. Children demonstrate task functions by providing the group with ideas and information and by summarizing, clarifying and evaluating group progress, whereas maintenance functions are those tasks that help the group work well together. Children show that they understand these functions as they give praise to other members of the group and help to relieve tension within the group. Through children's involvement in both group functions—task and maintenance—interpersonal skills are strengthened.

Monitoring

Monitoring is an essential part of cooperative learning. As the teacher monitors the groups, she or he is able to determine how effectively the children in each group are using positive interpersonal skills and to check on the subject matter or lesson content for each group.

Processing

Following each cooperative learning experience, the children in each group need time to reflect upon and react to the process that they have just experienced in the cooperative learning group. This processing is essential to the cooperative learning experience; without it the group work is less effective. Processing helps the children to develop their awareness of the skills and the purposeful function of the cooperative group learning experience, thus giving them positive feedback on their behaviors. Processing is a time when the pupils can reflect on the cooperative learning experience and discuss the process of working together.

Evaluating

In cooperative learning groups, the child is evaluated for content mastery as well as for interpersonal skills. Evaluation of content material mastery utilizes the usual types of evaluation instruments, such as reports, projects, homework, or examinations. Much of the evaluation of interpersonal skills takes place during the monitoring and processing stages mentioned in the preceding section. To assist the teacher in the evaluation of interpersonal skills, check lists and observation forms can be developed.

Cooperative Learning Procedure

The cooperative learning procedure will vary somewhat from classroom to classroom depending upon the age of the children and the experiences they have had. However, using this structured procedure will definitely make a difference in how successful the cooperative group procedure will be. Generally, the procedure incorporates the essentials of good problem solving and reflective thought in solving problems. Interpersonal skills will always be enhanced with careful monitoring by the classroom teacher.

Organizing the Groups

The size of the groups will be determined by the teacher. Usually small groups work best while the children are learning to work cooperatively in learning groups. The teacher can assign pupils to the groups, or self-selection can be done. The teacher should stress the rules pertaining to the cooperative learning experience to each group separately or all of the groups at one time. Important interpersonal and group skills are reviewed for the children to use during the experience. Such skills as sharing, caring, compromising, communication, trust, and leadership are emphasized.

Identifying the Problem

The teacher decides upon a curriculum area and determines the structure of the cooperative learning groups that best aids in solving the problem. After the pupils are made aware of their need to determine more about the problem, the teacher allows the pupils to select the research group in which they wish to work. Learning groups can be self-selected (as in this example), teacher assigned, or randomly assigned. Using the concept "Geographical features and special land grants determined the early colonization efforts in the United States," the following problem might be evolved: "Why were certain areas in the United States colonized before other areas?" Different cooperative groups could be organized around each research topic. For example, one group could do research on Spanish grants of land for colonization; another group could research English grants; and yet another group could research geographical features that facilitated colonization.

Materials

The materials needed for the children to solve the assigned problem should be made available and planned for in advance. Each child in each group could have his or her own set of materials, textbooks, and other supplementary materials or only one set may be provided for the entire group. To build interpersonal communication in the group, a check sheet should also be made available so each member will be reminded of his or her role as leader, helper, praiser, asker, or recorder.

Teacher Role during Cooperative Experience

The teacher will consistently monitor each group to determine cooperative behaviors and problem-solving skills. It is often important to let the pupils understand exactly what cooperative behaviors you will be monitoring as you visit each cooperative learning group. As they understand fully your monitoring role, they will feel better during the observation.

Cooperative Learning Group Processing

Following the lesson in which the problem is solved, processing takes place within the group. The children examine their behaviors and rate them. This will make the group more effective the next time they work together.

Evaluation

The teacher evaluates each group's processes as well as the quality of the problem solved. The evaluation may suggest that the group membership be left the same for other problems or it may suggest that the group be changed. However, often the same groups working together for several different projects will add efficiency to the cooperative group experience.

Planning for the Cooperative Experience

As with all other methods or techniques mentioned in this book, careful planning by the teacher is necessary for the cooperative learning group to work effectively in developing good interpersonal skills and in solving problems cooperatively. The illustrated plan involves a problem-solving approach.

——————— **Lesson Plan Illustration (third grade social studies area)** ———————

Problem Why do we have rules and laws in our community, state, and nation?

Concept Rules and laws make living with others more orderly and pleasant.

Goals After this lesson, the pupil should understand that rules and laws make his or her life more orderly and pleasant, as evidenced by:

1. Ability to discuss the questions that are written on a sheet with other members of the cooperative learning group
2. Ability to come to a consensus on each question and be prepared to provide a rationale for the group's answers

Lesson Approach   Have you ever wondered what would happen if we had no rules for how we leave our classroom when the fire bell rings? What would happen if we had no rules for playing on the playground? Why do you think some rules are hard to follow? Does any one person have the right to choose which rules or laws they will obey? What responsibilities do you have to obey the rules and laws?

Today, we are going to work in cooperative learning groups of four children in each group. I have randomly assigned each one of you to one of these groups. Let's review how we are to work cooperatively in each group:

1. One set of materials for each group will require you to share the materials and one answer sheet will require each one of you to participate in arriving at the answer to be written on the sheet.
2. All of you in each group must participate in the discussion of each question.
3. Each one of you must seek to understand each response contributed by other members of the group.
4. You are expected to create a comfortable climate in the group. You may criticize the idea but not the person who gave the idea.
5. I will visit each group and provide assistance and help each one of you to maintain good interpersonal skills while staying on the problem.
6. After completing the answer sheet each of you will complete the process sheet and then share your responses with other members of the group.

Lesson Development   Now that we have reviewed the process for our cooperative learning group, your task is to read the handout materials on rules and laws. With your group, you will complete the question sheet.

During the cooperative learning group work, the teacher will observe and help when needed. The teacher will be there not only to help with the problem solving about rules and laws but also to keep good interpersonal skills and all children in each group working together.

Deriving Generalizations   From the questions answered, one major generalization seems evident:

Rules and laws make living with others more orderly and pleasant.

Evaluating Cooperative Learning Outcomes   The task assignment was evaluated in the preceding step, deriving generalizations. In this part of the lesson, the teacher evaluates how well the groups functioned. The evaluation should include (1) how well the pupils demonstrated cooperative skills, (2) any particular notes on individuals within the groups that may need extra attention, and (3) what changes should be done next time to make each group more effective.

The preceding lesson plan may be too detailed for some teachers and not detailed enough for others. The primary purpose of this plan is to demonstrate how the cooperative learning group could be utilized in solving a problem in social studies. The cooperative learning group lesson is also used for the development of interpersonal relationships and the development of a democratic classroom.

Values

- Cooperative learning groups need not be homogeneous, thus allowing a more flexible grouping procedure in the classroom.
- Children can belong to several different groups of various abilities and interests.
- Competition is kept at a minimum in the cooperative learning groups. Some children learn more effectively when competition is minimized.
- Isolation of the pupil in the learning process is negated in the cooperative learning group.
- Group goals and individual accountability will enhance achievement gains.
- Cooperative learning groups positively affect self-esteem, intergroup relations, and the ability to work with others.

Limitations and Problems

- If the children are grouped on the basis of ability only, many pupils experience an ego-deflating stigma when permanently assigned to the "slow" group.
- Some children enjoy competition in the classroom and like to work alone for the joy of being first, or right.
- It is not enough to merely put the children in a group and call it cooperative learning.
- Cooperative learning strategies are not equally effective for all children.

————————— **Cooperative Learning Illustrations** —————————

  I. Useful in the reading area (all grades)
     Grouping   Two pupils (random or teacher assigned; mixed-ability groups)
     Problem   Develop a set of questions the students feel will be answered in the story to be read. Predict the answers and then read the story together to discover whether their questions were answered or not and if their predictions were correct.

 II. Useful in mathematics area (middle grades)
     Grouping   Three pupils (teacher assigned; ability groups)
     Problem   Read ten story problems. Work out the mathematical problems and come to a consensus in the group for the correct answer for each of the ten. Each member must be able to explain the procedure in arriving at each answer.

III. Useful in the language arts area (all grades)
     Grouping   Three or four pupils (random, teacher assigned, or peer selected; mixed-ability groups)
     Problem   Show the children in each group a picture to be used as a story starter. Ask each group to discuss the picture and write a group-composed story.

 IV. Useful in the science area (upper grades)
     Grouping   Three or four pupils (teacher assigned; mixed-ability groups)
     Problem   Work together on one science experiment from your textbook. Set up the experiment and determine the results. Reach a consensus from the results of the experiment and write the report together.

Endnote

1. Based upon Joyce Gwilliam, Gayle Hughes, Denise Jenkins, Wes Koczka, and Lizabeth Nicholls, *Working Together, Learning Together!* (Saskatchewan: Department of Cooperation and Cooperative Development, Education Unit, Teaching Material Centre, © Saskatchewan Teachers' Federation, 1983), pp. 15–67.

Chapter 15

Peer Tutoring Procedures

Overview

Key Concepts

- Peer tutoring is often beneficial to both tutor and pupil.
- Both academic and social-emotional benefits may be achieved through peer tutoring experiences.
- As in any method of teaching, peer tutoring must be planned carefully.
- Both same-age and cross-age tutoring have been used effectively.
- Peer tutoring is most effective in the realm of mental or motor skills.

Chapter Terms

- Peer tutoring: Use of one pupil to act as a teacher of another or of a small group in a given instructional activity.
- Cross-age tutoring: Use of an older pupil to act as a teacher of a younger child. The recommended age differential is usually placed at three years.
- Modeling behavior: Showing another person how to perform a task by doing it oneself.
- Tutor log: A record of each tutoring session, indicating lesson covered and an indication of social-emotional factors.

Using pupils to teach other children is certainly not a new concept. The one-room schoolhouse of Colonial times featured one teacher responsible for several grade levels. Older or more capable pupils were frequently given the responsibility of teaching younger or less able children on a part-time basis. The arrangement apparently worked.

Current interest in peer tutoring began in the 1960s in an effort to reach culturally different children. This often involved older pupils teaching younger children, more accurately labeled as cross-age tutoring. Recently, the emphasis has shifted to "same-age" tutoring arrangements.

Fundamental Properties

Peer tutoring, the use of one pupil to assist the learning of another child in the same class, must be carefully planned and executed. It is an instructional technique, like many other aspects of teaching. Prior to the actual tutoring experience, several aspects of the program must be carefully considered and developed. This section is concerned with these elements.

Appropriate Peer Tutoring

Peer tutoring is most effective when mental or motor skills are being emphasized. The technique is also effective in those instances when factual recall is stressed. Peer tutoring comes into its greatest use in helping pupils correctly apply skills for which they have already developed a basic understanding. It is not very effective in helping individuals learn new skills.

This instructional technique is beneficial to both tutor and pupil. When placed in a teaching role, the tutor is forced to continually review material already learned, thus adding to depth of learning. The process also forces the tutor to restructure learning, thereby contributing to a better grasp of the underlying structure. Furthermore, by preparing illustrations and examples, various applications are made. The learner, of course, has an opportunity to imitate or model another pupil who may better understand his or her way of viewing things. In effect, tutoring leads both tutor and student to self-development and self-discovery.

Tutor Selection

The notion that teaching merely requires a basic understanding of a subject or area has long been discredited. Likewise, a pupil who possesses a needed skill is not automatically qualified to tutor others. In addition to such qualities as dependability, trustworthiness, a cooperative attitude, and a concern for others, certain tutoring skills are important. Some of these include:

1. Avoiding making judgmental statements
2. Keeping the student on the task
3. Providing needed reinforcement
4. Guiding the learner into verifying his or her own responses
5. Establishing rapport
6. Developing clarity
7. Displaying interest and enthusiasm
8. Asking appropriate questions

Some teachers recommend that selected tutors be provided an opportunity to role play at least some of these skills prior to the actual tutoring experience. For example, in avoiding judgmental statements, the tutor should be able to demonstrate that for an incorrect response, the correct response should be provided and the pupil is then asked to repeat it. The amount of preparation needed is dependent upon the nature and extent of the tutoring process and the age of the tutor.

Tutor and Pupil Pairing

Pupils may be paired for tutoring for a variety of purposes. Perhaps the most popular occasion among teachers of older children is for individualization of instruction. Teachers are finding that they just cannot work effectively with thirty or more heterogeneously grouped pupils. Moreover, there is mounting evidence that, for many purposes, "partnership learning" may be just as effective as learning through conventional means.

When academic objectives are involved, most teachers prefer to pair a pupil with one who is less advanced in the area. However, a variety of combinations have been used, with varying degrees of success. Possible combinations are high-low, high-average, and average-low. Even combinations of average-average and pupil choice have been used with positive results. One point is made repeatedly: The tutoring arrangement over a period of time should provide for reversal of roles. Otherwise, there is a serious danger of stigmas. Children who always fall in the pupil role in the class may be assigned as tutors in a cross-age tutoring situation in a lower grade.

Younger children are often paired for purposes other than academic. In such instances, emphasis is placed upon the bond or relationship of the pair. Generally such factors as race or sex have no bearing on the arrangement. There are exceptions, however. For example, it has been found that Chicano boys often do not do well when the tutor is a girl. This problem is apparently a reflection of the cultural mores of the particular ethnic group.

Training

Tutors should be prepared to work with other pupils. The amount of training needed, however, is an issue of considerable controversy. Some argue that children tutor best when they are provided with minimal training, apparently holding to the notion that pupils are natural teachers and thus are sensitive to the needs of the learner. Others feel that extensive training in both content and personal-social skills is essential.[1] Just as the notion that "teachers are born, not made" has been discredited, so it would seem that tutors must be carefully prepared for their teaching tasks.

Typical tutoral training programs include the following points[2]:

1. Putting the student at ease
2. Clarifying the prescribed task
3. Showing the learner how to verify his or her answer
4. Directing the learner to read each problem aloud
5. Having the student respond overtly, marking or recording responses before the tutor provides feedback
6. Having the pupil verify each response
7. Avoiding any form of punishment
8. Providing a tangible reward when appropriate
9. Providing verbal praise when appropriate
10. On designated problems, evaluating all elements of mastery

Generally it is considered desirable to discuss and have each peer tutor play each behavior with another peer tutor. Each of these concepts should be treated as a ten-minute lesson. Training sessions should be as close to the actual tutoring sessions as possible.

Tutoring Procedure

The tutoring process represents a form of individualized instruction. As such, it must be carefully planned and executed. Since a number of pupils are usually involved, many of the activities will occur beyond the direct supervision and control of the teacher. In addition to content objectives, social and emotional considerations are of utmost importance. Thus the steps of the tutoring process, emphasized in this section, should be followed carefully.

Establishing Goals

Evidence clearly indicates that in a successful tutoring situation the tutor and learner may gain academically and in the social-emotional realm.[3] Thus participants are selected for various reasons. Sometimes, for example, a child who withdraws from an adult teacher may readily accept a peer tutor for certain periods of the day.

Ultimately, instructional goals for both tutor and student must be developed in specific, behavioral terms. In the academic realm, for example, it is not unreasonable to expect the tutor to gain at least one grade level in reading scores following the experience. If a warm, supportive atmosphere is expected, specific objectives could include the following:

> Exhibit reflective listening on at least 80 percent of observed occasions. Maintain eye contact while talking.

For pupils, of course, a primary objective is to help such persons master certain mental or motor skills. Those being tutored are seldom working at the same level as their tutors in content areas. Again, social-emotional needs must be considered. As with tutors, pupils frequently can relate better with their partners than with the teacher.

Obviously it is extremely hazardous to pair two "emotionally starved" individuals and expect immediate results. The specific needs of pupils must be thoroughly diagnosed. The pairing process, based upon all available evidence, is tentative at best. Careful observation during the first tutoring sessions may suggest the need for reassignment.

Diagnosis

Teachers who utilize peer tutoring have found pretesting a necessity. As tutoring generally has focused on the basic skills, standardized achievement tests are usually administered early in the school year. These are usually supplemented with informal tests, teacher observation, and so on.

Pupils selected as tutors must have a solid grasp of the specific skills needed. Hopefully at some point all children will possess sufficient grasp of materials to permit assignment as tutors. Sometimes a pupil may possess the needed skills but lack sufficient motivation to achieve; at other times a child may show deficiencies in organizing materials. Such individuals often make good tutors and frequently show remarkable improvement in their own areas of deficiency.

Tutor Guidelines

Most teachers prefer to provide the tutor with specific guidelines for tutoring. These can be grouped into categories of "Things to Do" and "Teaching Techniques." As experience is gained, such guidelines can be abbreviated or abandoned entirely. Ehly and Larson[4] offer an example that might be used in the area of spelling. Major portions of their illustration follow:

━━━━━━━━━   **Tutor Guidelines for a Tutoring Lesson on Spelling**   ━━━━━━━━━

Things To Do   First you should ask your partner friendly questions and do things that will make him or her feel comfortable with you.

Smile and speak in a friendly voice. Be careful not to speak too fast.

Read over the spelling words and sentences before you start the session. If you do not know how to pronounce a word or know the word's meaning, talk with your teacher before the session.

At the beginning, fill out your name, your pupil's name, and the date on the top of the lesson sheet and answer sheet.

Have your pupil spell out loud each word and then write it on the answer sheet as you present it. Be sure at the beginning of each session that your pupil knows that he or she must write down the spelling.

Teaching Techniques   You must follow the procedures listed below: Look over the lesson sheet for the day. There will be ten words to cover in the session. The sheet will have the same format every day.

Important things you can say to praise your tutee:

Very good,
Very, very good
You are really doing well.
You really know how to spell.
That's right.

Think of other ways to praise your tutee, so that you don't always say the same thing.

When you praise your tutee, speak clearly, and say it so that you sound pleased.

If the tutee does not spell a word correctly, do not say things like:

You are wrong.
Oh, no!
Why did you do that?

Sound positive. Emphasize exactly where the error is in the spelling, and that the tutee will be allowed to try to spell the word until he or she gets it correct.

Sample item from a lesson sheet:

"Grain. We gathered the grain in the field. Grain."

Read slowly and clearly.

"Grain. We gathered the grain in the field. Grain."

Repeat the entire sequence if the tutee asks you do so.

Tell the tutee to write down the spelling of the word you present (in the sample case, the word *grain*) onto the first section of the first line of the answer sheet.

If the tutee spells the word correctly, say, "That's right," or "Very good." Then go to the next word in the lesson.

But what if the tutee's answer is not right? You will point to the tutee's answer and say, "Everything you have written to the left of the vertical slash (you will put in the slash) is correct, but everything to the right of that slash is an error."

Here's how you put in the slash.

If the correct spelling of the word is	grain
and the tutee writes down	grane
you put in the slash like this:	gra / ne

Then you say, "Try spelling the word *grain* again."

The tutee will write down his or her second attempt in the second section of the line for that word *grain*. If the tutee spells the word correctly, say, "That's right" and go on to the next word of the lesson. If the tutee does not spell the word correctly, put a vertical slash at the point where the tutee made the error.

If the word to spell is	grain
and the tutee, on the second try, spells	graim
you put in the slash:	grai / m

Tell the tutee that everything to the right of the slash is an error and try to spell the word. If the tutee wants you to give the word in the sample sentence again, you may repeat the original sentence.

The tutee will write down the third attempt in the third section of the line for that word. If the tutee spells the word correctly, say, "That's right" and go on to the next word.

If the tutee does not spell the word correctly on the third attempt, show him or her the correct spelling. Write out the word on your scratch paper and let the tutee look at it. Tell the tutee, "We will be returning to this word in a little while, so you will get another chance to spell it correctly."

Go through the ten words in the daily lesson in the order that they are on the lesson sheet and follow the same procedures listed above.

After you have gone through the list once, allowing for up to three attempts at spelling a word correctly, you will have completed the first cycle of presentation.

You are then to go back to those words that were missed by your tutee in the first cycle. Follow the same procedures as before.

Notes to the Tutor   Lessons are planned so that you should take about thirty minutes to complete. If more time is needed, you may take longer.

If the tutee does not get the first letter of a word correct, help him or her to sound out the letter.

Your tutor log is to be filled out daily and turned in at the end of the week. Make sure to make note of the time you met with the tutee on a day. Just write down the time you started the session and the time you ended. Be sure to write down whether you were meeting for a regular or a makeup session. Also put down any comments about the tutee that seem important to you.

You must remember to praise the tutee every time he or she gives the correct spelling of a word.

By using such a guideline for each new area of instruction, beginning tutors can become effective teachers, knowing precisely what their tasks are. Feedback, in the form of a log, may be the only way the teacher can fully keep up with events. This applies especially when several pupil pairs are functioning at the same time.

Modeling

Often the pupil knows the skill but merely experiences difficulty in applying it correctly. Blocks to this application may be few or many; the difficulty arises from the pupil's inability to effectively analyze the source of difficulty. Thus the learner needs a pattern or model of a "better way" of completing the task. When compared with his or her own efforts, basic differences become readily apparent. To help a student, for example, in oral reading to develop proper enunciation and observe punctuation marks, the tutor can read orally as a model for the learner, observing the punctuation marks and developing proper speed and voice inflection. The pupil can then read the same selection as the tutor did.

Modeling can also consist of providing examples of correct solutions, as in math problems. It entails a step-by-step approach with a focus on important cues or prompts needed in the process. In the area of spelling, the tutor may say, "This is the way I do it" or "When I attempt to correct a misspelled word, this is how I think." It has been observed that the learner often behaviorally models the tutor. Realizing this likelihood, the tutor's behavior must carefully reflect specific goals of the program.

Practice

Acquisition of skills demands considerable practice. Deficiencies often arise from too little practice and, less often, from inappropriate practice. Often overlooked is a learner's mental state during practice exercises. For example, pupils may go through the motions but be thinking of more pleasant things. This especially applies to the practice of the mental skills.

The tutor's role during practice is to observe and to inquire of the learner's mental state at the time. It helps to relate his or her own thoughts during the experience also. For example, the tutor might say, "I kept thinking of the key words that our teacher placed on the chalkboard as she elaborated on pupil questions." Or, in learning to spell new terms, the tutor might suggest, "I concentrate on the syllables first and then tie the syllables together as a package."

The monotony of repeated practice can be minimized through the use of games. Some pupils almost intuitively develop their own games as cues in learning. One pupil, for example, was able to learn the nines of the multiplication table by envisioning nine spokes of a wheel as she practiced. Another pupil learned to spell a difficult term by relating it to a similar word. Such creative applications among better pupils are common. In many respects, the peer tutor is better qualified than the teacher to help a fellow pupil develop such skills; thus the expression, "To think like a pupil, one must be a pupil."

Teacher's Role

After clarifying the specific purpose and pairing pupils, the teacher serves as a resource guide. Suggestions for both tutor and learner are offered as needed. These may come in the form of suggested fresh approaches, clarification of difficult points, and so on. At all times, a spirit of teamwork is encouraged. Tutoring sessions should not be interrupted unless absolutely necessary.

When tutoring is used as a major activity over a period of time, the teacher and tutor should hold weekly sessions. Here tutors describe their experiences and draw upon each other and the teacher for help. It may be desirable to meet with pupils occasionally for similar purposes.

Values

- As classes have become more heterogeneous, individualization of instruction has become increasingly difficult. Peer tutoring offers considerable promise in this area.
- Peer tutoring is especially beneficial to the tutor.[5]
- Frequently a pupil can more readily understand another pupil's frame of reference than the teacher's framework.
- Serving in the role of tutor can be especially valuable to the able, unmotivated pupil.
- Peer tutoring often contributes to the social-emotional development of those involved.

Limitations and Problems

- The pairing process is critical. In some instances, re-pairing is necessary.
- If several tutoring teams are functioning simultaneously, it is difficult for the teacher to monitor both.
- There is some danger of stigmas when using pupils of the same age.
- Peer tutoring demands considerable training. Not all situations favor such a program.
- Peer tutoring is most effective in the realm of basic skills; it is less effective in the cognitive domain.
- Cross-age tutoring is often difficult to arrange. In effect, it reduces class time for the tutor.
- Many teachers subconsciously hold to the erroneous notion that "only teachers can teach." Thus they are unwilling to try the technique.

Dos and Don'ts

For this chapter, it seems appropriate to provide some "dos and don'ts" in the area of peer tutoring.

Dos

1. Permit each individual to serve the role of tutor and learner from time to time.

2. See that specific learning deficiencies are diagnosed before help is offered.
3. Try to establish a warm, supporting relationship with the learner.
4. Offer praise and encouragement frequently.
5. Provide the correct (or a better) procedure without criticizing.
6. Display patience and faith in the learner by both word and deed.
7. Call attention to the basic structure of steps involved.
8. Enlist the teacher's assistance when needed.
9. Help the pupil provide his or her own feedback (e.g., "How did you know that?").
10. Encourage extensive practice.
11. Review the skill or process frequently.
12. Make allowances for frequent lapses to undesirable habits or other behavioral patterns.

Don'ts

1. Don't create the impression that the tutor is "smart" while the learner is a "dummy."
2. Don't rush the learner.
3. Don't permit the tutoring session to stray too far from its purpose.
4. Don't criticize the pupil for errors.
5. Don't do the task for the learner repeatedly.
6. Don't get overinvolved with details.
7. Don't expect immediate skill development.
8. Don't let the pupil "slide over" habitual mistakes.

Endnotes

1. Keith Topping, "Peer Tutoring and Paired Reading: Combining Two Powerful Techniques," *The Reading Teacher,* Vol. 42, March 1989, pp. 488–494.
2. Stewart W. Ehly and Stephen C. Larsen, *Peer Tutoring for Individualized Instruction* (Boston: Allyn and Bacon, 1980), p. 53.
3. Ibid., pp. 33–36.
4. Ibid., pp. 88–95. Used by permission of the publisher.
5. Michael Webb and Wendy Schwartz, "Children Teaching Children: A good Way to Learn," *PTA Today,* October 1988, pp. 16–17.

Chapter 16

Inquiry-Discovery Method

Overview

Key Concepts

- Inquiry techniques are designed specifically for independence in problem solving.
- A set for inquiry is established when the pupil is guided into asking questions for which he or she has no logical answers.
- Inquiry processes may range in length from one or two hours to two or three weeks.
- Inquiry processes may be structured around several unit concepts.

Chapter Terms

- Inquiry process: An approach to learning that emphasizes pupil initiative and direction for generating and validating knowledge.
- Discovery lesson (episode): A short (often initiatory) experience designed to provoke a set for learning by "offending the learner's imagination" or otherwise prompting questions.

The new emphasis upon processes of "inquiry," or "discovery," or "inductive" teaching has created considerable confusion among teachers. Although often referred to as "a method," a perusal of the recent literature suggests many interpretations of meaning. It is generally agreed that the basic processes of inquiry are synonymous with Dewey's steps of reflective thinking, first published around the turn of the century.[1] The "new" emphasis focuses upon pupil self-direction as an outgrowth of a carefully planned situation. *How* a situation may be structured and *how* pupil self-direction may be structured provide most of the apparent confusion over methodology, suggesting not one but many approaches to the problem.

Fundamental Properties

Like most other instructional approaches, the processes of inquiry are representative of systematized problem solving. Unlike some other approaches, however, this technique is based upon current pupil needs and interests rather than upon organized bodies of subject matter as a starting point. Indeed, the processes of reflective thought are applied by the entire group.

The fundamental properties of the inquiry-discovery method are based upon a cooperative experience. This cooperative experience may be teacher-group or teacher-individual situations. In both cases, the classroom environment plays a vital role in the inquiry-discovery method. The fundamental properties of the inquiry-discovery method are treated within this general framework.

Teacher-Group Inquiry

The advocates of teacher-group inquiry feel that *interpretation* is best accomplished in group discussion, based upon a problem designed to encourage pupils to argue. The teacher as discussion leader plays the role of devil's advocate. The class as a group develops its own chain of reasoning as it seeks to *generalize* from the data provided. *Conclusions* are an outgrowth of pupil analysis.

The Individual Learner

Those who favor the teacher-individual cooperative experience suggest that it is the child who must be the active individual in his or her own learning process in the inquiry-discovery method. The learning activity must be both individualized and personalized to be effective, relevant, and enriching to the participant.

A fundamental property of the inquiry-discovery classroom is to provide pupils with an organized, improved method of thinking about and dealing with information. Thus the learning activities must be provided to allow self-direction for the pupil. Hence, each individual has some topic, problem, or question to investigate that has high interest appeal and about which he or she is curious. Findings, of course, are shared and evaluated by the entire class group.

Classroom Environment

A fundamental property of the inquiry-discovery method is a classroom climate that is open to queries. The children in the classroom must feel comfortable in asking questions. Each child should have the assurance that the teacher and classmates will listen and respect his or her questions and discovery activities.

The teacher must establish an environment in the classroom that will stimulate curiosity. A wide range of experiences should be provided in which the pupil is involved with concrete objects, printed materials, pictorial items, audiovisual devices, and creative and investigative activities.

Problem Focused

A fundamental aspect of the inquiry-discovery method is that it focuses on problems. These problems are defined and probed. Often in the inquiry method, the problems have the possibility of more than one correct answer. In working through the problem there is more than one way of arriving at answers; therefore, a range of alternatives is always possible for the pupil.

Questions Stressed

In the inquiry-discovery method, questions are stressed rather than answers. Emphasis is not on subject matter to be mastered, but rather on ways of examining and explaining processes and events. Indeed, there are no teacher-determined "correct" answers. Questions become the important aspect of the teaching act, and they are used to find out what the pupil knows and does not know. In addition, questions are asked to arouse interest, evaluate a pupil's preparation, develop insights, review and summarize materials, stimulate critical thinking, and evaluate the achievement of goals.[2]

Inquiry-Discovery Procedure

The inquiry-discovery procedure may vary somewhat from one situation to another; however, the major objective is to develop an experience in which the child is encouraged to explore, experiment, and discover facts, generalizations, and techniques. Preparation and planning, initiating activity, development of the lesson, concept development, and evaluating the pupil behavior are all necessary steps in the inquiry-discovery procedure.

Preparation and Planning

In planning for the inquiry-discovery process, the teacher must carefully select an area to be explored. The teacher collects documents and other objects, places books in the classroom, and arranges for full use of the available resources. If maps, diagrams, pictures, tables, and art objects are needed, then these resources should be made available.

In addition to getting the classroom environment ready for the inquiry-discovery process, the teacher must develop the behavioral objectives, questioning strategies, and planning activities well in advance of the lesson.

Initiating the Activity

Quite frequently the project is introduced with a "discovery episode" that serves as a springboard for inquiry and discussion. Be it a short poem in language arts or a short science demonstration, the objective is to stimulate thinking.

An example of a discovery episode could begin with the students observing the teacher with a bottle in which is found a liquid. From the bottle top a drinking straw protrudes. The teacher drinks from the bottle by sucking up through the straw. The teacher then seals the top of the bottle around the straw. When the teacher tries to suck liquid up through the straw, no liquid comes up through the straw after it is sealed. The discovery question is "Why did this happen?" The discovery episode ends at this point and the lesson development begins.

Development of the Lesson

The discovery episode is used to further develop the lesson and to induce perplexity and create the general attitude that the teacher is also an inquirer who has no absolute answers to offer. It is emphasized that points must be defended on the basis of data. This sets the stage for group work that follows. In short, the teacher prods pupils to explore and test new alternatives. Questions usually are redirected to the group. During time of impasses, the teacher may raise additional questions designed to help pupils see alternative ways of resolving an issue. Sometimes the pupil-question, teacher-answer technique may be employed. To refrain from supplying too much information, pupils may be restricted to questions that may be answered by yes or no.

The inquiry-oriented teacher encourages pupils "to play their hunches" and to conjecture. This activity may be considered the core of classroom instruction. Generally, the teacher's role may be described as dialectical rather than didactic, inasmuch as it is assumed that pupils will learn more when provided opportunities to discover ideas and relationships for themselves.

During the development of the lesson, the pupils are expected to ask questions, formulate hypotheses, search for additional data, draw conclusions, and learn concepts. Concept formulation may be learned by grouping or classifying those facts that have common properties, labeling each group, listing specific pieces of information from a larger whole, or generalizing from the facts presented. From the conclusions developed by an individual child or a group of children, a concept could also be formulated. During the inquiry-discovery method, concepts are not only learned but also must be put to use in observing, classifying, generalizing, and other processes.

Evaluation

The evaluation of the process of inquiry-discovery should be continuous. Throughout this method, the teacher should observe how children go about their tasks of inquiry as well as the end product of their work. Inasmuch as the inquiry-discovery method is a cooperative activity, much of the evaluation can be done through joint pupil-teacher evaluation.

Pupil behavior that can be evaluated would include the type of questions the child asks and how well the pupil identifies problems, organizes information, and proceeds through the inquiry-discovery process to a hypothesis and concept.

Planning for Inquiry-Discovery

A major problem that causes poor inquiry-discovery lessons is the lack of planning on the part of the teacher. One of the greatest changes a teacher should make when using this method is in the preparation and planning stages. The following lesson plan is only a guide to an inquiry-discovery classroom experience. Many other approaches to this method could be just as appropriate.

———————— **Lesson Plan Illustration (science—fifth or sixth grade)** ————————

Unit Matter—Its Changes
Concepts
1. Matter has different volume depending upon its state.
2. Atmospheric pressure is exerted upon matter.
3. Heat can be conducted.
4. Vapor exerts a pressure.
Problem Does matter change its volume when it changes its state?
Goals After this lesson the pupil should have furthered his or her understanding of one of the preceding science concepts, as evidenced by:

1. Ability to identify the problem through asking questions
2. Ability to organize information
3. Ability to develop a hypothesis
4. Ability to generalize and learn a concept

Initiating the Activity

The Discovery Episode

"What do you see here on the science table?"

(The following responses may be made by the pupils.)

"A can with a screw-down cap."

"A Bunsen burner."

"A beaker of water."

"I am putting one inch of water in the can. Now as I heat the can with the water in it, what will happen?"

(The pupils may give various responses.)

When the water begins to boil, the cap is screwed on tightly. After the water has boiled and the cap is secured tightly, a stream of cold water will be poured over the can. The can will then collapse.

Lesson Development

The Discussion Episode   Some possible questions are as follows:

1. Why did the can collapse?
2. Why was it necessary to put water in the can?
3. Why was the can heated?
4. Why did the can need to be capped?
5. Why was it necessary to pour cold water over the can?

(During this time questions usually are redirected to the group.)

Deriving Generalizations or Concepts   From the demonstration, what big ideas seem to stand out? For example:

1. For the walls of the can to move inward, it is necessary that forces pushing in be greater than forces pushing out.
2. The atmospheric pressure pushing in on the can is constant throughout the experiment; therefore, the forces pushing outward must have decreased.
3. When water changes into steam, the volume is increased.

Values

- In the inquiry-discovery method the pupil assumes the central role in the educative process. The pupil becomes an active inquirer rather than a passive learner.
- Emphasis is upon problems that are defined, probed, and labeled as relevant to the learner.
- The inquiry-discovery method's aim is the development of judgment-making ability. A range of alternatives is always available.
- In effect, the method shifts the role of the teacher from that of supplying answers to one of asking questions.
- Every individual's belief system of values and attitudes is considered important. Expanding and developing that system is a major goal.
- The teacher, too, is an inquirer. At no time does the teacher assume to know all that is being learned.
- Emphasis upon competition for grades is removed. The pupil is working with goals that are his or her own.

Limitations and Problems

- In a group inquiry-discovery session, not all pupils may be involved in the actual process. One pupil may make all the decisions and another pupil may merely record the decisions.
- There is a danger that the inquiry-discovery method may become a ritual rather than a true problem-solving approach.
- The time factor is an important aspect in the inquiry-discovery method. There is a decided tendency to "rush" pupil responses. Critical thinking takes time.
- There is a tendency with some pupils to provide answers or solutions to problems the pupil feels are the teacher's preconceived solution. Sometimes such a session may evolve into a "game" to ascertain what the teacher has in mind.

─────── **Illustrated Inquiry-Discovery Problems** ───────

I. Useful in the social studies area (primary grades)
   Unit   Community Helpers
   Concept   Police officers are needed in our community.
   Problem   Why are police officers needed in our community?
   Discovery Episode   From a picture of a police officer, the following questions may be developed:

1. What do they do?
2. Why do they carry a gun?
3. What might happen if our community did not have them?
4. What makes a good police officer?

II. Useful in the study skills area (middle grades)
Unit   Map Reading
Concept   Geographic features and natural resources affect the growth and location of cities.
Problem   Where should the largest city be placed on this map?
Discovery Episode   After reading various maps of the same area, each pupil may develop the following questions for inquiry:
1. How will rivers and lakes affect the size of cities?
2. How will mountains, valleys, and other land forms affect the growth of cities?
3. How will climate affect the city size?
4. How will mineral deposits affect the size of the city?

III. Useful in the reading area (any grade)
Unit   Critical Reading
Concept   Drawing conclusions from facts read are processes of critical reading.
Problem   How could this story end?
Discovery Episode   After reading a third of a selection, the following speculative questions may be developed:
1. What inferences can be drawn from the reading?
2. What conclusions can be made from the material read?
3. What could be the story plot?
4. What is the likely outcome for the story?

IV. Useful in the health area (upper grades)
Unit   Foods Useful for People
Concepts   Modern technology has made it possible for people to eat food grown in all parts of the world.
Problem   How is modern technology changing people's eating habits?
Discovery Episode   After viewing a filmstrip about technology and food, the following questions may be developed:
1. What are some kinds of food grown in some areas of the world and not in other areas?
2. What would happen if the transportation system of today stopped immediately?
3. How can technology make it possible to eat food from all areas of the world?
4. Why can food be produced in an area that does *not* have the proper geographic requirements?

5. Why does the availability of food make a difference in people's eating habits?

Endnotes

1. John Dewey, *How We Think,* rev. ed. (Boston: D.C. Heath and Co., 1933).
2. J. T. Dillon, "The Remedial Status of Student Questioning," *Journal of Curriculum Studies,* May–June 1988, pp. 197–210.

Chapter 17

Explicit
Instruction Method

Overview

Key Concepts

- Facts, rules, and action sequences are taught effectively and efficiently through the explicit instruction method.
- The explicit instruction method is mainly teacher-centered instruction.
- Children in both whole-class instruction and small-group instruction can benefit from explicit instruction.
- Allocated time, academic engaged time, and success enhances student learning during the explicit instructional lesson.

Chapter Terms

- Direct instruction: The teacher tells, shows, models, demonstrates, and teaches the skills to be learned in the most direct, quickest route. Another term used for this teacher-centered strategy is *explicit instruction*.
- Allocated time: The length of time allocated for instruction in any one particular subject matter area.
- Academic engaged time: That portion of allocated time when a student is actually attending to the task at hand.
- Monitoring: The ability of the teacher to check for student understanding, to provide feedback, to reteach if necessary, and to ensure that the assigned task is completed by each student.
- Schema: An image held in the mind that serves to associate various elements of knowledge into a coherent whole.
- Apperception: The process of understanding something perceived in terms of previous experiences.

Fundamental Properties

In the professional literature explicit instruction has been referred to in many different ways. For example, it has been called direct instruction, active teaching, teacher-directed instruction, and teacher-scripted instruction. In its generalizable term, explicit instruction has come to mean some

196

form of explicit, intensive teacher-led instruction.[1] In the context of this chapter, explicit instruction is considered teacher led with many opportunities for the students to still become involved in the learning process. The properties described here are basic to the explicit instruction method of teaching.

Teacher-Led Instruction

Teacher-led instruction begins with the teacher discussing experiences that build background for the children. The lesson objective is stated and a reason is given why the materials to be learned are important to them. The direct explicit instruction by the teacher may proceed through several possible routes. One route could involve the teacher telling them certain facts or details. The teacher could describe or model a certain behavior or skill needed to be learned. Whatever route is followed by the teacher, the students are given directly, and in the shortest way possible, the information that is needed for the lesson.

Gradual Release of Responsibility[2]

In the process of gradual release of responsibility, the teacher assumes the responsibility at the beginning and then slowly relinquishes that responsibility to the children in the classroom. This process begins with the teacher, then moves to joint responsibility (teacher and students during group practice and checking for understanding), and finally to the children, with full responsibility by the children taking place during independent practice. From the teacher leading the lesson discussion to the students in independent practice, the gradual release of responsibility takes place so the children are actively participating in the learning process. During the group practice, checking for understanding, and independent work, the teacher is constantly monitoring the children in their work.

Allocated Time

The amount of time allocated to an academic subject is directly related to the amount of student learning. Therefore, it is evident that the teacher must schedule the proper amount of time the children will need to learn the objectives of the lesson. In addition to allocated time, the on-task behavior of the students will also make a difference in the amount that is learned. This on-task behavior is referred to in the professional literature as academic engaged time. Not only must the time be allocated for learning to take place, but also the more the students are academically involved in the task, the greater the effect on learning the lesson objectives. Another factor to be considered is that the students need to be successful in their pursuit of the task to be learned. The combination of these elements certainly will aid the student's learning process. The teacher should work toward dealing with these three elements in developing his or her explicit instructional lesson.

Explicit Instruction Procedure

Although it varies greatly from one teacher to another, the explicit instruction procedure as mentioned in this chapter consists of six steps: (1) building background, (2) lesson objective, (3) input and modeling, (4) group practice and checking for understanding, (5) independent practice, and (6) evaluation.[3]

Building Background

In this part of an explicit or direct instruction lesson, the teacher introduces the new materials that will be taught during the instructional period. Background is developed through activating the child's schema. To activate the students' schemata, the teacher attempts to match the children's past experiences with the subject to be taught in the lesson. This is called *apperception*. It is the job of the teacher to begin with the experiences the students have already had, in other words, to talk about the things the students know. Then the teacher makes a transfer or comparison from that which is known to the new material to be studied in the lesson. This in turn will help the children to understand the material to be studied.

Lesson Objective

The purpose of the lesson is clearly stated by the teacher. The students are also informed how the materials to be studied or the particular skills will help them.

Input and Modeling

The teacher tells, shows, models, or demonstrates how the skills or the subject matter material can be learned. During this part of the lesson responsibility for the skill is gradually released from the teacher to the students. The teacher continues to constantly check if the students understand what is being taught.

Group Practice and Checking for Understanding

During this part of the lesson, the students are asked to locate data, make items, write out answers, and read to find answers under the teacher's supervision. At this stage the teacher continues to monitor the childrens' progress very closely to determine which students may need further help or reteaching.

Independent Practice

Students work independently of the teacher. This practice could be, for example, reading silently, completing worksheets and charts, writing answers to questions, or following the steps to solve a science or mathematical problem.

Evaluation

Together, the teacher and students check the information collected during the independent practice. Any errors or misinformation can be cleared up at this time. Evaluation is made of the final product generated from the lesson.

Planning Explicit Instruction

Inasmuch as the explicit lesson is a formal one, it must be carefully planned. The plan that follows indicates one way to teach an explicit reading lesson in comprehension. The specific comprehension skill to be taught to the children is drawing conclusions while reading.

─────────── **Lesson Plan Illustration (reading area — fourth grade)** ───────────

Building Background   Read to your students a very short, exciting story or chapter from a book. Stop before you get to the conclusion. Over their cries of objection, ask them what they think is going to happen next. Discuss it. Tell them that you will read the end of the story later on in the lesson.

Lesson Objective   Tell the children that today they are going to be learning about anticipating outcomes, which will help them in becoming conclusion-drawing detectives.

Input and Modeling   Discuss with the children why it is important to be able to predict outcomes. Tell them that as they are reading, they should constantly be looking at the story and trying to anticipate what is going to happen next and checking to see if what they thought is correct. Model this process as you continue reading the story used in the background section of the lesson. Stop periodically and predict what might happen next in the story. Then continue reading to determine if the prediction was correct. As you model for the children, think out loud why you are making these types of predictions based upon what is read.

Group Practice and Checking for Understanding   Have children practice predicting outcomes with comic strips. Using a series of action strips such as Superman or Spiderman, read with the class a section of it. Several places in the story, stop and discuss what they think is going to happen next. Read on to see how they did in predicting these action strips.

Independent Practice   From a Sunday newspaper, cut out several comics, leaving out the last frame. Give to each child a strip with which to work. Have the child write what he or she thinks is going to happen next in the strip. After a few minutes, have the children exchange strips, until they have all worked with each one.

Evaluation   Discuss their answers for each strip, and then share with them the actual ending from the paper. Discuss the value of predicting the outcome of stories as it helps them to comprehend what they are reading.

Values

- Explicit instruction gives the teacher immediate feedback, so she or he can make corrective changes during the lesson for increased student understanding.
- Instructional and curriculum materials can be adjusted and modified to meet the individual differences of children in the classroom when planning explicit instruction.
- Although at the onset of an explicit instructional lesson the teacher takes the larger responsibility, through gradual release of responsibility the students become actively involved in the learning process.
- Explicit instruction lends itself to well-planned, systematic, and intensive instruction when needed in teaching children in the classroom.

Limitations and Problems

- Some explicit instruction lessons are scripted in such a way that the teacher simply delivers the lesson with very little, if any, instructional decision making.
- Instruction should be child centered rather than teacher centered.
- Explicit instruction exerts too much control over students and teachers.
- Educational means rather than ends are emphasized in explicit instructional lessons.
- Explicit instruction models are not appropriate in all instruction nor in all subject matter areas of the curriculum.

Illustrated Explicit Instruction Plans

I. Useful in the reading area (first grade)
Lesson Objective   Children will be taught main ideas in lists of words. Tell the children that finding the main ideas will help them in reading comprehension.
Input and Modeling
1. Prepare a list of five or six words under a main idea word.
2. Compare the list of words to the legs of an octopus. The list of words supports the main idea.
3. Produce several other lists of five or six words related to a main idea.
4. Let the children select a main idea word that tells about the whole list. Each word in the list must support the main idea.

II. Useful in the mathematics area (third grade)
Lesson Objective   Children will be taught three-digit addition. Tell the children that learning how to do three-digit addition will help them when they start working with more complicated mathematical problems.
Input and Modeling
1. Add ones and then regroup.
2. Add tens and then regroup.
3. Add hundreds and then regroup.

III. Useful in the science area (fifth grade)
Lesson Objective   Children will understand that plants and animals are made of cells. Tell the children that this introduction is necessary at this point because it is the foundation of our study of living organisms.

Input and Modeling
1. Explain that plants and animals are alike in one important way. They are made of cells.
2. Explain that because of their size, cells could not be seen until someone discovered the microscope.
3. Explain that the size of an organism is related to the number of cells it contains.

IV. Useful in the social studies area (sixth or seventh grade)
Lesson Objective   Children will understand how changes in various landforms over the ages have shaped the earth as it is known today.
Input and Modeling
1. Describe the physical makeup of the earth.
2. Explain how changes occur in the earth's surface.
3. Describe the various landforms that make up the earth's crust.

Endnotes

1. James F. Baumann, "Direct Instruction Reconsidered," *Journal of Reading,* May 1988, pp. 712–718.
2. P. David Pearson, and M. C. Gallagher, "The Instruction of Reading Comprehension," *Contemporary Educational Psychology,* 1983, pp. 317–344.
3. Paul M. Hollingsworth, and D. Ray Reutzel, "Prior Knowledge, Content-Related Attitude and Reading Comprehension," *Journal of Educational Research,* March/April 1990, pp. 194–200.

Chapter 18

Oral Reporting Techniques

Overview

Key Concepts

- For many years the oral reporting technique has been misused in many schools.
- The oral reporting technique is basically a means of clarifying or expanding information; other supplementary methods must be employed to complete the reflective process.
- The oral report is short, usually running less than fifteen minutes.
- The oral report essentially involves telling them what you are going to tell them, telling them, and telling them what you have told them, for example, the initial summary, detailed information, and final summary.
- The oral report is usually more effective when hearing is supplemented with visual experiences.

Chapter Terms

- Oral report: A short presentation designed to inform or clarify points that may be temporarily impeding the process of reflective thinking.
- Initial summary: The technique of foreshadowing major points for the learner.

Strictly speaking, there is no single oral reporting method. Rather, the term encompasses several allied techniques. When the teacher or pupil informs others by telling, explaining, or showing, this is oral reporting. The traditional (formal) lecture method, first popularized in the medieval university, was designed as the basic instructional approach for a school system that emphasized knowledge as an instructional end. As emphasis shifted from the acquisition of knowledge for its own sake to the *use* of knowledge to solve meaningful life problems, the formal lecture fell into disrepute.

Oral reporting in the elementary school is designed to expedite pupil problem-solving activities. It may be employed for varying lengths of time at any point in the learning process when it becomes obvious that pupils can profit from outside assistance. Frequently oral reports are used to provide pupils with essential background information for subsequent learning experiences. Often the procedure will involve use of certain films or demonstrations.

Fundamental Properties

There is nothing sacred per se about the size of a class group in which a pupil learns. Learning results from a combination of listening, viewing, reading, and talking activities. The size of a group is most appropriately determined by the purposes or objectives being sought. Likewise, the choice of instructional method will depend upon what must be accomplished. It has been assumed throughout this book that the bulk of major learning activities should be so organized as to accommodate critical thinking. The fundamental properties of oral reporting are treated within this general framework.

Objectivity

In evaluating evidence, the learner must have access to the pertinent facts. Since the teacher, pupil, or resource person may represent the major source of information, an objective, unbiased presentation is essential. The demonstrator or reporter must clearly label private opinions if they must be stated. The reporter will state his or her knowledge sources and indeed will encourage further investigation when controversy is evident. Whenever possible, a report is avoided in highly controversial areas.

Visual Aids

Oral presentations are difficult to understand and to remember unless supplemented liberally with visual aids. Use of the chalkboard, pictures, color transparencies, diagrams, and the like can greatly enhance the effectiveness of oral presentations. An effective reporter, for example, will frequently outline major points on the chalkboard or chart and then proceed to develop each point by offering numerous illustrations and examples. With the use of visual aids, the pupils are better able to remember and understand the main ideas in the report.

Repetition

Repetition provides another useful means of supplementing the spoken word. It is characterized by an initial summary, periodic summaries along the way (if the oral report is of considerable length), and a final summary. A teacher once expressed the idea in these words: "Tell your listeners what you plan to say, tell them, and then tell them what you have said." Such planned repetition seems more vivid, thereby providing a much needed structure for retention of major points.

Feedback

Feedback is an essential aspect of the instructional process.[1] Teachers quite naturally accept and sometimes elicit questions during difficult explanations. Teacher or pupil oral reports and demonstrations are usually short, providing opportunities for clarifications immediately after the experiences. Sometimes the question period may even exceed the length of the original presentation. It is only through such feedback that the reporter or demonstrator is able to discover blocks to communication and learning.

Supplementary Techniques

When learning is conceived as a process of critical thinking, it is obvious that the oral report cannot stand alone. Psychologists have emphasized repeatedly the importance of an overtly active learner. Whenever the oral report is employed, it merely serves the function of providing data and background information needed for resolution of an important problem. Thus the oral report must be supplemented with additional learning activities germane to a given problem.

Time Limitations

The elementary school age is an active one. The pupils usually experience difficulty in concentrating on a problem for a long time. They need to move about, ask questions, and express themselves frequently. Thus oral presentations should be limited to a period of not more than ten to fifteen minutes. With small children, even the teacher has difficulty keeping the children's interest over fifteen minutes. Even so, they must be interspersed with extended periods of activity. If the oral report must be longer, it should be broken into two time periods separated by a lively question-and-answer session.

Oral Reporting Procedure

As has been indicated, oral reporting procedures vary somewhat from one situation to another. For example, a report or demonstration may vary from one or two minutes of spontaneous explanation to an entire class period. The frame of reference utilized in this section is the preplanned presentation (by the teacher or by the pupil), which usually ranges from ten to fifteen minutes. Generally the procedure will incorporate the essentials of oral reporting and demonstration procedures. Important differences in these techniques are noted.

Identifying the Problem

The oral report problem usually is formulated as a question of fact. Such problems are characterized as "is" or "are" questions. A fifth grade pupil, for example, might be asked to prepare an oral report on the American buffalo. When formulated as a question of fact, the problem might be "What factors contributed to the virtual extinction of the American buffalo (bison)?" Although oral reports often are assigned as topics, pupils limit and clarify problems by formulating specific factual-type questions.

Problems of a highly controversial nature are usually not handled as oral reports. Sometimes a teacher will find it necessary to report on such a problem, but different points of view must be presented as objectively as possible.

Organizing the Presentation

Oral techniques are ineffective unless the speaker captures the imagination of the listeners. One can do this by beginning the presentation with an unusual or startling statement. One pupil, for example, who was reporting on the effects of fluoridation on teeth began the presentation with "I hate dental appointments."

When the topic is of considerable interest to the group, one may go into it directly. This is best accomplished by reference to the main theme or purpose. For example, the teacher who finds it necessary to interrupt other class activities to give a needed explanation usually will plunge directly into the points to be clarified. Many times, however, the group will not be especially concerned with the subject. They may not understand how a presentation relates to the ongoing class activities. Most reports and demonstrations fall into this category. In addition to a catchy title designed to arouse curiosity, an *attention-getting* opening is needed. A startling statement, question, or unusual illustration at the very beginning can gain immediate attention. The pupil who is to present a report on the effects of fluoridation on teeth might open with these words:

> Your teeth are as old as a thirty-year-old person. An individual who has lived thirty years has lived almost one-half of his or

life; a tooth that has lived twelve years has lived approximately one-half of its life. But with the help of fluoridation the average tooth may chew well for you. . . .

This pupil made an unusual comparison and then explained how the information could be of value to those listening to the report.

The attention and needs set the stage for that which is to follow. Usually three or four statements will suffice. The speaker must carefully avoid extending this part of the presentation beyond its usefulness.

It is in the *satisfaction* phase of a presentation that one states references and presents the main points of the talk. The individual can greatly increase the effectiveness of this phase of the presentation by adhering to a simple outline.

1. Initial summary: This consists of a brief enumeration of the main points to be made. For young people especially, it is desirable to write these points on the chalkboard.
2. Detailed information: Here the speaker brings in supporting facts, examples, and illustrations to clarify the issues. It is desirable to show the relationship between the major points.

    Some individuals have difficulty in determining what the main points will be. The reporter can consider breaking his or her topic into such categories as time sequence (past, present, future), cause-and-effect relationships, interested parties involved, and anticipated problems and their solutions.

    The speaker completes one point before proceeding to the next. By referring to the original points listed on the chalkboard, the speaker is able to move from one area to another without losing the listeners.
3. Final summary: The speaker concludes by restating main points and important conclusions that have been developed.

The pupil who reported on the effects of fluoridation on teeth broke the presentation into three parts—causes of tooth decay, effects of fluoridation, and permanence of fluoridation treatment. After placing the main points on the board for the benefit of the class, the pupil presented facts and examples designed to clarify each of the main points.

Listening Techniques

One of the most difficult problems facing a teacher involves ways and means of educating a group to listen effectively. It is easy enough to spot the pupil who is overtly disturbing, but much of the time it is practically impossible to detect the individual who has let his or her mind wander to other avenues of thought. On the other hand, some individuals who attempt to listen carefully have difficulty forming the mental images essential for comprehension.

In many life situations, listening is voluntary or purposeful. Often this is not the case in ordinary classroom situations. Many times members of the audience are captive listeners. (In most states, youngsters are required to attend school and participate in programs in which they have no genuine interest.) Attention, however, is enhanced *when the listener realizes that he or she is to become directly involved in subsequent activities.* For example:

1. A teacher explained an arithmetic problem, involving principles necessary for doing the assignment.
2. The teacher issued final instructions before the start of an extended field trip.
3. Mary gave a report on the mountain rattlesnake, which the group was likely to encounter on a science excursion.
4. An individual demonstrated techniques of artificial respiration prior to practice by each pupil.

Listening is also enhanced when the speaker is sincerely interested in what he or she is saying. Frequently this is lacking in assigned reports. The pupil may see the task as just a job to be done. The speaker who makes the presentation almost a life or death matter is likely to hold the listeners.

Thus far, consideration has been given to the speaker's efforts to gain the attention of the audience. However, communication is a joint process between the speaker and the observer. The listener has definite responsibilities other than merely placing oneself within hearing range of the speaker and assuming the proper listening pose.

One who listens pays attention to what is being said. This state of mind suggests that one is focusing faculties on what he or she expects to receive from the experience. An individual *listens with a purpose.* The person who listens in a vague sort of way is likely to receive little benefit from the presentation. In an expository type of presentation the audience is interested in the soundness and relationships of the facts and ideas presented. This in turn will help them organize their listening for a purpose. After all, there will always be reports and demonstrations that are poorly organized. However, it may still be possible to profit from the experience despite the speaker's limitations.

Presenting the Oral Report

The effective presentation of an oral report or demonstration embodies all the characteristics of effective speaking. First of all, the speaker must be heard. One must vary voice and pitch in such a way as to drive home the important points. The good speaker is enthusiastic about what he or she has to say and looks directly at the listeners—talking *to* them rather than *at* them.

Techniques of delivery will be found in almost any communications textbook. The following elements of effective communication are basic. The reporter should:

1. Speak in a conversational manner.
2. Closely observe audience reactions.
3. Maintain poise at all times. (Some teachers violate this rule by sitting on the desk or leaning on a speaker's stand. In an attempt to appear casual or relaxed, they appear to some pupils as sloppy or lazy.)
4. Avoid annoying mannerisms. (One may develop little habits that detract seriously from what is being said. Often the teacher is unaware of these annoyances. Some teachers periodically provide pupils an opportunity to indicate the nature and extent of such annoying mannerisms. Anonymity is essential for valid suggestions.)

Entertaining Questions

The question or discussion period following an oral report or demonstration is of utmost importance. The report, being designed to inform the group, usually needs some clarification. This can come only from the group, as the speaker cannot know the type of mental images the discourse has produced. Three to five minutes usually will suffice for a fifteen-minute report.

The teacher then leads the class in a brief *review* of the main points made and brings them to bear upon the solution of a problem. The reader will recall that an oral report is meant to be a *basis* for problem solving. It is concerned with the data-gathering (factual) step. There remains the evaluation of the data and their bearing upon an appropriate solution of the problem under consideration. In the process of review both pupils and teacher can bring related information to bear upon the problem.

A concomitant outcome of an oral report can be valuable training in evaluation of data. Pupils need training in assessing the validity and reliability of both the spoken and written word. Fallacies, improper deduction, and outright distortion of facts are among the most prevalent weaknesses of oral reports. Young pupils are especially prone to confuse the issues by expressing their own value judgments along with the facts.

Most demonstrations are performed to help pupils visualize how conclusions are reached. Frequently the class is expected to form certain conclusions on the basis of evidence produced by the demonstration. Teachers violate sound scientific principles, however, by encouraging pupils to conclude too much on the basis of *one* experiment.

Evaluating Oral Presentations

To assist pupils, especially the older elementary school children, in improving their oral reporting techniques, an evaluation is an essential ingredient. However, one of the most difficult and controversial aspects of oral presentations involves evaluation. Indeed, some teachers attempt to judge such presentations on the basis of purely general impressions. Some authorities would seriously question or even deplore such a technique. Whether or not we like it, evaluations of oral discourses are highly subjective. Thus they are affected by certain predispositions of the evaluator. The personal factor involved can be substantially reduced by establishing a number of bases for such an evaluation. At least three bases that can be used are the following:

1. A presentation can be judged on the basis of the response of the group. Do pupils seem interested in the report during the actual presentation? Are there a number of appropriate questions following the report? Do pupils keep referring to the speaker's points in the follow-through session?
2. A presentation can be evaluated on the basis of the techniques of presentation. Was there evidence of planning or of proper body and voice control? Was eye contact maintained throughout?
3. A report can be judged on the basis of the adequacy of content coverage. Did the speaker present the facts fully? Was the speaker able to maintain his or her role as impartial observer?

The fallacy of using audience reaction as a sole basis for evaluation is readily apparent. Many reportorial topics, for instance, may provoke enthusiasm because they are of immediate concern to the group. Or they may happen to support previous convictions of many of the listeners. Sometimes the reporter will be especially well liked by the group. Enthusiasm expressed under such circumstances can be high even though the content is poorly stated or even invalid.

The immediate disadvantage of relying solely on techniques of delivery is inherent in the purpose of the talk. A report is designed to inform a group of people. Although recommended speech techniques correlate with effective communication, it is possible that the criterion of objective techniques will not be an effective measure for a particular individual.

The third criterion for evaluating a report is the adequacy of the content. The completeness and accuracy of content can be lost if oral communication is ineffective; therefore, the report *cannot* be judged solely on facts presented. The oral report is dependent on adequate communication of ideas.

It can be seen, then, that all three bases of evaluation are needed. Few teachers can maintain a very high degree of accuracy by relying on general impressions only. Many teachers utilize rating scales that can be checked during and immediately following oral presentations.

The rating scale for oral presentations, which follows, illustrates the essentials of such a measure. It will be noted that all three of the bases for evaluation previously described are included in the rating scale. In addition, there is a dimension for "general effectiveness." Different teachers, of course, favor different evaluation forms.

Rating Scale for Oral Presentations

Directions   Pupil will be marked with a check (√) on a continuum from one end of the line to the other. A check within the broken lines will be roughly equivalent to an average rating.

I. Delivery
  A. Lesson Beginning

| Attention-getting, indicative of general content. | Beginning apparently planned, but effectiveness somewhat lacking. | Beginning poorly given; rambling statements; apologies. |

  B. Audience Contact

| Looks directly at listeners. | Depends heavily on notes, apparently does not "see" the listeners. | Reads from notes or looks above heads of listeners. |

C. Enthusiasm

| Intensely interested in topic. Stress is "natural" or "spontaneous." | Some interest evident. Occasionally lapses into a monotone. | Lack of interest; just another job to be done. |

D. Use of Communication Skills (voice, posture and gestures, grammar, spelling, penmanship)

| Communication skills above reproach. | One or two of the communication skills need further development. | Several communication skills need immediate attention. |

II. Content

A. Major Points

| Major points stressed and supported with pertinent examples. | Major points not very clearly defined and developed. | Content of the presentation confusing or extremely vague. |

B. Objectivity

| Distinguishes between "facts" and opinion. | Sometimes difficult to distinguish between facts and opinion. Tends to overemphasize own opinions. | Facts and opinions generally indistinguishable. Apparently unaware of projections. |

III. Audience Reaction

| Pupils attentive and ask pertinent questions. | Some audience interest evident. Questions are brief. | Little evidence of interest. Few questions. |

IV. General Effectiveness

High overall effectiveness. Appropriate "balance" maintained.	Presentation reasonably effectively.	Presentation generally ineffective. Lacks needed "punch."

Planning for the Oral Report

Techniques of informing others must be carefully planned. Pupils are painfully aware of teachers who "cannot explain very well" or those who "are confusing or difficult to follow." Likewise, pupils and teachers recognize the difficulties that many pupils experience when asked to present oral reports. Most of these difficulties are related to inadequate planning. It is hoped that the illustrated plan that follows will clarify the problem somewhat. The plan is suggestive only.

Lesson Plan Illustration (useful in the health area — fifth or sixth grade)

Concept   The outer, middle, and inner ear are involved in conducting sound waves as we hear.

Problem   What are the functions of the outer, middle, and inner ear?

Goals   After this lesson, the pupil should further understand how we hear, as evidenced by:
1. Ability to relate the function of the outer, middle, and inner ear
2. Questions asked in the subsequent discussion: What are the functions of the outer, middle, and inner ear?
3. Application of the basic demonstration concepts to a subsequent pictorial drawing

Lesson Approach
1. Attention getting: (Pop a balloon.) Did you hear something? How does one hear the pop? All of us hear something all the time; so we seem to take hearing for granted.
2. Initial summary: How we hear is dependent upon the function of the outer ear, the middle ear, and the inner ear. (Write these three on the chalkboard: 1. Outer Ear, 2. Middle Ear, and 3. Inner Ear.) Sound waves are necessary for us to hear, too.

Lesson Development
1. Slides and transparencies: Through the use of slides and transparencies show how waves and frequency play their part in hearing.
2. Tuning fork: Discuss sound vibrations per second.
3. Show ear model: Use the model of the ear to demonstrate the various parts of the ear and their function.

Deriving Generalizations   From the foregoing demonstration a number of generalizations seem evident. These are a few illustrations:
1. Sound vibrations (waves) moving through the air are received by the ear.
2. The ear is divided into three separate sections — the outer ear, the middle ear, and the inner ear.
3. The outer ear catches sound waves from the air.
4. When sound waves strike the outer surface of the eardrum, it vibrates and these vibrations are mechanically transmitted through the middle ear.
5. The round window membrane transmits vibrations into the inner ear.
6. Vibrations in the inner ear are received by nerve cells that carry the impulses to the brain.

The preceding lesson plan is more detailed than many teachers prefer; perhaps it is not detailed enough for others. The primary purpose of this plan is to provide information not readily accessible. The information is useful (along with six basic concepts) in providing a factual *basis* for resolving fundamental issues in the health area. Certain aspects of the oral report undoubtedly touched upon in text materials were *reorganized* and re-presented. These aspects, of course, merely would be mentioned in the presentation.

Values

- Oral reporting is economical in terms of time and materials.
- The method serves to channel thinking of all pupils in a given direction.
- Demonstrations enable the teacher to utilize activities that would be too dangerous for pupils themselves to perform within the ordinary classroom.
- Oral reports and demonstrations are easy to prepare, as they are usually based on specialized knowledge of the leader.

Limitations and Problems

- Information-giving methods can encourage the retention of facts as ends in themselves.
- The method, in and of itself, is inadequate for teaching certain types of concepts. (Attitudes, feelings, and skills, for example, are not learned through pure telling or showing procedures.)
- Some teachers have difficulty adapting their presentations to the comprehension levels of their pupils. (A passive audience is less able to indicate its lack of understanding.)
- Social learnings are minimized during oral presentations.
- This approach to teaching tends to encourage acceptance of the teacher as a final authority. Because of this factor, a teacher's biases and prejudices may be accepted at face value.
- Exposition processes are extremely difficult to adapt to individual differences among pupils. Superior pupils, for example, frequently complain of boredom "after about the fifth explanation." Similarly, less able pupils often charge that oral reports present too much information too quickly.

Illustrated Oral Report Outlines

I. Useful in the science area (primary grades)
   Unit Space
   Concept Oceans occupy space.
   Problem How large a space do oceans occupy?
   Main Points
   1. Ocean basins are very large.
   2. If all the land above the sea was pushed into the ocean basin, it would not be filled.
   3. The Pacific Ocean basin is believed to be almost the same size as the moon.

II. Useful in the social studies area (middle grades)
   Unit Construction
   Concept The construction engineers build dams for many reasons.
   Problem What are the reasons for building dams?
   Main Points
   1. Dams are used to prevent floods.
   2. Dams are built to conserve water.
   3. Through the use of dams, power and energy can be developed.

III. Useful in the reading area (upper grades)
Unit Reading Comprehension
Concept The good reader must perform specific activities while reading.
Problem What must a reader do to comprehend and read well?
Main Points
1. A good reader must remember the essentials of what is read.
2. A good reader relates the details to main ideas.
3. A good reader is able to place story events in a proper sequence.
4. A good reader understands the author through literal and/or interpretive comprehension activities.

IV. Useful in the arithmetic area (middle grades)
Unit Approximate and Estimate
Concept Estimation is used to avoid gross errors in arithmetic problems.
Problem What methods can you use to avoid making gross errors in arithmetic problems?
Main Points
1. An estimate of the answer is made before computation.
2. An estimate is a close guess.
3. After the computation, the answer and estimate are compared.
4. Estimates are used as a quick way to determine whether or not an answer is too small or too large.

V. Useful in language arts area (middle and upper grades)
Unit Oral Language
Concept Standards for giving reports will increase the effectiveness of oral reports.
Problem What are the standards for reporting in the classroom?
Main Points
1. Speak to the entire class.
2. Speak so everyone in the class can hear.
3. Stay on the topic for the report.
4. Use gestures and movements when necessary.
5. Use visual aids to enhance the report.
6. Mention where you read or acquired the information.
7. Use proper and correct language.
8. Do *not* use run-together sentences.

Endnote

1. James A. Kulik and Chen-Lin C. Kulik, "Timing of Feedback and Verbal Learning," *Review of Educational Research*, Spring 1988, pp. 79–97.

Chapter 19

Film and Television Analysis

Overview

Key Concepts

- Instructional media do not, in and of themselves, teach; they merely assist in the instructional process.
- Film and television are comparable to most other instructional methods involving reflective thinking.
- A film or television program, by spanning time and space dimensions, may be superior in many respects to the actual experience.
- Film and television can (and frequently do) distort reality to meet the bias or whims of the producer.

Chapter Terms

- Single-concept film: A short film that presents one idea, concept, or principle. It may be used to set the stage for reflective thinking.
- Documentary film: A film that dramatizes actual events related to an issue of social significance.
- Simulated reality: The staging or editing of events to emphasize selected aspects of a situation for instruction or entertainment.
- Sponsored film: A film made by an agency or industry to communicate its purposes or products.

Almost all teachers make use of motion pictures. Too often, however, educational films and television have been misused. Although a film may create considerable interest, there is no assurance that a film used alone will result in any worthwhile learnings. Since films are abstractions designed to highlight selected elements of reality, *misconceptions* are all too common.

Like dramatic play and simulation games (treated in Chapters 11 and 12), a film is a simulation of reality. As such, it is ideally suited for capturing time and space problems. As with other instructional methods, the learner must be guided in appropriate processes of critical thinking. The film analysis that follows is suggestive only. Its use is limited to those films designed to develop basic instructional concepts. The same procedures are generally applicable to the selection and use of television programming.

Fundamental Properties

Although some educational films and television programs have been used by enterprising teachers for many years, the full impact of their value is just beginning to be realized by the great majority of teachers. Certainly the unbelievably rapid progress in the direction of automation has been felt. In some cases, increased use of instructional materials has become a fad. However, the major impact of educational films and television can be attributed to a new concept of the final goal of education. Teachers are beginning to realize that the final goal of education is not memorized information; it is a changed individual who lives differently because he or she has learned.

Teacher's Role

An educational system that hopes to change behavior must do much more than provide facts. It must deal with personal perceptions—with individual meaning. Meanings exist within each individual and cannot be manipulated or controlled. Thus the teacher's role becomes one of helping youngsters explore and discover for themselves the personal meaning of events in films. The teacher's task, then, is one of creating a favorable climate for learning. Bridging the gap of time and space for *personal meaning* often demands the use of films.

Single-Concept Films

At the present time several types of films are available for class use. The most popular of these are the single-concept film, the documentary, and the sponsored film. The *single-concept film,* of recent origin, is usually short—ranging from three to fifteen minutes in length. Like other simulations, its function is to introduce a problem without attempting to solve it.

Documentary Films

The *documentary film* is designed to portray the everyday world in a manner that emphasizes relationships and meaning. Its aim is to provide new insights and new understandings, but it does express a given point of view. Most documentary films appearing on television screens today, for example, present a vigorous treatment of some issue of social significance. Others are designed especially for those contemplating extended vacation trips.

Sponsored Films

The *sponsored film* is commercially produced for the purpose of presenting a given point of view. Some such films may be produced as a part of broad advertising and public relations programs. The advertising message does not necessarily render such a film inappropriate for class use. In fact, some commercial film producers design films especially for class use, their major purpose being to inform. Nevertheless, they should be previewed carefully for bias and distortions.

Film and Television Analysis Procedure

Although films serve different purposes, they should all contribute to critical thinking. Even those that may be employed as motivational devices should enable the learner to relate content material to life experiences. Films can be so designed as to lull one into accepting a point of view that could not withstand critical examination. Just as pupils are prone to accept a point of view because "it said so in the text," so are they often prone to believe something because it was offered in a film or seen on television.

Preplanning for an Instructional Film

The teacher must arrange to preview those films that may serve his or her purposes. Today most schools have special facilities available for this function. A critique of every film previewed, whether used or not, is useful for future reference. A preview is essential to the development of an adequate film analysis.

Effective timing is another critical aspect of preplanning. At what point during the instructional process should a film be introduced? Some films, for example, are most effectively used to introduce a lesson, others should be used as or along with the heart of a lesson, and a few may be useful as culmination activities.

Scheduling the Film

Usually films must be scheduled several days in advance. How is one to predict the precise progress of pupils? Obviously, this is an impossibility! All the teacher can do is to predict as accurately as possible and then adjust accordingly. Some schools are producing their own single-concept films as one way of overcoming some of the timing problems. Sometimes a film does not arrive as scheduled, occasionally a film projector breaks down, and so on. Thus it is imperative that alternative activities be prepared for every scheduled use of a film. This is not a particularly difficult task, but one that is frequently neglected by many teachers.

Introducing the Film or Television Presentation

The teacher can greatly influence the effects of a filmed or televised presentation by the things he or she does before, during, and after the showing. Preliminary preparations include arranging physical conditions such as room darkening and screen or monitor placement in order that all pupils can see and hear in comfort and without distraction.

The introductory comments preceding the showing of a film are designed to prepare the pupil for the experience. Usually two or three key questions should be posed. Rather than emphasizing facts, the questions should focus upon relationships, application, or hidden meaning. Sometimes certain problems or problem situations should be noted. At other times, new terms or new ideas should be pinpointed. Too many questions or points to look for may be confusing.

Normally, key points to look for in a film are put on the board for further reference. Pupils should be discouraged from taking notes during the showing of a film. A film may be stopped for emphasis and discussion; it may also be rerun in slow motion.

Follow-Through Discussion

The follow-through discussion is designed to determine how well the original questions or problems can be answered. This leads to resolution of the problem. As with any other method, various possible solutions should be posed and evaluated. If a single-concept film is used, this is a natural outgrowth of the experience. If a documentary or sponsored film is utilized, considerable guidance may be necessary.

Attention must be directed to incorrect notions or unanticipated misunderstandings that may have resulted. Sometimes differences between the film and information from other sources may conflict or at least appear to do so. Above all, pupils should be encouraged to pose their own questions for reflection. Sometimes pupils' questions will suggest the need for a second showing of the film or they may suggest the need for other class activities.

Deriving Generalizations

As a culmination of the learning experience, the derivation of ideas, concepts, or generalizations should be encouraged. These may evolve from the film itself, or they may be an outgrowth of activities that may have preceded or followed the film. If film bias is noted, this will become a part of the summation process.

Preparing for Television Experience

From the standpoint of their instructional function, television and motion pictures are the same. Both types of media are capable of displaying events and manipulating time and space. Much of the programming broadcast on commercial television is in fact filmed material that is simply distributed through the television medium.

From a logistical standpoint, the two media are quite different. Films, for example, may be previewed prior to scheduled use at the teacher's request and may be shown repeatedly if desired. Broadcast television, on the other hand, cannot be previewed prior to the broadcast, is scheduled by the local station, and is very seldom rerun. Broadcast television is not under the control of the teacher and, as such, is more difficult to coordinate and integrate with other instructional activities.

The classroom teacher who wishes to use television broadcasts to extend teaching will have to adopt a different instructional strategy from that employed in using films. Through such publications as the *Teacher's Guide to Television* and *TV Guide,* the teacher can become aware of appropriate programming to be scheduled during the school year. If arrangements can be made to videotape broadcast presentations for later playback in the classroom, then many of the obstacles to using broadcast television programs can be overcome. A videotape may be used in essentially the same manner as a film. When videotaping is not available, the teacher may recommend that pupils view a commercial program at home. To *require* that all pupils view a program at home is unrealistic; some homes may not have television receivers, the required program may conflict with a parent's favorite program, or some pupils may forget or have conflicting activities scheduled.

Planning for Film and Television Analysis

Audiovisual materials and resources are so common and so varied that little effort has been made to specify specific uses. Several aids, such as the chalkboard, the overhead projector, still pictures, and the like, are used as tools to enhance the instructional effectiveness of other methods and techniques. Films also find their place in this manner. Frequently, however, a film represents the method itself. There is an all too common tendency to assume that the film itself can teach. *When used as an instructional method, a film must be planned within a framework of problem solving.* The lesson plan that follows is based upon a single-concept film. Such films are ideally suited for this purpose.

Lesson Plan Illustration (useful in the reading area — primary grades)

Unit   Abraham Lincoln
Concept   Honesty is an essential part of a person's character.
Problem   What policy should one follow when one finds money that belongs to someone else?
Goals   After this lesson, the pupil should have furthered his or her ability to perceive the relationship between honesty and dishonesty, as evidenced by:
  1. Comments and questions during the follow-through discussion of a single-concept film
  2. Ability to derive generalizations from the experience.

Lesson Approach   Through the story of Abraham Lincoln, we have discussed how Abraham Lincoln walked several miles to return a few pennies that belonged to someone else. We have discussed what satisfactions he received from being a very honest individual. Today, through a short film, we will look at another approach to honesty.

Lesson Development
  A. Film description (not to be given to pupils)
     Film: *The Dollar Bill* (3 minutes)
          A young boy has been given a grocery list and several one-dollar bills. After leaving his house, he reads through the grocery list and counts his dollar bills. The boy places the list and money in his pocket and in doing so he drops one dollar. A second boy comes upon the scene and finds the one-dollar bill. The film should be stopped at this vital point, and the problem becomes a matter of group discussion, or one child may analyze what he or she would do in this situation.
          The film poses two different approaches to the problem. Within the film three key questions are given. These questions may be placed on the chalkboard.
     Key Questions
     1. What will he do with the found money?
     2. What would you do?
     3. Why should you do it?

B. Show the film without comment.
C. Follow-through discussion (first direct attention to the last two of the above questions)
   1. What would you do if you found some money and you did not see anyone lose it?
   2. To what extent must one go to get money or a lost article to the proper owner?
   3. What do you think of the saying, "Losers weepers, finders keepers?"
D. Weighing alternatives: In view of our analysis, what policy should one follow when finding a lost item or money?
E. Example solutions
   1. Return the item or lost money to the individual you see lose it.
   2. If you do not know to whom it belongs, advertise in the paper.
   3. Take the lost money or item to the police and seek their help in finding the owner.
   Discuss advantages and disadvantages of each solution as it is posed.
F. Deriving generalizations (suggestive only)
   1. Honesty is a good policy to follow.
   2. Ideals of honesty can be goals for which to strive.

It is evident from the foregoing lesson illustration that the film was used as a means of bringing human interest into a problem situation. Dramatic play or even class discussion could have been used with possibly the same effectiveness. However, the film had the advantage of economy of time and a carefully staged setting specifically designed to further the lesson objective. The impact of the lesson rests with the entire experience— not just the film itself.

Values

- Use of educational films and television can effectively bridge time and place in demonstrating concepts, attitudes, and skills.
- Films may be economical of time and energy.
- Film media can present different sides of a story. They can present the normal along with the spectacular.
- Films can contribute to critical thinking.
- Educational film media can relate content materials in textbooks to life experiences.

Limitations and Problems

- Films have been widely misused. When using film, a decision must be reached relative to its probable effectiveness as compared with other available modes of instruction.
- Films have the disadvantage of being costly to rent or buy.
- Availability and scheduling are always a problem with films. Alternate activities must be planned in case the film does not arrive.
- Documentaries and sponsored films do not always present a true picture of the events portrayed. There is a tendency to capture the sensational.
- Simulated reality, of necessity, distorts reality. This is especially true of educational films and "live" broadcasts. Thus the editor or the broadcaster can introduce bias while maintaining the appearance of objectivity.
- Use of such media seldom provides adequately for individual differences. A film or televised lesson, for example, may be too difficult for some pupils and too easy for others.

━━━━━━━━━━ **Illustrated Film and Television Uses** ━━━━━━━━━━

I. Useful in the science area (middle grades)
   Unit   Conservation
   Concept   People, animals, and plant life all depend upon one another.
   Problem   What policy should one follow concerning wildlife in the forest?
   Lesson Development
   Film: *Patterns of the Wild* (26 minutes)
         (Sponsored film: U.S. Department of Agriculture, Forest Service, State Fish and Game Department and the National Wildlife Federation)
   Key Questions
   1. Why can't all animals survive in the forest?
   2. How does one harvest the forest in the area of timber and wildlife?
   3. Why does forest life depend upon death?

II. Useful in the social studies area (upper grades)
   Unit   The Presidents of the United States
   Concept   World events shape the destiny of man.
   Problem   What world events and preparation made it possible for Dwight D. Eisenhower to become president of the United States?

Lesson Development
Film: *A Place in History* (28 minutes)
> (Documentary film: National Archives, General Service Administration, Washington, DC)

Key Questions
1. Why did World War I change Eisenhower's life?
2. What events of World War II placed Eisenhower in a leadership position?
3. What human qualities did Eisenhower have that endeared him to the people of the world?

III. Useful in the science area (elementary grades)
Unit Space Travel
Concept The scientific knowledge of many people made it possible for men to walk on the moon.
Problem What made it possible for men to walk on the moon?
Lesson Development
Film: *Eagle Has Landed* (30 minutes)
> (Documentary film: National Space and Aeronautics Administration, General Services Administration, Washington, DC)

Key Questions
1. Why was governmental action necessary in order that men might walk on the moon?
2. What scientific preparation was necessary?
3. Why were people of the world brought closer together because of the moon walk?

IV. Useful in the health area (primary grades)
Unit Foods
Concept The diet of bears is like that of humans in that it is unusually varied.
Problem Why is the diet of bears similar to that of humans?
Lesson Development
Film: *Brown Bear Diet* (4 minutes)
> (Single-concept film: Walt Disney Nature Library, Ealing Films, Cambridge, MA)

Key Questions
1. What protection does the brown bear have against bees when gathering honey?
2. How does the diet of the brown bear compare with that of humans?

V. Useful in the language arts area (kindergarten and primary grades)
   Unit Reading (Word Attack)
   Concept Relationships exist within word families.
   Problem What relationship exists within word families?
   Lesson Development
   Television series: "The Electric Company," "Sesame Street"
   Review: Relate to what was discussed and seen on the show.
   Follow-up: Place words in contextual situations for overlearning.

Chapter 20

Review Methods

Overview

Key Concepts

- Although recall is a basic aspect of review, it merely sets the stage for the extension of original learnings.
- A review emphasizes application of concepts to related problems.
- Related problems in a review are merely *identified;* they are not analyzed extensively.
- Reviews often are used informally in conjunction with other instructional experiences. A carefully planned culminating review is an essential experience, however.
- Review is most effective in increasing retention of that which is learned.

Chapter Terms

- Review: A new look at previous learnings for the purpose of guiding the learner in applying original learnings to new situations.
- Initial learnings: Previously learned concepts (ideas) that form the basis for review.
- Retention: One's ability to remember (and use) that which is learned.

The term *review* is almost as ambiguous as the term *class discussion.* Teachers speak of reviewing for a test, reviewing the results of a test, reviewing important words or terms, reviewing the major points of a lesson, and so on. Too often a review is little more than repetitive practice or drill. While there is a definite place for such an exercise, when drill is substituted for review, the results must be disappointing. Review, literally, means a re-view or a re-look at something. This review might be better called a new view, that is, a view of some problem from a new angle. It is a technique of guiding the pupils in the application of original learnings to related situations.

Fundamental Properties

In addition to enhancing transfer of learning to related life situations, review may contribute substantially to the permanence of that which is learned. Unlike class discussion that focuses attention to one particular problem, review emphasizes the recognition of many, related problems. Its widespread misuse reflects a general misunderstanding of the essential properties involved.

Initial Learning Requirements

Before an individual can take a *re*-view of a situation, he or she must have viewed it at least once before. There is a tendency to assume adequate initial learning when the pupil has read the text or is able to verbalize answers to factual questions. Thus one loses sight of the basic nature of the learning process—that of coping with basic educational *problems*. The products of each educational experience consist essentially of centralized ideas, generalizations, or concepts. These in turn become the necessary data for review lessons. If previous experiences have emphasized the acquisition of knowledge only, it is logical (but fallacious) to conceive review as a mere repetition of these facts. Generalizations *must* be derived prior to effective review.

Recall

Recall is a fundamental aspect of review. Basic unit generalizations are brought together in one lesson for the first time. By recalling some of the methods and techniques employed during the original learning experience, the learner may develop associations that will enhance one's recall of basic ideas. Although some clarification of generalizations is often necessary, the primary objective is to bring the ideas together for further analysis.

Extending Associations

Once basic, previously derived generalizations have been brought before the group, their application to related problems is emphasized. Although specific lesson generalizations, like facts, may not apply readily to broad problems, it is relatively easy to combine them into broader concepts for this purpose. Review is most effective when generalizations are somewhat comparable in scope to unit concepts. They are most effectively utilized, however, when pupils themselves derive the concepts. Processes of reflective thought reach their peak as pupils identify related problems to which previous learnings apply.

Review Procedure

Once an individual has resolved an issue (facilitated through some other teaching method), a review can help him or her acquire new meanings, understandings, and attitudes from original concepts or generalizations. Psychologists tell us that transfer of learnings to related situations occurs to the extent that the learner is able to recognize identical or similar elements in both situations. *Review, then, is a technique for guiding the pupil in the application of original learnings to related situations.*

Although it is recognized that a *re*-view or *re*-look is important at any point during a lesson, the emphasis in this chapter is on review lessons that occur at the culmination of a unit or block of work. The basic essentials can be readily applied to other review situations.

Recalling Basic Unit Generalizations

Each lesson should be culminated with one to five pupil-derived generalizations. Collectively these generalizations embody a major lesson concept upon which the lesson rests. In a review lesson, pupils are expected to recall most of the generalizations derived during the unit. There is a natural tendency to expand specific lesson generalizations into broader concepts. This process should be encouraged. To illustrate from an art lesson concerned with color relationships:

Lesson Generalizations

1. Light, bright colors evoke a happy, gay mood.
2. Dark, somber colors generally evoke a depressing mood.
3. Different colors have different emotional impacts. (Red, for example, is happy and exciting.)
4. Colors symbolize ideas. (Blue, for example, is associated with loyalty and honesty.)

In recalling these generalizations, pupils might be encouraged to evolve the following concept: Color may be used to create mood and symbolize ideas. In this manner the major unit concepts (usually four or six) are clarified and written out for the benefit of the entire group of children.

Recalling Generalizations

Basic unit concepts are related to other problems through a skillful process of questioning. The objective is to help pupils realize the wide applicability of that which has been learned. The process often is initiated by asking questions of advocacy. Such questions usually begin with the word *should.* An advocacy question directs attention to one particular solution to a problem. Sometimes "how" or "could" questions are useful in this respect. To illustrate from an art lesson, Color Relationships: "Should (*or* How could) we use color to improve our homes?" Possible responses might include the following:

1. Bright-colored walls would make the room gay.
2. Light colors in a small room would make it look larger.
3. Dark colors may be used to make a large barnlike room appear smaller.

Each suggested application is discussed briefly for the purpose of clarifying the idea. No effort is made to resolve issues in a review lesson, as the function is merely that of *recognizing related problems for expansion of knowledge.* (In some instances, of course, such problems may reveal the need for further consideration of basic issues. In such cases, other appropriate techniques will be employed.)

In a review lesson, pupils should assist in the recall of basic generalizations and derivation of concepts; they should bear the major responsibility for extending these learnings to related areas. It may be necessary for the teacher to offer a few suggestions as a means of preparing pupils for further analysis. There is a decided tendency to rush pupils through a review lesson, assuming that most of the important relationships are obvious. The evidence quite clearly suggests that pupils transfer learnings only to the extent to which they are taught to transfer. Several hours might be profitably devoted to such activities.

Evaluating the Experience

An appropriate review generates considerable enthusiasm and creativity. When individuals begin to understand how their school experiences can be applied to out-of-school problems, they tend to develop and maintain a high degree of interest. Such behaviors will be apparent in other class activities as well. The teacher will become more conscious of the importance of transfer of learnings to related situations.

The review lesson, designed to extend learnings to related problems, is closely akin to evaluational experiences. Test items, for example, serve a similar purpose. However, test item situations must include problems other than those introduced during reviews. The purpose is to determine if individuals can make such associations and relationships on their own.

Planning for Review

A major factor contributing to poor review lessons is inadequate planning. Teachers quite naturally are interested in clarifying facts and principles; oddly enough they are often less interested in extending them to real-life situations. Yet it is through extension and association of ideas that adequate understanding is best revealed. The following plan represents that review which is usually introduced at the culmination of a unit.

——————— **Lesson Plan Illustration (art area — middle grades)** ———————

Unit   Drawing

Concept   Will involve all the unit concepts as an essential aspect of the lesson.

Problem   How can we relate what we have learned about drawing to different situations?

Goals   After this lesson, the pupil should have furthered his or her understanding of the basic principles of drawing, as evidenced by:

1. Ability to identify related problems in class review.
2. Ability to apply basic principles to related problems.
3. Ability to draw parallels with problems previously studied.

Lesson Approach   During the past two weeks, we have emphasized the principles of drawing and we have pointed out how drawing can be an important tool of education. We have seen that drawing is a very important aspect in our world. Today we will take a look at some of the areas where drawing can be used to solve problems.

Lesson Development

I. *Analysis of the previous unit experiences:* What generalizations or big ideas evolved during our study of this unit?
   A. Quantities can be compared through drawings.
   B. Relationships can be shown through drawings.
      1. Organization charts can show relationships.
      2. Comparison drawings can show relationships.
   C. Drawings can be used as attention-getting devices.
   D. Ideas can be expressed through drawing.

II. *Recalling how the major concepts were derived*
   A. Each child created a drawing to depict quantities or amounts. For example stick figures were used to represent people and coins were drawn to represent money.
   B. Each pupil executed two drawings expressing (1) organization relationships and (2) comparison or contrasts.
   C. To illustrate an attention-getting device, each child made a drawing to move the observer to action.
   D. Each child made comic-strip-type drawings to express an idea.

III. *Extending unit concepts to related problems:* With our ideas before us, let us briefly consider other areas to which they may apply. For example:
   A. Should we use drawing to improve arithmetic?
      1. Drawings can show proportion.
      2. Percentages can be shown through drawings.
      3. Circle graphs could be used in arithmetic.
   B. Might we use drawings to improve business?
      1. As attention-getting devices, drawings could be used to advertise what businesspeople want to sell.
      2. Drawings can be used to tell people who cannot read what the businesspeople want to tell them.
   C. How could we use drawings to improve oral reporting?
      1. Drawings attract the attention of those listening.
      2. Drawings can be used to condense ideas.
      3. Drawings can show comparisons, contrasts, and relationships to help people understand the presentation.
   D. Could we use drawings to improve communication?
      1. Expression can be shown through drawing.
      2. Drawings can clarify meaning.
      3. Drawing can evoke interest.

IV. *Deriving generalizations:* From our treatment of related problems, what big ideas seem to stand out?
   A. Drawings are capable of improving every area of the curriculum in school.
   B. Drawings can be utilized to improve many areas in our world outside of school activities.

Values

- Review facilitates application or transfer of learnings to related situations. It has long been recognized by psychologists that individuals apply or transfer learnings to new experiences to the extent that they are taught to make this transfer. Review is designed for this purpose.
- The formulation of new associations and relationships, through review, renders more permanent learning.
- Review enables the teacher to correct misconceptions and misunderstandings that inevitably arise in group learning situations.
- Review procedures are extremely flexible. They may range from the informal five-minute review to extended reviews of several hours.

Limitations and Problems

- Review has been widely misused. Often mistaken for review are recitation sessions in which the learner has been expected to recall specific facts for a test.
- Prior to initial learning, review is a waste of time. To make a *review* of learning not thoroughly understood in the first place results in chaos.
- Review is deceptively easy. Even when review is used for the purpose of expanding learning, it is extremely easy to get bogged down on some related issue. If this occurs, review purposes may be impossible to achieve.
- Review is extremely difficult to conduct. The major factor contributing to poor reviews is inadequate planning.

Illustrated Review Problems

I. Useful in the physical education area (upper grades)
   Unit   Teamwork in Sports
   Problem   How can we relate what we have learned about teamwork to our lives?
   Unit Concepts
   1. We are on teams all our lives.
   2. Each player has a responsibility to the team.
   3. It is important to bring others into team participation.

Extending concepts to related areas:

1. How may teamwork be used in research groups in the classroom?
2. How can we use teamwork in Girl Scouts or Boy Scouts?
3. How might we use teamwork principles in our family?

II. Useful in the language arts area (primary grades)
Unit Discussion Techniques
Problem How can we relate what we have learned about discussion techniques to everyday situations?
Unit Concepts

1. Speak on the question or subject being discussed.
2. Explain ideas so they are easily understood.
3. Tell only one fact or idea at a time.
4. Make explanations simple by avoiding too much detail.

Extending concepts to related areas:

1. Is it possible to use discussion techniques in other school activities?
2. How could discussion techniques be used at home?

III. Useful in the social studies asrea (middle grades)
Unit Interdependence of States
Problem How can we relate what we have learned about interdependence of states to practical aspects of living?
Unit Concepts

1. People in our state depend upon services, products, and food from other states.
2. Our state exports minerals and products to other states.
3. People of all states depend upon one another.

Extending concepts to related areas:

1. Is it possible to find interdependence in our homes?
2. How may it be possible to have such a variety of food to eat, clothes to wear, and products to buy?
3. How can we use the principle of interdependence in our classroom?

IV. Useful in the science area (middle grades)
Unit Machines
Problem How can we relate what we have learned about machines to other situations?
Unit Concepts

1. A machine is anything that makes work easier or transfers a force.
2. A machine can gain either force or speed (distance) but not both at the same time.

3. Six simple machines make up all compound machines.

Extending concepts to related areas:

1. How might machines be used in your home?
2. How could simple machines help you if you were lost and without modern conveniences?
3. Is it possible that simple machines might be used in future inventions?

Chapter 21

Teaching through Field Trips

Overview

Key Concepts

- The field trip should be planned in relation to ongoing unit activities.
- Field trips enrich children's study by involvement in a learning situation that is not easily visualized through reading or discussion.
- A field trip should meet the needs of the children involved and be of interest to them.

Chapter Terms

- Learning environment: All aspects of the child's personal world.
- Learning milieu: Those people and institutions that have a direct effect upon the child.
- Socializing skills: Those skills the child learns for effective interaction with various groups of people.

At some time many pupils and teachers have been involved in a field trip or excursion. It has been a part of almost every teacher's schedule, but all too often the learning experiences inherent in such an outing are not fully explored or planned. Many times such a trip may be seen by the pupil as a holiday from school and by the teacher as a series of management difficulties with thirty children. Through adequate preplanning, however, a field trip or excursion can be an invaluable learning experience for all.

Fundamental Properties

The quality of any field trip rests upon a number of basic properties; for instance, it makes it possible for children to expand their learning environment. The constrictive qualities of the school building and classrooms as a learning environment are well known; therefore, through field trips the children's learning milieu is greatly expanded.[1] Other fundamental or basic properties necessary for field trips are the organizational patterns, relatedness to ongoing classroom activities, point of interest, and socializing skills.

Organizational Patterns

Two basic organizational patterns may be used in field trips: teacher directed and pupil directed.

Teacher Directed
In the teacher-directed field trip, the teacher selects the problem, directs the pupils in observing and collecting the data, and assigns the children responsibilities for reporting aspects of the outing.

Some advantages of the teacher-directed organizational pattern are that more detailed observations are made, trial and error is eliminated, and an efficiency of time is achieved. The teacher can introduce more concepts to children in a teacher-directed excursion than in a pupil-directed outing.

Many disadvantages also are apparent. The range of observation for the children is limited by the teacher's ability to select items for discovery. Also in a teacher-directed field trip there is little opportunity for the pupil to select relevant material or reject irrelevant information.

Pupil Directed
The teacher's role in a pupil-directed organizational pattern for field trips is to establish the location and date for the excursion. Also the teacher would motivate the pupils and prepare them for the learning experiences as well as be involved in the follow-up activities.

The pupils would clarify the tasks to be done on the field trip as well as plan how they might communicate their findings to the class following the excursion. The pupils would plan how they might solve the problems posed on the field trip.

The advantages of this approach are many; for instance, it provides for *maximum application of creative thinking and problem solving* among the children. The pupils also may pursue areas that interest them. The pupil-directed pattern of organization makes it possible for the pupils to be involved in all areas of *problem solving*.

Some possible disadvantages could be the level of maturity of the children who are doing the planning and the ability of the group to make adequate plans. Depending upon the grade level of the children and the problem to be studied, modifications could be made in the organizational pattern from the teacher-directed organizational pattern at one end of the continuum to the pupil-directed organizational pattern at the other end with many levels in between.

Relatedness to Ongoing Activities

If field trips are to be important and valuable to the children, the excursions should be *planned in relation to ongoing unit activities*. Field trips can be a means of enriching the children's study by taking them to a learning situation that is not easily visualized through reading or discussion. Some field trips may be taken near the beginning of the unit for gathering information on specific topics or problems. Other field trips may be taken during the unit so that the pupils may get new motives or different directions for their studies. A field trip may be taken at the end of a unit as a culminating activity. Whenever the field trip is taken, it should be related to the classroom activities and unit requirements.

Point of Interest

A central point of interest is a necessary ingredient for a successful field trip. No matter where the excursion may be, it is important that the trip meet the needs of the children involved and be of interest to them.

For younger children a short trip may be made to the fire station, police station, school nurse's office, dairy, local museum, library, park, and other similar places. For older children, the field trip could be to an assembly plant, factory, planetarium, newspaper office, national forest, and other places where more complex activities may be observed.

Socializing Skills

Many different values are achieved from field trips aside from gathering facts and observing firsthand activities. To some children, the many activities engaged in as they work together and socialize with one another are important values. Therefore, a fundamental property of field trips is the socialization that takes place among the children as they discuss, write about the activity, sit together on the bus, or ask questions of the guide. This, too, is an important aspect of a field trip; however, this alone is *not* an adequate purpose for a field trip.

Field Trip Procedure

An effective field trip or excursion involves *far more than the actual outing*. Careful preplanning, establishing problems to solve, evaluating the outing, and deriving generalizations from the data gathered are all essential for an effective field trip. The procedures outlined in this section are included to assist the teacher in planning an effective field trip.

Problem Identification

After the teacher has clearly identified the basic concepts to be taught, he or she selects an instructional method or technique that seems most appropriate for concept attainment. The field trip method is especially useful in that the guide can present to the children a sequentially planned series of field experiences that will lead to the development of one or several concepts. Generally, the basic concepts are first approached through textbooks or other reference materials and then extended and applied to the learner's own life through the excursion. An example from the science area — A Study of Living Things — suggests that living things are in constant change. From this basic concept children on an outdoor field trip could be asked to find as many examples as they can showing change in living things.

Preplanning

Children must be *involved in planning* the trip if it is to be successful. This planning must include developing the purpose for the trip; when, where, and how to make the excursion; and follow-up activities. Children in the upper grades can take more responsibility in the preplanning stages; however, it is obvious that primary grade children may need much more direction. Nonetheless, *all* children at *any* grade level should be involved in some of the planning.

Transportation may be necessary for some excursions. The school bus usually is the preferred transportation because of insurance regulations and liability laws. If the bus tour is lengthy, plans should be made to occupy children's time while traveling. Valuable learning and language arts experience may be accomplished while riding on the bus. For example, children may keep a log of their trip complete with departure time, weather conditions, road conditions, points of interest en route, and such other items they wish to include.

Several weeks prior to leaving on the field trip, it is necessary to communicate with the people at the place of visitation so that they will be available for guide service or that permission to visit will be acknowledged. Often it is appropriate for the teacher to visit the place in advance to determine exactly the nature of the trip and any problems that might arise when the children arrive. Not only should guide service be considered in the preplanning stage, but restroom facilities and food services must be considered too.

Parental written consent is a necessary prerequisite for a child to participate in most trips. If parents understand the nature and purpose of the field trip, there should be no problem in securing permission.

In the preplanning stage not only should the children discuss the forthcoming excursion, but also some prereading on the subject is necessary. Concepts. and purposes should be developed so that the children *know exactly what they are looking for* on the tour.

The Visitation

For a field trip to be successful, the children must be directly involved in what is to be seen or heard. It may be necessary to divide the children into smaller groups. If this is necessary, then several guides may be required and the children will see the same things but at different times.

If questions have been sent to the guides in advance, the tour will be focused upon what the children and teacher wish to see or hear. Of course, the children will see and hear much more than might have been anticipated. Older children may want to take notes or write down some information. Smaller children may need paper bags for the collection of items while on the field trip. Paper and pencils, bags, and other necessary equipment should be made available at the visitation site.

Evaluation

After the trip is over and you are back in the classroom, an evaluation of the activity should be made. Several questions should be answered. Was the field trip a success in the sense that it fulfilled its aim, purposes, and objectives? Was the time spent from the classroom worthwhile or could as much be accomplished in the same amount of time in the classroom? How did the children feel about the excursion?

Many different forms of evaluation may be used by the teacher. Some children may wish to write a class story concerning their impressions, and other children may wish to use the tape recorder. Some pupils may wish to write a short play, design a bulletin board, set up a display, make a diorama, write a report, or become involved in some other activity based on the trip.

In the evaluation, attention is directed toward the basic concepts that were identified to be taught. The evaluation activities should help the children to understand, to develop more clearly, and to reinforce those concepts.

Deriving Generalizations

As a culminating activity, pupils are encouraged to derive generalizations from the field trip experience. These are basic ideas pupils are expected to transfer to related situations. At this point, field trip evaluation materials are related to the basic content materials and relationships are formed.

Planning for Field Trips

In addition to careful preplanning for a field trip or excursion, a lesson plan must be developed. Major emphasis will be directed to the essential steps in a lesson plan for a field trip. The illustrated plan involves a problem-solving approach.

Lesson Plan Illustration (kindergarten or first grade social studies area)

Problem   Why are rules, railroad signals, and signs needed at railroad crossings?

Concept   Rules, signals, and signs at railroad crossings are very important for our safety.

Goals   After this lesson, the pupil should have furthered his or her understanding of safety around trains and railroad tracks, including rules, signals, and crossing signs, as evidenced by:

1. Proper use of these devices during the field trip
2. Ability to discuss the purpose and meaning of signals and crossing signs on the field trip and follow-up activity in the classroom
3. Ability to write down the purpose under each sign
4. Participation in writing an experience story on safety rules

Lesson Approach   Now that we have discussed the importance of railroad transportation to us and our country, what should we know about safety around trains? Have you ever been riding in a car and the car was stopped so a train could cross the road? What would happen if the car did not stop? Why do we need rules for crossing the railroad tracks? What do these signs and signals mean? If no signs are by the railroad tracks, what safety rules should one follow?

Signs, signals, and rules of safety around railroad tracks are very important. We need to know these rules and what the signs and signals mean so we will not be involved in an accident or get hurt.

Preplanning   "What plans are necessary before we can take a field trip?" the teacher asks. The pupils would be guided to suggest necessary steps such as the following:

1. Where could we see these railroad signals and signs?
2. How could we get there?
3. What could we do at the railroad tracks?
4. When does the train pass by there?
5. Who could tell us about the safety rules and railroad signals and signs?
6. How can we tell our parents asbout an excursion?

These questions and others could be discussed in the preplanning stages. The children would be divided into groups and assigned specific tasks at this time.

Visitation   The visitation will be made to a railroad station or depot. The guide will focus discussion at the visitation site on safety rules and the purposes for the railroad signs and signals. The children will be able to see how the signals and signs are used when trains approach. The children will demonstrate safety rules around trains and railroad tracks.

Evaluation Activities
1. Follow-up discussion concerning the purposes of rules and signals.
2. Label each sign by giving its purpose.
3. Write an experience story concerning the field trip emphasizing safety rules and the purposes of railroad signs and signals.

Deriving Generalizations   Why are rules, signals, and signs necessary at railroad crossings? When do we need rules, signals, and signs in school situations? Some examples might be as follows:
1. Rules are needed so everyone will know what to do at certain times.
2. Signals and signs are like punctuation marks in our writing. They direct others how to read what is written.
3. Rules help us to live better with one another.

Values

- A field trip is realistic. The children have an opportunity to view and be a part of the real thing.
- Inasmuch as the visitation makes the experience real to the child, the field trip captures the interest and imagination of the learner.
- By seeing and analyzing real problems, the pupil is able to bridge the gap between school and real-life experiences.
- It is possible through field trips to develop many language arts experiences.

- Field trips reduce the constrictive qualities of school buildings and classrooms.
- Learning situations that are not easily visualized through reading and discussion may be developed into a field trip.

Limitations and Problems

- The field trip is time consuming. If used extensively, it will definitely limit the content material that can be covered.
- Field trips may not be as successful as they might be because teachers develop inflexible habits of thinking about the teaching process involved in excursions. Many teachers may look at the field trip as thirty children clustered together receiving a lecture.
- The difficulty encountered in managing and directing a group of children in a new and unfamiliar setting is a limitation of field trips.
- Sometimes field trips are visualized by the children as a holiday from school. Excellent preplanning activities with the children involved in these activities should eliminate this feeling.

—————— **Illustrated Field Trip Plans** ——————————

I. Useful in the science area (kindergarten or first grade)
Unit Our Autumn World
Problem What happens to leaves of trees and bushes and grass in the autumn?
Concept The leaves of many trees, grass, and bushes change in autumn.
Visitation With a child's decorated bag, take a discovery walk about the playground or nearby neighborhood. Observe the change in leaves from trees and bushes and grass. Put samples in the bag for further activities in the classroom.

II. Useful in the social studies area (fourth or fifth grade)
Unit Life during Colonial Days
Problem How was life different in colonial days compared to our life today?
Concept During the Colonial period in U.S. history, the people had to make by hand many of the items they needed in their homes and shops.
Visitation Museum depicting life during colonial days. The clothes worn, machines used, and magazines and books read bring the child closer to visualizing the Colonial period.

III. Useful in the reading area (upper grades)
Unit Newspapers for Information
Problem What processes are necessary to print a newspaper?
Concept Many steps and processes are necessary in printing a newspaper.
Visitation Visiting a newspaper plant where the newspapers are printed can help the child see the processes in printing a paper from news reporting to printed paper and delivery person.

IV. Useful in the science area (fifth or sixth grade)
Unit Living Things in Our Environment
Problem Do living things depend upon one another? Find evidences that they do or do *not* depend upon one another.
Concept Living things are interdependent upon one another in our environment.
Visitation A park or any outdoor area would provide ample opportunities for pupils to find many examples of how living things are interdependent.

V. Useful in the music area (any elementary grade)
Unit Music Listening
Problem How many musical numbers can you identify?
Concept Music with which the child can identify will aid in one's music-listening skills.
Visitation A young people's concert at the concert auditorium provides excellent opportunities for the children to apply good music-listening skills. Music is played that appeals to them.

VI. Useful in the art area (upper grades)
Unit Art Communicates
Problem How do these masterpieces of art communicate?
Concept Art is a method of communication.
Visitation An art gallery can provide children with an opportunity to visualize how art communicates. Allow each child to determine how various art pieces communicate; then have the guide explain how the various art masterpieces communicate.

Endnote

1. Cleo B. Greenslade, "A Walk Back," *Social Studies,* March–April 1988, pp. 47–50.

Chapter 22

Using Games and Kits

Overview

Key Concepts

- School curriculum games offer possibilities for "action" in the learning process with problem solving and intuitive thinking.
- Games may involve mental, physical, and emotional activities on the part of the player-learners.
- Games include three major parts—the players, objectives or outcomes for the game, and rules under which the play takes place.
- Games should be designed for maximum participation by children and very little, if any, spectator activity.

Chapter Terms

- Self-competition: Competition with oneself whereby a child strives to improve his or her previous performance. This is especially appropriate for children who are not as successful or challenged in the direct one-to-one competitive games.
- Rewards: Self-satisfaction through inner drives, winning in the game activity, or reaching the goal of the game.

The intellectual capacities, curiosities, and interests of our present-day pupils demand that the teacher go beyond the traditional textbooks for learning in the classroom. Thus games and specialized learning kits are becoming another aspect of the elementary school curriculum. In the school curriculum, games offer various possibilities for action in a learning style that is chiefly mental yet includes freedom, intuitive thinking, problem solving, and reactive responses of physical movement.[1]

Fundamental Properties

Games and kits embody the fundamental aspects of a pleasurable activity, which is simple in operation and involves mental, physical, and emotional activities on the part of the player-learners. Another fundamental property of the game is the competitive or noncompetitive aspect the game can have as determined by the teacher.

Pleasurable

Games add fun to learning for almost everyone including elementary school children. An enjoyable way to transmit knowledge is to make a game of the subject matter under study. Because of the pleasure games give to the child, the game activity reinforces learning. Children are willing and anxious to learn tedious skill drill activities if they are in the form of a game. The game becomes pleasurable to the pupils because they are *relating to and with their peers*. Therefore, a fundamental property of a game or kit *must* be its pleasurable nature.

Simple

Games should be relatively simple. If the game has simplicity, it will help to build self-confidence within the pupils playing the game. Simple game activities will allow each child to compete equally with all other children in the classroom and allow enough chance in the game so that any pupil or team can win. The simplest aspects of a game will include three major parts — the players, objectives or outcomes of the game, and rules under which the play takes place.

The game activity should be compatible with the child's level of maturity. Forcing early practice or asking the child to play a complex game before one's maturity level is adequate will have a deleterious effect. The game selected should be both simple and appropriate for the children that will be playing it.

Mental

Another fundamental property of a game is that it involves mental activity on the part of each pupil. The child who is involved in a highly imaginary play situation is building readiness for analyzing, hypothesizing, and developing generalizations. Mental and creative reasoning is fostered and practiced in playing a game. The mental activity when playing a game both directly and subtly increases the child's confidence in adapting to and choosing among various alternatives. These types of mental activity lend themselves to solving problems in many areas of the elementary school curriculum.

Physical

The exercise of motor functions involved in game and play activities is a physical benefit children acquire while playing games. In coping with problems in games, children are actively involved with their environment and the challenges of the game. They are individuals who *do* and who *act* in the game situation. Thus, the physical aspect is another fundamental property of game activity.

Emotional

Games also can be used to satisfy emotional needs. A game play activity provides for a safe release of tension or aggression that a child may feel or develop in the regular school routine. Games interspersed at frequent intervals during school activities will aid the child who is tense and needs opportunities to relax. A game that will provide an emotional outlet for children is still another fundamental property to be considered.

Competition

The nature of a game implies that there may be pupils who win and pupils who lose; yet a game should be so constructed and organized that all those who play learn. If individual competition is to be minimized, group competition can be in the game plan. Self-competition is for those children who are not as successful in the direct one-to-one competitive games. Of course, direct competition for many pupils can be highly motivating. Another approach to more evenly match children for games is to give a child who is less successful in direct competition a handicap. The handicap could be worked on points, scoring, or some other method of measuring progress. In the old-fashioned spelling bee, the child who needed the practice most was the first child out of the game. The competitive aspect of a game should be so organized that the child who needs the most practice gets it.

Game and Kit Procedure

Game activities can take many forms, occurring informally between two individuals or as an activity involving opposing teams. The games can involve the entire class or they can be played in small groups. Whatever the organization for the game, there are certain procedures a teacher should follow. These game procedures are discussed next.

Identifying the Problem

In using games in the classroom, the teacher first decides the teaching objectives and the scope of the subject matter he or she wishes to have included in the game activity. The teacher must identify the problem and then select a game that would help the children in understanding the concept to be taught in the game. All too often, teachers select a game to be played, and *hope* the children will learn *something.* In the proper use of games, the problem is identified and is taken from the ongoing classroom activities. The game should be used as an *effective teaching device,* not just something to fill the day's activities. For example, the teacher may find that during the reading lesson, children are having difficulty in the discrimination of vowel sounds. He or she then selects the game activity Vowel Lotto, which helps children to discriminate the vowel sounds.

Game and Kit Rules

Before children begin game activities, they need to know the rules and regulations for the game. Often many children become frustrated and unhappy because the game rules have not been fully explained. Usually it is helpful for the teacher to play the game first. Then he or she can better explain the game to the children. With young children the game's scoring activities and rules should be very simple. More mature children can be involved in elaborate games with many rules. The important element to remember in game rules is to *keep them simple* no matter what age the children may be.

Pupil Involvement

All children need to be involved in the game activities. Most educational games are designed for maximum participation by the children and very little, if any, spectator activities. A helpful way to get pupils involved might be to start a pair or group in the game activity and then divide the group and add to the two groups people who have not played the game. Dividing the groups and adding new children to the game activity can be continued until all children are involved. This technique also will help children who have difficulty in understanding the rules because the rules will be taught, or at least reinforced, as the children enter the group with children who already know how to play the game. Pupil involvement is an essential ingredient for game activities whereby children can *learn by doing.*

Rewards

Many games are constructed in such a way that children can *win* or, at least, reach some *reward* or *goal.* For many children the reward seems to be learning the subject matter in a nonthreatening activity. If the game is organized with winners and losers, even the loser has the reward of reinforcement of skills, understandings, or other learning processes while playing.

Values

- Games and kits are effective in stimulating pupil interests and involvement.
- Motivation and pupil interaction in the classroom are greatly improved through the use of games.
- Games are especially successful in focusing the pupil's attention on a particular set of concepts. The attention span of children is appreciably lengthened because of the excitement surrounding the playing of the game.
- The immediate feedback that games provide to pupils helps them judge their own performance.
- Games are versatile in that both the fast and slow learners can be involved simultaneously in the activity.
- Many areas of the curriculum that are not otherwise demonstrable in the classroom may be presented through the use of games.

Limitations and Problems

- No formal studies offer proof that educational games are more effective than conventional classroom procedures. Some educators feel games should not be used in the classroom because children do not learn as they are too busy having fun during the game activity.
- In games it is often difficult to establish evaluation criteria as to what the game is actually teaching.
- It may be especially difficult to transfer learning from game situations to the actual ongoing class activities.
- Games may place more emphasis on the child winning the game than upon learning the concepts involved in the game.
- The competition that many games generate may have a bad effect upon the slow learner.

Sources of Educational Games and Kits

Useful in the Language Arts Area

1. *Media Kit.* This kit helps students examine subtle ways in which mass media shape our lives. A. W. Peller and Associates, Inc., Educational Materials, 210 Sixth Avenue, Hawthorne, NJ 07507.

2. *Photosearch: A Library Skills Detective Game.* This game provides experiences for time-traveling detectives and helps students to identify the who, what, when, and where of old photos found in an attic. A. W. Peller and Associates, Inc., Educational Materials, 210 Sixth Avenue, Hawthorne, NJ 07507.

3. *Classroom Filmstrip Kit.* This kit encourages self-expression by allowing students to create their own filmstrips. A. W. Peller and Associates, Inc., Educational Materials, 210 Sixth Avenue, Hawthorne, NJ 07507.

4. *Guess My Name Game.* This game encourages children to talk and listen. Lakeshore Curriculum Materials Co., 2695 E. Dominguez Street, P.O. Box 6261, Carson, CA 90749.

5. *Versa-Tiles Language Arts Lab 1, 2 and 3.* These kits develop reading comprehension. Educational Teaching Aids, 199 Carpenter Avenue, Wheeling, IL 60090.

6. *Comprehension Games: Main Idea Travel, Context Clues, Drawing Conclusions, Fact or Opinion, and Reading for Detail.* These games are written for specific reading abilities with each game focusing on a special comprehension skill area. Educational Teaching Aids, 199 Carpenter Avenue, Wheeling, IL 60090.

7. *SRA Reading Laboratories.* Nine kits designed for grade levels 1–14 with ten different difficulty levels of reading in each kit. Science Research Associates, Inc., 155 North Wacker Drive, Chicago, IL 60606.

8. *Cliffhanger: Story Completion Kits.* This kit gives the students an opportunity to complete the story by writing an ending after reading an expertly written beginning story that builds to a rousing climax. Opportunities for Learning, Inc., 20417 Nordhoff Street, Dept. KA 2, Chatsworth, CA 91311.

Useful in the Mathematics and Science Areas

1. *Primary Dinosaur Kit.* Children are transported back to prehistoric times through this kit. A. W. Peller and Associates, Inc., Educational Materials, 210 Sixth Avenue, Hawthorne, NJ 07507.

2. *The Cell Game.* This game helps children to learn the basic cell structure and some aspects of cell function. A. W. Peller and Associates, Inc., Educational Materials, 210 Sixth Avenue, Hawthorne, NJ 07507.

3. *Food Webs Game.* This game helps students to recognize the interdependence of plants and animals within the food web. A. W. Peller and Associates, Inc., Educational Materials, 210 Sixth Avenue, Hawthorne, NJ 07507.

4. *Computational Skills Development Kit.* This kit pinpoints children's weaknesses in mathematics and then students can work independently to correct these weaknesses. Science Research Associates, Inc., 155 North Wacker Drive, Chicago, IL 60606.

5. *Early Childhood Science Kit.* In using this kit, children can become interested in basic science concepts. Educational Teaching Aids, 199 Carpenter Avenue, Wheeling, IL 60090.

6. *Number Fun Games Box.* This box is filled with exciting games that help children to learn not only math concepts but also that math is fun. Lakeshore Curriculum Materials Co., 2695 E. Dominguez Street, P.O. Box 6261, Carson, CA 90749.

8. *The Allowance Game.* With this game students gain practical experience in making change and learn how to handle their own money. Lakeshore Curriculum Materials Co., 2695 E. Dominguez Street, P.O. Box 6261, Carson, CA 90749.

Useful in the Social Studies Area

1. *Exploring Your World Geography Game.* Map and social studies skills are reinforced by this game. A. W. Peller and Associates, Inc., Educational Materials, 210 Sixth Avenue, Hawthorne, NJ 07507.

2. *Archaeology Kit.* The children carefully excavate pieces of pottery and assemble or restore these ancient vessels by gluing the fragments. A. W. Peller and Associates, Inc., Educational Materials, 210 Sixth Avenue, Hawthorne, NJ 07507.

3. *World Map Carpet Game and U.S.A. Map Carpet Game.* Students answer questions about locations and places on the maps. Lakeshore Curriculum Materials Co., 2695 E. Dominguez Street, P.O. Box 6261, Carson, CA 90749.

4. *Map and Globe Skills.* In using this kit, children develop interpretive and study skills in social studies. Science Research Associates, Inc., 155 North Wacker Drive, Chicago IL 60606.

5. *NewsLab.* This kit helps children read and interpret the newspaper. Science Research Associates, Inc., 155 North Wacker Drive, Chicago, IL 60606.

Useful in the Elementary School Curriculum

1. Betty P. Cleaver, Barbara Chatton, and Shirley V. Morrison, *Creating Connections: Books, Kits and Games for Children* (New York: Garland Publishers, 1986). A resource book for many games and kits that can be used in the elementary school.
2. Many games with educational value may be purchased in toy stores, school supply houses, and general merchandising establishments. These games can be used as developed or they can be adapted to fit the objectives established by the teacher in the classroom.

Endnote

1. George W. Bright and John G. Harvey, "Games, Geometry, and Teaching," *Mathematics Teacher,* April 1988, pp. 250–259.

Chapter 23

Testing Techniques

Overview

Key Concepts

- A valid test must be reliable; a reliable test, however, may not necessarily be valid.
- Specified behavioral outcomes derived from instructional goals and basic concepts provide the basis for measurement and evaluation.
- Tests generally should emphasize the higher levels of cognition.
- Multiple-choice items tend to be superior to other types of test items.
- Test-taking behavior involves definite skills that may have a marked impact on test scores.

Chapter Terms

- Measurement: A quantitative amount of some experience, such as a test score.
- Evaluation: The quality of an experience, often based upon some measure.
- Validity: The trustworthiness of a measure. For example: "Does it measure what it is supposed to measure?"
- Reliability: The consistency of scores on a given measuring instrument.
- Situational test item: An item that thrusts the pupil into a contrived situation. It is designed to determine how well learnings may be applied.
- Performance test item: An item that requires the learner to actually do (perform) a specified skill.
- Modified or qualified test item: Usually a supplementary item so designed as to probe depth of understanding or frame of reference.
- Subjective test item: An item open to more than one type of response, based upon the frame of reference of the individual involved.
- Objective test item: An item that can be scored objectively.

Tests are designed to provide the teacher with a quantitative measure of some experience. On the other hand, the quality of a test is an assessment of the value of the quantity being measured. Since evaluation, to a substantial degree, is based upon the tests that teachers themselves produce, this chapter is designed specifically for those who desire to improve the quality of test items. It is recognized that other measurement and evaluation tools, such as rating scales, checklists, and anecdotal records, must be used in conjunction with tests.

Fundamental Properties

Measuring instruments and devices are often difficult to construct and score. They are as much a part of the instructional process as any other aspect of teaching, however. In fact, measuring instruments often determine the nature of learning that will occur when pupils study for tests. Thus a thorough understanding of their fundamental properties is essential if measuring instruments are to be effective.

Concept Application

Learning for what? This is a basic question all teachers must ask themselves repeatedly. Teachers and pupils quite naturally become engrossed in the content details of subject matter. A mere acquisition of specific facts, however, may provide a rather poor means of assessing the usefulness of the learning experience. It has been established that pupils quickly forget specific details. They may remember basic concepts (big ideas), however, for an indefinite period of time. Basic concepts, then, become the fundamental ingredients for subsequent experiences. Many test items are designed to determine if such concepts can be applied appropriately in related situations.

Reflective Processes

It seems reasonable to assume that a substantial portion of school learning is based upon an orderly process of critical or reflective thinking. In short, when confronted with a difficulty, an individual will assess the situation in terms of the available facts, will consider possible solutions or courses of action to take, and will finally select or act upon the solution that seems most compatible with the data available. Instructional methods are viewed as different approaches to the reflective or problem-solving situations. They may be new to the individual but involve application of definite concepts gained from the educational experience.

Validity

A valid test measures what it is supposed to measure. For example, if ten major concepts have been identified and emphasized during a unit, the test must be based upon these concepts. While it is appropriate to include some items dealing with specific facts pertaining to concepts, major emphasis must be focused on the learner's ability to *use* the concepts in related situations.

The number of test items pertaining to any given concept should correlate with emphasis given to the concept during the instructional program. If several hours of instruction were given to one concept while only one hour of instruction was devoted to a second concept, three times as much test emphasis might be placed on the first concept.

Reliability

Every teacher is concerned with the trustworthiness or consistency of test results. Does Johnny's poor mark indicate a general lack of understanding in the area, or might it merely reflect errors due to chance and poor test items? How much would the score change if the test was administered several times without the influence of the previous test experiences?

Although it is impossible to eliminate all chance error, a simple item analysis will reveal those sources of inconsistency due to poor and/or ambiguous items. An accurate index of item difficulty and discrimination between good and poor pupils can be obtained by determining how well a given item is related to success on the test as a whole.

Objectivity

A test item is said to be objective if it is clearly stated. Most words have several meanings. Therefore, it is important for a teacher to clarify intended meanings so that pupils will understand the question in the same way. Both essay- and objective-type items run the risk of being misunderstood. The qualified essay item described later in this chapter may greatly increase objectivity. Likewise, modified multiple-choice and true-false items enable the pupil to indicate his or her particular frame of reference when responding to the item.

Another aspect of objectivity is associated with scoring procedure.

Use of a scoring key reduces the effect of personal bias. A scoring key usually consists of acceptable responses and the various weights to be assigned to each item.

Difficulty Range

The difficulty range of criterion-referenced items used to determine mastery level must be interpreted quite differently from that of norm-referenced items. In the former, pupil achievement is assessed in terms of type of behavior or performance a pupil is capable of demonstrating. Level of performance, usually predetermined, is stated as a part of each instructional goal and behavioral outcome. In this manner an absolute standard *(criterion)* is established for assessing an individual's achievement. *One's position relative to other pupils in class is not a factor.* In testing for minimum essentials, mastery within reasonable limits is expected. Thus a spread of scores is not expected. The difficulty of a test item (or task) should correspond to the difficulty of the performance task described in the specific learning outcome.

The range of difficulty becomes an important concept in all norm-referenced measures. Such measures are used with developmental objectives. Here one is interested in the pupil's relative standing in class. Achievement is assessed in terms of how the learner's achievement compares with that of other pupils in class. Thus a spread of scores becomes important. Since complete mastery is not expected, a range of item difficulty is needed if one is to assess relative degree of progress toward a given objective.

Norm-referenced items chosen for maximum discrimination will tend to have a range of difficulty of approximately 50 percent, that is, one out of two pupils will respond incorrectly to the item. Allowing for chance clues and the like, the point of maximum discrimination usually is placed slightly higher. Although an item ideally will be answered correctly by 50 to 60 percent of the pupils, it may be desirable to include a few easy items (for encouragement) and a few hard items for the purpose of discriminating among top pupils. Since a few easy items and a few hard items are included, the minimum level of about 70 percent is usually considered a "passing" level.

A criterion-referenced test must accurately determine the range of criterion behavior involved. Rather than give pupils such a test before the learning experience begins, teachers often arbitrarily determine the range themselves. Perhaps a better technique would be to administer the test both before and after the learning experience. Although only a few pupils would be expected to answer any given item correctly on the preassessment test, most of them should respond correctly on the postassessment test. An overall score of 80 percent or higher should be expected.

Time Limitations

Tests are of two types with respect to time: power and speed. A power test provides the pupil with ample time to respond to all items, whereas a speed test limits the amount of time allowed for separate sections and/or the total test time. Most teacher-made tests are designed as power tests. In attempting to include as many items as possible within a specified time limit, tests are sometimes too long for slow pupils. Thus a power test, in effect, becomes a speed test for *some* pupils. Such a condition may produce unreliable test results.

In those areas in which criterion-referenced items can be used, the problem becomes especially critical. A representative sample of a pupil's performance within a given area is necessary. If numerous skills are involved (as in arithmetic), each separate skill must be adequately tested. As a rule of thumb at least ten items for each instructional objective should be included. Thus in order to keep such tests of reasonable length, pupils' tests involving a week or two of class time may become necessary.

Testing Procedure

The construction of effective tests demands careful attention to content, purpose, and level of goal achievement expected. Thus testing procedures vary considerably. Those that follow, however, should provide the teacher with a useful guide that is consistent with the other instructional strategies presented in this book.

Identifying Concepts and Goals

If the instructional process rests upon basic unit concepts (as advocated in this book), then testing procedures must be based upon such a foundation. The reader will recall that the first step in the instructional process is concept identification. Each unit concept (usually four to six per unit) provides a basis for development of unit goals, with their accompanying behavioral outcomes. When behavioral outcomes are first identified, the teacher is most interested in those *intermediate* behaviors indicating progress *toward* goal achievement and concept attainment. The following example illustrates this point:

> After reading the story about an immigrant family, the pupil should further appreciate the social inequalities as evidenced by (1) realistic *responses* in a class discussion on the problem, "What should be the U.S. policy with respect to immigrant

people?" (2) willingness to examine feeling reactions resulting from a dramatic play designed to portray feelings in a specified social situation, and (3) greater cooperation in school with children who dress differently or speak with an accent.

It will be noted that outcomes 1 and 2 are to be elicited *during* the instructional process. Although the third outcome is a *terminal* behavior, it can hardly be used for evaluational purposes in its present form.

To be most useful for evaluational purposes, behavioral outcomes must be redefined as *terminal* behaviors, and they must be much more explicit than the intermediate behaviors. The first outcome from the previous illustration, for example, reads: Realistic responses in a class discussion on the problem, "What should be the U.S.' policy with respect to immigrant people?" As a result of the class discussion, what specific outcomes might be expected? From such an experience one might expect (among other things) the learner to evaluate evidence in the area and to draw warranted conclusions from the evidence available. The unit concept, "social inequities may exist with immigrants," is used as a guide for constructing test items designed to determine how well the learner can evaluate evidence and draw warranted conclusions in the area. Likewise, the second outcome, concerned with the learner's willingness to examine feelings portrayed through a dramatic play experience, must be more specifically stated for evaluational purposes. The teacher should determine what will result from this examination of feelings. Perhaps it will be increased empathy or increased skill in interpersonal relationships. Test items and other evaluational tools are then constructed for assessing progress in this direction. The third outcome, although already stated as a terminal behavior, must be more specifically qualified if it is used for evaluational purposes. (As a terminal behavior it does not directly serve instructional purposes.) Further refinement of the outcome can be achieved by specifying the important *conditions* under which "greater cooperation with children who seem different" might be expected. For example, one condition might include the learner's willingness to accept such pupils in specific group activities. Such an outcome is probably most appropriately evaluated through direct observation.

Selecting Test Levels and Types

After the terminal behaviors for each unit concept have been explicitly identified, the teacher must decide which of these can best be examined through the use of test items and then ascertain the level of goal achievement expected. In terms of the actual instructional experience(s), the teacher decides what level of goal attainment might be expected. If, for example, oral reports were employed as the basic means of attaining a given concept, the teacher must judge how effective they were. If they were not as effective as anticipated, test items dealing with the specific concept(s) involved might be restricted to the knowledge or comprehension levels of the cognitive domain.

Identification of the goal achievement level provides a sound basis for ascertaining the type of test item to be employed in each case. As indicated in the following sections, different test types correspond broadly to goal levels as identified in each of the three instructional domains.

Constructing Performance Test Items

For many years one of the leading controversies in the area of test construction has focused on the level of item difficulty needed to determine progress toward goals. Some teachers have assumed that a knowledge of the essential facts in given areas should be sufficient evidence of goal achievement. Others, pointing out the wide gap between knowledge and application, have suggested that more than retention is needed. Although some indication of learning can be ascertained from how well one knows the facts, most teachers would readily agree that the best indication of learning is application in real-life situations.

In many areas, especially in the area of motor and mental skills, it is relatively easy to provide test situations that demand actual life applications of the concepts involved. The illustrations that follow suggest the wide applicability of performance test items to different areas of specialization.

1. Adds fractions correctly
2. Prepares and delivers persuasive reports effectively
3. Recognizes plant species in the local area
4. Summarizes effectively
5. Selects art objects that portray a given mood
5. Plays music according to directions
7. Analyzes current events in terms of selected concepts gleaned from social studies

It is evident from the foregoing illustrations that performance test items can be employed in most subject areas. In skill areas, some tests may be entirely concerned with performance. Items are relatively easy to construct once the desired application has been identified. The major task is to establish the conditions and criteria of acceptable performance. For example, how many plant species in the local area should a pupil be able to identify and under what conditions? How well must the student speak and under what circumstances?

Constructing Situational Test Items

Unfortunately, it is not always possible to measure behavioral changes directly. In the first place, the teacher may not have an opportunity to see each pupil in a realistic situation that demands a direct application of the learning involved. Frequently the outcome will not be applied to any real-life situation for several weeks or even months, simply because the learner will not be in a situation demanding such application. In an effort to determine the degree of understanding, the teacher will be obliged to resort to less direct measures. In such instances one can do no better than *simulate* an experience involving an appropriate application. For example, in a unit on first aid, one evidence of understanding the principles involved would probably be "The pupil recognizes and administers first aid properly in case of shock." It is impractical to induce a case of actual shock for test purposes; however, it is possible to simulate or act out the experience. Since it is impossible to objectively evaluate such an experience for all thirty pupils in a class, a written description of a realistic situation may be as close to reality as is possible. Thus pupils are measured on the basis of what they would *plan* to do in the situation rather than on their *actions* in the situation. Such a procedure obviously is a compromise with what is desired, because people do not always behave the way they plan to behave. For instance, in the previous illustration one might describe a fully adequate plan of action, whereas in the actual situation he or she might become hysterical and do nothing. Despite the exceptions, however, an indication of what one *thinks* he or she would do in a lifelike situation is a reasonably sound prediction of what the individual actually would do. It is for this very reason that people plan ahead.

Multiple-Choice Test Item
The multiple-choice item can be readily adapted to the problem-solving situation. Many of the most difficult problems involve making choices between known alternatives. The choices made in relatively simple problem situations often materially affect one's degree of success and/or happiness in life. This is not greatly different from the problem of a pupil choosing between alternatives on a multiple-choice item. Experience over many years has convinced test developers of the generally superior versatility and convenience of multiple-choice items. Although other forms can be used effectively in special situations, the multiple-choice test is more widely applicable and generally effective.

The multiple-choice question consists of a base question or statement and four or five responses, one of which is the best answer. The other answers are usually referred to as foils or distractors. In essence, the base item poses the problem situation and the possible answers represent the alternative solutions. The pupil "solves" the problem by making a choice. All the foils or distractors should be plausible to those who lack the necessary understanding of the concept application involved. Some teachers include distractors that all seem quite acceptable; that is, they represent accurate statements. Only one of the possible answers is best, however, *in terms of the situation posed.* In general, the possible answers should include one *preferred* answer, a distractor that is almost the correct answer, and another that is clearly erroneous. The remaining distractors tend to fall some place between these two extremes. Teachers sometimes make use of the distractors "all of these" or "none of these." These responses can be used effectively only when the question calls for a highly specific answer that is either completely correct or incorrect.

There are likely to be a number of reasons why pupils make inappropriate selections on multiple-choice tests. They could misunderstand the base item or any one of the distractors, they could interpret the question in a unique way, or they simply may not possess an adequate understanding of the concepts necessary for the application. If the first two reasons are involved, the item is not valid for *that particular individual.* Sometimes a teacher desires to achieve greater validity by giving the pupil an opportunity to qualify or otherwise justify his or her answer. This enables the teacher to give credit for a choice that might have been justifiably selected *from the pupil's point of view,* even though it ordinarily would have been considered incorrect. Ultimately, however, the teacher must decide whether or not the reason is sufficient to warrant full credit for the response.

A modified situational form of the multiple-choice item follows:

Subject matter area	Social studies
Concept	Pueblo Indians built homes to protect themselves from their enemies.
Item	A. In what way was the Pueblo Indians' home like a fort? 1. It was made of logs. 2. It was square. 3. It was for protection. 4. It was entered through a small opening. B. Defend your answer.

If, during the instructional process, the teacher did not use the specific situation employed in the item, then the test question will probably demand knowledge of the facts *in addition to* application of a basic idea (concept). Thus the pupil must "go the second mile" to respond properly to the question. The "defend your answer" part of the item serves to probe still further one's depth of understanding.

Essay Test Item

Like the multiple-choice item, the essay item is readily adaptable to a specific situation. Unlike other test item types, it may elicit a detailed written response involving the making of complex relationships, selection and organization of ideas, formulation of hypotheses, logical development of arguments, and creative expression.

The essay item is particularly vulnerable to unreliability, especially in terms of how it is scored. To some extent, a pupil's mark on such an item is dependent on the reader rather than on the actual quality of a response.

The essay item can be made more reliable if constructed to elicit an application of learnings or different situations. Test reliability can be improved by giving directions concerning the structure of the answer expected. Sometimes this is called the *qualified* essay question. An illustration of the *situational* essay, in which the answer is somewhat *qualified*, follows:

Subject matter area	Social studies
Concept	Pueblo Indians built homes to protect themselves from their enemies.
Item	Pueblo Indians built their homes where they were hard to find and out of reach for protection from their enemies. Discuss what the pioneers, moving West, did that was similar to the Pueblo Indians.

Scoring reliability is substantially improved if the teacher develops an answer key in advance of marking the questions. Sometimes it is desirable to underline or otherwise call attention to key points. Pupils may also be asked to underline key phrases. In addition, scoring reliability can be increased if the teacher does not know whose paper is being marked. This may be accomplished by asking the individual to enter his or her name on the back of the test paper. The practice of marking all pupils on each essay item before proceeding to the next one and completing the process without interruption may greatly enhance one's scoring consistency.

Constructing Recall Test Items

Sometimes teachers assume that if pupils can recall the important facts in an area, they will make actual applications when needed. Using an illustration cited earlier, one could assume that a pupil who could describe the symptoms and appropriate treatment for shock could be reasonably expected to apply that knowledge. Considerable evidence, however, indicates that a broad gap exists between *verbal* understanding and application of that understanding.

True-False Item

True-false testing has lost much popularity within recent years. There are many serious limitations associated with its use. Among the most serious is a tendency for the user to emphasize isolated facts that often hold slight validity in relation to the unit objectives. Contrary to popular belief, the true-false item is so dificult to construct that it has little meaning. This type of question tends to penalize the pupil, since he or she is more likely to think of an exception that can alter intended meaning. Furthermore, test makers tend to make more items true than false, to use specific determiners (all, never, entirely, etc.), and to use textbook language.

It is possible, however, to improve the true-false item substantially so that it can serve a useful function. For example, in emphasizing broad concepts and selection of alternatives on a test, one might also test for specified data. In this context the true-false test item becomes quite useful. The item can be substantially improved by encouraging pupils to apply a minor concept or generalization in some way. To illustrate in the social studies area:

Concept	Pueblo Indians built their homes to protect them from their enemies.
Item	Pueblo Indians built their homes <u>on the plains</u> so they could protect themselves better from their enemies.

One of the most important means of improving the true-false item is to modify it by asking pupils to correct all items in such a manner as to render them true statements. In order to guard against the addition or deletion of something like the word *not* as a means of correcting an item, it usually is necessary for the teacher to underline certain key clauses or phrases. The pupil is asked to change the underlined portion in such a manner as to make the statement correct. If change is necessary, the pupil should alter the underlined portion only. Pupils may be allowed some credit for the mere recognition of a true or false statement and additional credit for their ability to make appropriate corrections.

Completion Test Item

The completion test item also has been overemphasized. Like the true-false item, its answer was easy to defend merely by referring the pupil to a particular page in the textbook. As a consequence, specific details and, all too often, meaningless verbalisms were emphasized. The objectives of the unit were often forgotten when tests were being constructed. The inevitable result was a tendency to gear the entire instructional process to memorizations. Likewise, pupils realizing they would be tested in such a manner tended to study only specific details and terminology. Thus, cramming for tests became popular.

Despite the inherent weaknesses of this measurement, there are occasions when the meaning of a term is important enough to employ completion items on a test. In fact, most tests will contain a limited number of such items. As its name implies, the item is answered by the completion of a statement. There is an ever-present danger, however, that a statement will be so construed that the respondent will be unable to understand the meaning intended. For this reason, some teachers have changed the uncompleted statement to a question form. The following example illustrates the item.

Subject matter area	Social studies
Concept	Pueblo Indians built their homes to protect them from their enemies.
Item	Pueblo Indians built their homes in hard-to-find and out-of-reach areas for _____.
	Why did the Pueblo Indians build their homes in hard-to-find and out-of-reach areas? _____.

Although both forms elicit the same information, the second one is probably easier to answer because it is worded as a complete thought. Furthermore, the answers can be placed in a column to facilitate marking.

Matching Test Item

Like the completion item, the matching question is of relatively minor importance. It is used when teachers desire pupils to relate such things as dates and events, terms and definitions, persons and places, or causes and events. Its chief disadvantage is that it does not adapt very well to the measurement of real understandings. Because the separate items in the exercises should be homogeneous in nature, there is the likelihood that test clues will reduce their validity. Multiple-choice items should be used whenever possible to replace the matching test item.

Appropriate use of the item is facilitated by (1) having at least five and not more than twelve responses, (2) including at least three extra choices from which responses must be chosen, and (3) using only homogeneous items or related materials in any one exercise.

Utilizing Test Results

Tests are utilized for two distinct purposes: results and processes. The teacher must determine how well basic concepts can be applied in life or lifelike situations. Test results may also provide the teacher with clues to deficiencies in the learning experiences and the need for reteaching certain concepts. Using tests as a basis for ascertaining weaknesses in the instructional process is a sound but frequently neglected technique.

A pupil who responds incorrectly to a given test item is in effect communicating evidence of a learning deficiency. By examining all items devoted to each concept, the teacher may obtain a reasonably sound basis for remedial instruction. If all or most of the group displays similar problems, special group activities may be provided. However, most deficiencies will be of an individualized nature. This necessitates individualized remedial instructional processes. Generally, each individual utilizing the test paper as a basis should be provided additional opportunities to make conceptual applications in areas of deficiency. Eventually this may take the form of a subsequent test or it may merely entail informal written statements pertaining to areas of deficiency. When the teacher is satisfied that deficiencies have been corrected, at least partial credit may be allowed for the purpose of evaluation.

Values

- When used appropriately, test items offer a sound measure of the learner's ability to apply what has been learned.
- Diagnostic tests help both the teacher and the learner identify areas in which relearning and reteaching are needed.
- The quantitative nature of test results accommodates group evaluation. Thus test results are often more valid than results obtained through other measures.
- Test items are extremely flexible. By using various types, the teacher can assess almost any level of goal attainment. This applies especially to the cognitive domain.
- When used appropriately, tests can motivate the learner to greater effort. Pupils must be assured a reasonable chance of success, however. Competition with able, or even average, pupils for grades is self-defeating for the less able pupil.

Limitations and Problems

- A pupil's achievement on teacher-made tests is often *inappropriately* assessed in terms of all other pupils in class. Mastering testing must be made independent of class standing.

- Tests that demand mere recall of information tend to relegate learning to memorization. While some items appropriately should test recall of facts, more items should test the achievement of important class goals through problem-solving techniques.
- Passing tests often has become the end of education, at least in the minds of many pupils. While tests should measure progress toward more basic goals, *the intent to remember and to apply beyond the confines of a test* is an extremely important psychological principle.
- Tests, as often used in today's schools, tend to encourage cheating and other forms of dishonesty. Also involved may be the development of some form of status order that often is closely related to community social class lines.
- When overemphasized, evaluation tends to be made at the expense of other, more effective instructional procedures. Furthermore, the difficulty of evaluating certain basic educational goals (e.g., affective goals) tends to limit the extent to which they will be taught and achieved.

———————— **Illustrated Test Items** ————————

Multiple-Choice Items

I. Useful in the science area
   Unit Weather
   Concept Moisture is in the air.
   Item
   A. If a glass jar is filled with ice and some water and the jar is left in the classroom on a sheet of paper, which of the following would happen?
      1. The paper would become dryer.
      2. Nothing would happen to the paper.
      3. The paper would become wet.
      4. The paper would change color.
   B. Support your answer.

II. Useful in the arithmetic area
   Unit Percentages
   Concept Percentages can be expressed in many different ways.
   Item
   A. If the tax on your property is 4 percent of its value, which one of the following would represent the tax?
      1. 40¢ per $1.00 value.
      2. 40¢ per $10.00 value.

    3. 40¢ per $100.00 value.
    4. $4.00 per $1000.00 value.
  B. Support your answer by computing a 4-percent tax for your properties, which are valued at $1.00, $10.00, $100.00, and $1000.00.

III. Useful in the social studies area
    Unit   The State of California
    Concept   Climate has always been important to Los Angeles.
    Item
    A. In what way did the climate of California bring the movie industry to Los Angeles?
       1. The movie industry stars wanted good sun tans.
       2. Electric lights were too bright and caused discomfort for the movie stars so they wanted to be outside.
       3. Movie directors could depend upon sunlight for picture taking almost every day of the year.
       4. The movie people wanted to be away from movie fans on the East Coast.
    B. Defend your answer.

IV. Useful in the language arts area
    Unit   Telephone Procedures and Proper Use
    Concept   A person should respect the rights of others when using the telephone.
    Item
    A. If you are not sure of the telephone number you wish to call, what should you do?
       1. Dial the number you think is right.
       2. Ask someone else if he or she can remember the right number.
       3. Try several numbers hoping one will be the right number.
       4. Look up the number in the telephone directory.
    B. Give your reasons for selecting the answer you did.

Essay Items

  I. Useful in the physical education area
    Unit   Teamwork
    Concept   Teamwork is an excellent method for attaining goals.
    Item   John and five of his classmates have been assigned the task of reporting the life of Babe Ruth. John feels the other members are not putting forth a very effective team effort. Discuss the steps that John should take to ensure effective teamwork for this group.

 II. Useful in the reading area
    Unit   Interpretation of Characters in Stories

I. *Concept*   Characters in a story will arouse emotional reactions on the part of each reader.
Item   After reading the book *Lentil*, how would Lentil have felt if Old Shep had *liked* his music?

III. Useful in the spelling area
Unit   Studying Words for Spelling
Concept   How to study spelling involves a definite technique.
Item   How to study spelling independently involves a definite technique. Explain each step involved in the technique.

IV. Useful in the science area
Unit   The Plant Kingdom
Concept   Plants need three major things to make food.
Item   State in your own words what is needed for plants to make their own food.

True-False Items

II. Useful in the social studies area
Unit   Pioneer Period
Concept   Pioneers adapted themselves to their environment.
Item   In the prairie lands, pioneers built their homes out of logs because there were many trees nearby.

II. Useful in the reading area
Unit   Phonics
Concept   A consonant blend is a combination of two or three consonant letters used to represent two or more consonant sounds in a series.
Item   The letters *bl* in blue are a consonant blend.

III. Useful in the language arts area
Unit   Choric Verse
Concept   The rhythm of the poem should be maintained to produce an effective choric verse.
Item   Choric verse should be done in a sing-song voice.

IV. Useful in the arithmetic area
Unit   Division Problems
Concept   To find the average of two or more numbers, add the numbers and then divide the sum by the number of items added.
Item   To find the average of 44, 33, 71, and 14, you would add all four numbers and divide by 4.

Chapter 24

Parent Involvement

Overview

Key Concepts

- Closer ties between the home and the school is an important need.
- Parental involvement in the school is for the mutual benefit of the children.
- Communication between home and school is an important ingredient for parental involvement.
- Parents are a strong teaching force for their children.
- Parents working as volunteers have an effect on teachers and schools as much as on themselves and their children.

Chapter Terms

- Role clarification: The process of clearly identifying the expected behavior pattern each person is to perform in a given relationship or organization.
- Role modeling: A person serving as an example for imitation or emulation, for example, a teacher or parent.
- Aide: A person who acts as an assistant.

As one looks historically at parent involvement in schools, a drastic change has taken place. In earlier times, education for children was viewed in terms of parental rights. From the one-room schoolhouse where the curriculum was prescribed by the parents to the multifaceted school systems of today where many parents have left curriculum planning to professional educators, many changes in parental involvement have been made. Because of the need for more communication between schools and the home, attempts have been made to reach out to parents so as to involve them more in their schools.

Fundamental Properties

Involving parents in the school is certainly not a new problem. Teachers, school administrators, and parents have recognized the need for closer ties between home and school for many years. Communication is a very important human need, especially in home-school relationships. Fundamental properties necessary in positive parent involvement in the schools are the needs for interest, cooperation, role clarification, and expansion.

Interest

Certainly a fundamental property of parent involvement in the school is interest in home-school involvement on the part of the participants—parents, teachers, and administrators. School administrators may want parent involvement; however, unless parents and teachers also have an interest in home-school involvement, very little success will be achieved. Many parents may have the desire to be more involved in the school program yet need to be persuaded to participate more fully.

Interest and desire by the parents, teachers, school administrators, and school-governing boards all need to be engaged together to actually develop parental involvement in the schools. Once interest is there among all the participants, a planned program to induce this involvement is also necessary.

Cooperation

After interest and desire are established, probably the biggest stumbling block to parent involvement in the school is the lack of cooperation. The ability to act or work together as teacher and parent is a very important fundamental property. Of course, the importance of parental involvement in the school is to bring about a mutual benefit for the children. When cooperation is lacking, the child usually suffers.

A common effort is necessary to achieve the cooperation needed to make the parental involvement work. Communication between the participants is imperative. Written plans outlining the parameters of school-home involvement are necessary. Once cooperation is established and maintained, working together for the common benefit of the children becomes a reality.

Role Clarification

Cooperation is enhanced when roles are clearly understood by all concerned. Role clarification early in the parental involvement programs is a very important step toward working together in harmony. It is essential that each role is identified and made clear so all may understand. Each role that the parent, teacher, school administrator, or others may be assigned should be defined in the socially expected behavior pattern as determined by the assignment in the school and home. Many problems will be eliminated if this fundamental property for parent involvement in the school is carefully planned and determined.

Expansion

A fourth fundamental property for parent involvement in the schools is expansion of home-school activities into the environment. For example, the first teacher of a child is the parent in the home. These first teaching experiences will be brought to the school whether they were good or bad. Also, teaching experiences in the school will be brought to the home and the total environment of neighborhood, community, country, world, and even into space.

Parents can help the school widely expand the children's understanding of the community and world they live in through books, newspapers, magazines, field trips, and the like. Parents can expand and reinforce many of the activities taking place in the school.

Types of Parent Involvement

It has been a recognized fact that the parent is the child's first and continuing teacher. Whether or not the parent will be considered the most influential teacher will depend a great deal upon what the parent will do.[1] Therefore, as a teacher in the home the parent may significantly influence how the child views education in general and to what extent he or she participates in the learning process.

Parents, then, are involved in the school in many different roles. Parents are seen not only as the first and continuing teacher in the home but also in such roles as decision makers, an audience, paid employees, and volunteers in the school. Figure 24-1 illustrates the parent roles emanating from the important task of a teacher in the home.

Parents as Teachers in the Home

Parents are teachers both directly and indirectly as they train or teach the child in various learning situations. Young children are constantly observing their parents and using them as role models. Parents are indeed a strong teaching force for their children in early life as well as later.

Much work done by a teacher in the school can easily be undone by parents in the home. The values in education held by the parents will often reflect in the child. Educators have come to understand more forcefully today than ever before the importance of the parent as a teacher as

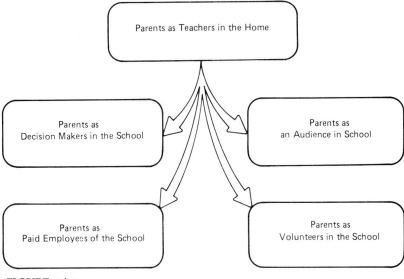

FIGURE 24-1

well as a learner for the improvement of teaching their children in the home. A good example of parents learning to be better teachers in the home is found in the many federally funded projects that require parents to learn how to be more effective as teachers in the home so that their children may be enrolled in the federal programs.

Parents as Decision Makers

In many school districts today decision making by parents is far removed from the parents. Usually their only decision may be in voting for bond issues, tax levies, or the governing school boards, which are still very important, but the decision making needs to be on the individual school level as well.

However, in some schools, principals have organized parent involvement committees or parental advisory committees. These new involvement committees are in addition to the traditional PTA and PTO organization groups. Parent involvement committees or parental advisory committees usually function with a chairman elected by the committee members. The committees are formed with teacher representative(s), the school principal, and parents. This committee advises the principal on pertinent issues involving the community and school. Problems that the school may be having with communication with parents on certain curriculum areas and other common problems are discussed at these committee meetings. Participation in these committees gives parents more opportunity for decision making in the school.

Many federal programs do require parents' participation in decision making if their children are in a federal program such as Head Start and Follow Through. There is a trend toward more parental involvement in the decision-making process in the schools today, and we may yet see in the future much more parental decision making in each school.

Parents as an Audience

Parent participation as an audience is usually the most common role parents play in the school. This role is performed by parents as they visit the school during open house and for plays, demonstrations, musicals, and the like. Many times parents play the role of an audience at Parent-Teacher Association meetings usually held in the schools. The audience role is an important one that not only supports children as participants in varied programs but also informs the parents of school activities, needs, and coming events.

Parents as Paid Employees

There are several programs that pay parents to come to school to learn various techniques or methods of teaching or working with their own children in the home. Other school programs pay parents to work in the school as teachers' aides, secretarial aides, lunchroom assistants, and playground supervisors. Many parents can become paid employees in other school-related jobs, such as cooks, custodians, school nurses, secretaries, clerks, and the like. It is quite rare to hear of a teacher who does not feel the importance of these school-related workers and the influence they have upon the children in the school.

Parents as Volunteers

The parent volunteer program has been a great success throughout the country as parents and even grandparents have become active volunteers and aides. The various volunteer programs help the school do its job more effectively by increasing the adult-child ratio in the classroom, as well as providing a means of informing parents about classroom activities and educational programs. By bringing parents and grandparents into the classroom as volunteers and aides, teachers and schools are changed and parents and children are influenced.

Values

- Parental involvement in the schools enlarges the communication process among parents, teachers, and school administrators.
- Attitudes and behaviors of parents toward the school and their children as learners are enhanced through parent involvement in the schools.
- Active cooperative efforts by teachers, parents, and others have influenced the educational environment and experiences of children that resulted in increased academic achievement.
- Information received from the home-school partnership assisted the parents in their skills in working with children in the home.

Limitations and Problems

- Many federal programs are for the lower socioeconomic parents. Attempts need to be made to bring in parents not previously reached by these programs.
- The absence of a good home-school partnership seems to cause discontent among some of the community members the school is striving to serve, such as special interest groups, racial groups, and religious groups.
- An effective school-home partnership requires a great deal of effort by all concerned. Often the effort required is not viewed by many as worthwhile.
- School administrators feel especially threatened by parental involvement in decision making.

Sources for Further Information

I. Routledge Publishers
   29 West 35th Street
   New York, NY 10001

   At Home in School: Parent Participation in Primary Education,
   1988. Authors: Viv Edwards and Angela Redfern

   This book is divided into two parts. Part 1 describes a brief history of parents and school involvement. Part 2 discusses parents and school involvement from theory into practice.

II. Croom Helm Ltd. and Methuen, Inc.
   29 West 35th Street
   New York, NY 10001

Listening to Parents: An Approach to the Improvement of Home-School Relations, 1988. Authors: Janet Atkin and John Bastiani with Jackie Goode

This book illustrates the positive interaction that can be developed between home and school by listening to parents. This book has practical value in helping in the development of more effective home-school practices.

III. Teachers College Press
1234 Amsterdam Avenue
New York, NY 10027

Enhancing Parent Involvement in Schools, 1987. Author: Susan McAllister Swap

This manual gives many suggestions for improving communication between parents and teachers. In addition, case studies, parent conferences, and ways to involve parents in school are given.

IV. Nancy Barbour
Assistant to the Director
Center for Parenting Studies
Wheelock College
200 The Riverway
Boston, MA 02215

Crossing the Moat: Building Bridges between Home and School

This is a slide and tape program that describes barriers to communication and a way to overcome these barriers between parents and teachers.

V. Heinemann
70 Court Street
Portsmouth, NH 03801

Home: Where Reading and Writing Begin, 1989. Author: Mary W. Hill

Parents who want to explore and reflect upon the role they play in their children's literacy development will want to read this book. This book provides answers to many questions parents ask about what they can do to help their children in reading and writing at home.

VI. CTB/McGraw-Hill
Del Monte Research Park
2500 Garden Road
Monterey, CA 93940

Parents' Guide to Understanding Tests — Important Facts About School Testing

This pamphlet provides parents with a clear, basic introduction to types of tests that are given in the schools, the meaning of different scoring reports, and ways to help children prepare for tests. A free copy is available by sending a stamped, self-addressed no. 10 envelope.

Endnote

1. Paul M. Hollingsworth, Shane Templeton, and Kenneth W. Johns, *Back to Basics: How to Help Your Child Become a Success in School* (New York: Monarch Press, Simon and Schuster, 1986), p. 12.

Index

Paul M. Hollingsworth was born and raised in a small rural community in southeastern Idaho. He accomplished his university level work at Idaho State University, Utah State University, Brigham Young University, and Arizona State University. He taught elementary school in a variety of settings, thus experiencing a wide range of teaching situations. He taught Navajo Indian children in the four-corner area of Arizona, Utah, Colorado, and New Mexico. He taught migrant workers' children as well as children from the wealthy Scottsdale, Arizona, area. He has had teaching experience with all the major ethnic groups in the United States. During each year that Dr. Hollingsworth has been employed at the university level, he has also taught elementary children in small groups in the reading center.

He is married and the father of six children. Currently Dr. Hollingsworth is Professor and Chairman of the Elementary Education Department, Brigham Young University.

Kenneth H. Hoover completed his first two degrees at Louisiana State University and was awarded his doctorate degree at the University of Washington in 1955. He taught secondary school students in the state of Washington, and briefly taught at Montana State University. He taught at San Francisco State College before coming to Arizona State University, where he taught from 1956 until his retirement in 1988. Dr. Hoover has published sixteen books, most of which have been published by Allyn and Bacon. He is currently Professor Emeritus at Arizona State University, Tempe, Arizona.